Representing Disability
in an Ableist World

Essays on Mass Media

D1444386

Representing Disability
in an Ableist World

Essays on Mass Media

by
Beth A. Haller, Ph.D.

The Advocado Press
Louisville, KY

Representing Disability in an Ableist World: Essays on Mass Media

Published by The Advocado Press, Inc., P.O. Box 406781, Louisville, KY 40204
www.advocadopress.org

Some of the essays in this book appeared in slightly different form in the following publications and are printed here with their permission: "Researching media images of disability" in *Research in Social Science & Disability*; "Changing disability terminology in the news" in *Disabiity & Society*; "Not worth keeping alive?" in *Journalism Studies*; "Autism and inclusive education in the news media" in *Disabiity & Society*; "Disability media tell their own stories" in *Journal of Magazine and New Media Research*; "Pity as oppression in the Jerry Lewis Telethon" in *Journal of Popular Film and Television*; "The new phase of disability humor on TV" in *Disability Studies Quarterly*; "Advertising boldly moves disability images forward" in *Disability Studies Quarterly*.

COVER PHOTO CREDITS:

"Jerry Lewis NO OSCAR," copyright 2010 by Tom Olin, Disability Rights Center.

Mainstream magazine cover, copyright Exploding Myths, Inc.

Cartoon, copyright 1919, permission to reprint from J.N. "Ding" Darling Foundation.

Prosthetic leg photo by Stephanie Diani for *The New York Times*, copyright May 13, 2007 *New York Times*, permission granted to reprint.

Library of Congress Cataloging-in-Publication Data

Haller, Beth A.
  Representing disability in an ableist world : essays on mass media / by Beth A. Haller.
    p. cm.
  Includes index.
  ISBN 978-0-9721189-3-4
  1. People with disabilities in mass media–United States. 2. Disabilities–Social aspects–United States. 3. Sociology of disability–United States. I. Title.
  HV1553.H33 2010
  305.9'080973–dc22
                2010022441

For John Clogston (1954-1995),
the true pioneer of media and disability research.
It has been my privilege to continue the work he began.

Contents

Preface

Even though I had been a newspaper journalist who covered health and medicine in the 1980s, I had never thought too much about media representations of people with disabilities. I did do a bit of coverage of some disability issues: I wrote an award-winning series on Down syndrome and did a story about an invisible disability that few people still talk about – head injuries – but not much else.

My awareness grew when I landed in the D.C. area for a journalism master's program at the University of Maryland-College Park in the year following the 1988 Deaf President Now protests at Gallaudet University. With the Gallaudet Deaf community[1] literally down the road from me, I sought them out. First, I did an in-depth feature story for a writing class in which I profiled the life of an average deaf student. The student's openness about her life and the misunderstanding from her hearing family truly opened my eyes. I remember thinking, "If this young woman's hearing family knows so little about Deaf culture, imagine what the general public doesn't know." I also was taking a mass communication theory class in my master's program and began to dig into the little research that existed about media images of people with disabilities. I found almost nothing in my field of mass communication, but a few articles existed in education, rehabilitation, or social policy.

But as someone who sees opportunity where others see difficulty, I excitedly began delving into any research articles I could find. It turned out that I was starting my own media and disability research at just the right time. A number of seminal essays about media representation by important scholars like Douglas Biklen of Syracuse University and Paul Longmore of San Francisco State had just been collected in an early book on the subject called *Images of the Disabled, Disabling Images* in 1987.[2]

So, fired up about this emerging scholarly area, I got to work. My master's thesis at the University of Maryland focused on coverage of Deaf persons in *The Washington Post* and *The New York Times* both during and after the Deaf President Now protest. Then, while I was researching my master's thesis, I discovered the disability media and the academic area of Disability Studies. Someone gave me a feature story that was running on the news wires about *The Disability Rag*, one of the most important U.S. disability rights publications. I became a subscriber. In the announcements section of the magazine, a small notice talked about a meeting of the Society for Disability Studies in Rockville, Md.; again it was happening right down the road from me. At that meeting, I found an academic discipline that still serves as my "scholarly home away from home." I met many people whose research I would cite and made lifelong connections – people who have become my friends, mentors, and scholarly collaborators.

I moved on to Temple University to work on my Ph.D. in Mass Media and Communication and again found myself at the right place at the right time. Temple University has an active Institute on Disabilities, which provides advocacy and academic programs as well as technological support and leadership development for people with disabilities. I took a graduate class called "Disability Rights and Culture," which was a great advantage to me because there were few Disability Studies classes available at U.S. universities at that time. And I happened to be at Temple when it began offering C2P2, Competence and Confidence: Partners in Policymaking, a leadership training program that teaches people with disabilities, their families, and graduate students about local, state, and national issues facing the disability community. As a participant, I gained much knowledge about disability rights issues. I continued my mass media research in my Ph.D. work, culminating in a dissertation that investigated elite news media coverage of the 1990 Americans with Disabilities Act, which had passed the year before I started at Temple.

It was during my time at Temple that I delved into the theoretical concepts that would inform my research – stigma,[3] ableism, social constructionism,[4] and

ii

the minority rights model of disability policy.[5] The concept of ableism is particularly germane to media studies and it is why I wanted the term in the title for this book. Although most people who undertake mass communication research have not heard of the concept, it is well-known in disability rights and disability studies circles.

I believe that the media narratives that ignore, devalue or misrepresent disability issues reflect the ableism of society through those narratives. Media content is shaped by dominant societal beliefs about disability that come from the power of the dominant able-bodied culture, which defines and classifies disability. When these dominant beliefs ignore or represent disabled people with stereotypes, this is known as "ableism."[6] The ableism within media content presents people with disabilities as inferior to able-bodied people, as "defective" or as having a worthless status. "Ableism causes pain because it convinces us that there is something fundamentally wrong with us, that we are not acceptable just as we are," Joy Weeber explains.[7] Ableism creates a societal meta-narrative in which "society perceives disabled persons to be damaged, defective, and less socially marketable than non-disabled persons"[8] Fortunately, the disability rights movement has tried to create an oppositional frame to these ableist media presentations, arguing that these stigmatizing representations lead to the further oppression of disabled people.

One group, the anti-assisted-suicide organization Not Dead Yet, which will be discussed in Chapter 4, has made one of its goals confronting "ableism." According to Not Dead Yet, the cultural beliefs that feed ableism engender public acceptance of deadly practices like assisted suicide. The organization says legalized assisted suicide represents bigotry against disabled people made life-threatening: "It's called ableism. Like racism, bigotry against people with disabilities can be deadly. [Jack] Kevorkian's ableism is as extreme as the racism of the Ku Klux Klan. . . . Why is society creating a double standard based on a person's health? Why don't disabled people receive the same suicide prevention that others can take for granted? If Kevorkian's assisted suicide is really 'voluntary,' then why isn't it available to anyone? . . . While ableist bigots like Kevorkian are showered with public attention, the real experts are never asked: How does someone with significant health impairments achieve a good quality of life?"[9]

Methodologically, I have used quantitative or qualitative content analysis to research mass media representations of disability issues. Content analysis allows me to assess what the news media say about disability through the sources they use, the language they use, the images they use, and with what effect.

Researchers can delineate the characteristics of a particular culture by investigating the content of its mass media. "The basic assumption is that both changes and regularities in media content reliably reflect or report some feature of the social reality of the moment. . . The purpose of the cultural indicator analysis is often to test propositions about effects from media on society over time, but it is also a method for the study of social change in its own right and for the comparison of different national societies and cultures."[10] Content analysis works within an understanding that most Western societies are now mass-mediated cultures in which its citizens understand "reality" through personal experience and mass media information. As media content researcher Pamela Shoemaker and Stephen Reese explain: "If we assume that the media provide most of the 'reality' that people know outside their own personal experience, then studying media content surely helps us assess what reality it is that they consume"[11]

Analyzing the content of the media has allowed me to understand the values of the media in representing people with disabilities and their concerns. This, in turn, helps assess the societal status of people with disabilities and determine whether there are changes in the social culture regarding their issues. I believe media content to be especially important because of the many societal barriers that still exist for many people with disabilities which limit interpersonal interactions between disabled and nondisabled people. I argue that most nondisabled people still learn about disability issues through the media, rather than through interactions with people with disabilities.

This book is the culmination of almost 20 years of research exploring how people with disabilities and their political, social, and civil rights issues are represented in the mainstream U.S. media. After developing the theoretical and methodological skills to begin my research career, I began studying all kinds of media content, from advertising to news to entertainment television to film. This research has been my passion since 1991. I have had two major collaborators in several of these research projects: Sue Ralph, Ph.D., of Northhampton University in the UK, and Bruce Dorries, Ph.D., of Mary Baldwin College in Virginia. Many of the chapters in this book come from previously published research, but all have been rewritten and updated in the form of essays.

I believe this essay collection brings together media studies and disability studies in a unique way. Given the surge in interest in both these areas, I would like students, researchers, and activists to find guidance from this book when pursuing their own interest in media and disability topics.

Here's an overview of what each chapter addresses: Chapter 1 looks at the surge of disability-related Internet content in the last several years. I see this growth as an empowering event for the disability community. No longer must people with disabilities put up with only the mainstream media defining their issues. Through blogs, Facebook, YouTube, etc., disability activists have a forum in which to make their arguments and discuss their issues for all the world to see. As traditional news media face a crisis of their own, disability activists can seize this opportunity to control the message and even drive the conversation about disability issues.

Chapter 2 explains the research methods I used in several of these studies and provides some guidance for those readers who want to do their own research on media images of disability. I walk readers through the process of conducting both a quantitative and qualitative content analysis of news media content.[12] It is my hope that this book of essays will not only enlighten its readers but encourage others to begin their own media and disability research projects.

Chapter 3 addresses the changing language about disability as reflected in the news.[13] Language has been a site of contention since the beginning of the modern disability rights initiatives, and many in the news media have never understood the importance of empowering language versus stigmatizing word choices. But through lobbying efforts, many in the disability community have been successful in changing the language local, state, and federal governments use when referring to disabilities. In some cases, that has helped educate the news media.

In Chapter 4, I look at how the U.S. news media have covered one of the most important issues for disability rights activists – assisted suicide.[14] An overarching theme has long been imbedded in much of American media coverage – that a human being is better off dead than living life as a disabled person. The media coverage of the high-profile Jack Kevorkian assisted suicides and the advent of the Oregon assisted suicide law are explored in this chapter.

Chapter 5 investigates one of the most covered disabilities in today's media environment: autism. This chapter is based on a case study[15] at a point when the news media was beginning to take notice of autism in educational settings and in society in general. A high-profile case in Virginia pushed the topic of inclusive education to national media attention in the mid-1990s. Beginning in 1995, *Hartmann v. Loudoun County Board of Education* tested whether or not schools must include severely disabled children in regular classrooms. Because of their three-year legal battle in Northern Virginia, the Hartmann family and the inclusion movement became almost synonymous. Mark Hartmann, who is autistic,[16] became a symbol in a national debate over whether, and how often, disabled youngsters should be educated alongside their non-disabled peers.[17] Using a narrative analysis, this chapter investigates the variety of arguments for and against inclusive education that made it into media coverage.

In Chapter 6, I look at the vibrant media by and for people with disabilities.[18] This study grew partially out of a comprehensive exam question for my Ph.D., in which I was asked to research how disability media fit within the journalism traditions of the alternative press and the ethnic press in the U.S.. After answering that question, I had an excellent literature review, and a few years later, it served me well when I began working as a consultant for the editors of *Mainstream* magazine, Cyndi Jones and Bill Stothers, who received a federal grant to create the Center for an Accessible Society, which tried to focus public and media attention on disability and independent living issues. I conducted several research projects for them and one looked at disability media and their coverage of their community. Many of the issues that the disability media cover are central to the disability rights movement and are often ignored by the mainstream news media.

Chapter 7 investigates the "pity party" that is the Jerry Lewis Telethon.[19] This chapter grew originally from a paper I wrote for a communication studies class during my Ph.D. program, in which I did a textual analysis of the 1992 Muscular Dystrophy Association Telethon. Through my ongoing immersion in reading about disability rights issues, I became aware of the controversy and protests surrounding the annual Labor Day fundraising event for the Muscular Dystrophy Association. Disability rights activists have long been trying to show society the hurtful stereotypes that telethons perpetuate. In 1981, Evan Kemp, a disability rights activist who served as EEOC chairman under President George H. W. Bush, explained that society views disabled people as "childlike, helpless, hopeless, nonfunctioning and noncontributing members of society, and the Jerry Lewis Muscular Dystrophy Association Telethon with its pity approach to fund raising, has contributed to these prejudices." Kemp adamantly stated that "the very human desire for cures . . . can never justify a television show that reinforces a stigma against disabled people."[20] In my study of the telethon, I teased out several claims made within the telethon's discourse about people with disabilities: that disability is intrinsic to the body itself – it is a physical attribute that turns into a social category; that the audience is "a threatened family" who must put its fear of affliction to work to help others; that Jerry Lewis – virtually equated with the telethon – serves as an oddball parent-child through intertextual relations to his career as a film star/comedian.

Chapter 8 illustrates how much better TV representations of people with disabilities have become. Thanks to cartooning work of John Callahan, who is quadriplegic, a cable network aimed at children took a chance on a show that featured a kid who used a wheelchair, "Pelswick," in 2000. This chapter argues that Callahan's more subtle approach to disability issues in the cartoon series had persuasive power with its young audience because Pelswick's portrayal comes across as a smart, cool 8th grader who gets into the usual scrapes with his friends. "Pelswick" both normalized and demystified the disability experience for its audience. The show focused on Pelswick's interactions with others and the world around him, not his disability. Through this revolutionary new portrayal, the cartoon ushered in a new phase of disability humor, one that focuses on normalcy, equality, and "bold honesty."[21]

Building off of this improvement in disability representations, Chapter 9 looks at the recent media advocacy surrounding film images. I call this the "Million Dollar Baby" effect, because I think this film's content ramped up disability rights protests of film portrayals of disability. In addition, the disability activists were taking on a critically acclaimed film and one that subsequently won four Academy Awards, including Best Picture. The protests also dovetailed with existing advocacy by groups like Not Dead Yet against assisted suicide, which was a prominent aspect of "Million Dollar Baby." Not Dead Yet said the film "promotes the killing of disabled people as the solution to the 'problem' of disability." Although primarily a movie about a female boxer trying to achieve her dream of a boxing title, it features an important plot point in which one character assists another to die after that person becomes quadriplegic. "It's a pro-euthanasia movie," according to Not Dead Yet. "But they don't want you to go in expecting that to be the main message. But it's the romanticized killing at the end that makes the movie 'great' for most of the critics."[22] It was these protests that acted as the catalyst for the subsequent media activism against "Tropic Thunder" in 2008 and the current R-word campaign nationwide to convince Americans to drop the word "retarded" from their vocabulary.

One form of media has long had an influential and persuasive place in American society – advertising. In Chapter 10, I explore the idea that advertising has actually moved disability images forward. Because advertising's goal is making money, it doesn't want to offend people. And because of U.S. truth in advertising laws, it can't "fake" disability and has to hire disabled models, actors, and athletes for its campaigns. This chapter discusses some improvements that have occurred in advertising images of disability, such as the themes of empowerment (Cingular ad campaign) and the themes of disability pride and inclusion (Doritos ad campaign). But the chapter also looks at several ad campaigns that still embrace antiquated themes that stigmatize disabled people, such as campaigns for Nuveen and Bank of America.[23]

As a writer, I wanted these essays to be extracted from an academic format and the sometimes convoluted academic jargon found in that format to be transformed into a more readable style that would be accessible to students in undergraduate and graduate college classes in media studies or disability studies, as well as scholars in those fields. I hope this book also will be of interest to disability rights activists, who have a growing interest in media advocacy.

Notes

1. In following the style from Deaf Studies, I use "big D" Deaf to refer to people who are part of Deaf culture, and "little d" deaf refers to people who have the condition of deafness. See Carol Padden and Tom Humphries, *Inside Deaf Culture.* Cambridge: Harvard University Press, 2005.

2. A. Gartner and T. Joe, *Images of the Disabled, Disabling Images.* N.Y.: Praeger, 1987.

3. Erving Goffman, *Stigma, Notes on the Management of Spoiled Identity.* Englewood Cliffs, N.J: Prentice-Hall, 1963.

4. Claire H. Liachowitz, *Disability as a Social Construct: Legislative Roots.* Philadelphia: University of Pennsylvania Press, 1988.

5. Simi Litvak, "Disability studies vs. Disability Policy Studies," *Disability Studies Quarterly,* 1994, 14:2.

6. Lennard Davis, "J'accuse!: Cultural imperialism – Ableist style," *Social Alternatives,* 1999, 18, pp. 36-41,; Simi Linton, *Claiming Disability: Knowledge and Identity.* N.Y.: NYU Press, 1998; and T. Hehir, "Eliminating Ableism in Education," *Harvard Educational Review,* 2002, 72:1, pp. 1-32.

7. Joy Weeber, "What could I know of racism?" *Journal of Counseling & Development,* 1999, 77, pp. 20-24. P. 21.

8. Marilynn J. Phillips, "Damaged goods: The oral narratives of the experience of disability in American culture," *Social Science & Medicine*, 1990, 30, pp. 849-857. P. 850.

9. Not Dead Yet, "Not Dead Yet! Disabled civil rights activists protest assisted suicide epidemic," notdeadyet.org/ablism.html, May 12, 1997.

10. Denis McQuail, *Mass Communication Theory*. London: Sage, 1989, p. 178.

11. Pamela J. Shoemaker. and Stephen D. Reese, *Mediating the Message, Theories of influences on mass media content*. N.Y.: Longman, 1996, p. 28.

12. Beth Haller and Sue Ralph, "Content analysis methodology for studying news and disability: Case studies from the United States and England," *Research in Social Science and Disability*, 2001, 2.

13. Beth Haller, Bruce Dorries and J. Rahn, "Media labeling versus the U.S. disability community identity: A study of shifting cultural language," *Disability & Society*, Jan. 2006, 21:1.

14. Beth Haller and Ralph, Sue "Not Worth Keeping Alive? News Framing of Physician-assisted suicide in the United States and Great Britain," *Journalism Studies*, 2001, 2:3.

15. Beth Haller and Bruce Dorries, "The News of Inclusive Education: A Narrative Analysis," *Disability & Society*, 2001, 16:6.

16. I use the term "autistic" because it is the preferred term of the autistic rights movement.

17. Debbi Wilgoren and Peter Pae, "As Loudoun goes, so may other schools," *The Washington Post*, Aug. 28, 1994, p. B1.

18. Beth Haller, "Content & Character: Disability Publications in the 1990s," *Journal of Magazine & New Media Research*, Spring 2000, 1:3.

19. Beth Haller, "The misfit and muscular dystrophy," *Journal of Popular Film and Television*, 1994, 21:4, pp. 142-149.

20. Mary Johnson, "A Test of Wills: Jerry Lewis, Jerry's Orphans, and the Telethon," *The Disability Rag*, 1992, raggededgemagazine.com/archive/jerry92.htm.

21. Beth Haller and Sue Ralph, "John Callahan's Pelswick Cartoon and a New Phase of Disability Humor," *Disability Studies Quarterly*, 2003, 23:4.

22. Not Dead Yet, Press Release, January 14, 2005, notdeadyet.org/docs/bigotpr.html.

23. Beth Haller and Sue Ralph, "Are disability images in advertising becoming bold and daring? An analysis of prominent themes in U.S. and UK campaigns," *Disability Studies Quarterly*, Spring 2006, 26:3.

1.

The changing landscape of disability 'news'

Blogging and social media lead to
more diverse sources of information

With the advent of the Internet's new media – blogs, Facebook, YouTube, disability-specific social networking sites, and Twitter – disability information may finally get some of the attention it deserves. Using these resources, disabled people, their parents, and disability organizations are taking control of the information about disability available to the general public. Everyone can now have access to significant disability topics from a disability perspective. Disabled people are able to tell of their experiences themselves so anyone with an Internet connection can bypass traditional news sources and read about their issues directly. And sometimes the information from these disability Internet sources even filters into traditional news sources.

It's become increasingly clear that information distributed via the Internet is becoming *the* way that those in the world who have access to computers will be getting their information from now on. According to statistics from 2009, Facebook passed the 400 million user mark, Twitter use surged to 50 million tweets per day, people viewed 1 billion videos per day on YouTube, and there are 126 million blogs. Additional data show: "There are 1.73 billion Internet users worldwide as of September 2009. There are 1.4 billion e-mail users worldwide, and on average we collectively send 247 billion e-mails per day. (Unfortunately 200 billion of those are spam e-mails.) As of December 2009, there are 234 million websites. Facebook gets 260 billion pageviews per month, which equals 6 million page views per minute and 37.4 trillion pageviews in a year."[1]

Blogs

Blogs are a kind of participatory journalism,[2] and their growing use by all facets of society has changed the news, as well as what is being covered in the news. In the area of media and disability, past research has shown that the news only rarely covers the crucial topics significant to the disability community.[3] But through the many blogs begun by disability organizations, disability rights activists, and individuals with disabilities themselves, the landscape of news about disability topics has shifted to one in which people with disabilities have control over their presentation within Internet information sources.

The term "blogging" reportedly began in 1997, but this type of online diary, or just online musings on a variety of topics, was difficult to produce without content management software, according to a report about the history of blogging on Mashable, The Social Media Guide.[4] Blogging software like Blogger came onto the scene in 1999 and led to the growth of much more blogging.[5] By 2005, mainstream media had embraced blogging and podcasting, and 32 million Americans were reading blogs.[6] But many tech watchers predict that within the next decade blogging may disappear or not look like its current form. Microblogging programs like Twitter and social networking sites like Facebook allow people to create brief online diaries daily. And that brevity may be all that readers want.

But others say blogging won't die because it has always been wrapped up in social networking, even before the term existed. Evan Williams, co-founder of Blogger and head of Twitter, says stand-alone blogs still have use: "There are still many advantages to a stand-alone blog: Your own brand, domain, design, etc. Creating a meaningful, independent voice on web, on which can be launched a movement, a brand, a career, or simply a good story, is best done with a stand-alone blog." Social media analyst Charlene Li says, "If you think of blogging as a 'mindset,' then it's not only healthy, but growing by leaps and bounds. In this way, I distinguish between a corporate blog that does nothing more than publish their press releases (but has no comments) and a blog written from a personal perspective but clearly associated and benefiting a company. . . . In the end, blogging grew because people used it as a way to connect with people and develop relationships. If it 'evolves' into new formats, then it's staying healthy, rather than stagnating."[7]

For the disability community, blogs have a significant role in activism, so they may last longer than typical personal diaries or musings-style blogs. The disability studies program at Temple University set up a blogroll of all the disability related blogs it could find, which was last updated in May 2009.[8] At that time, more than 250 disability blogs were listed on the blogroll. An unscientific study of some of these blogs in March 2010 showed that about 70 percent of them had recent posts from the past weeks or months. So the disability community appears to be continuing to put its thoughts out into the blogosphere.

William Peace, who blogs as Bad Cripple, says he believes blogging by disability activists, disability studies scholars, and people with disabilities generally is an antidote to the history of bad media reporting about disability issues. "In the disability community, it is rich (and) diverse, with real first-rate scholars doing great work," he says.[9]

Peace notes the specialized nature of disability blogs. The range of blogs available covers a wide variety of disabilities, from autism (Autism Street[10]) to blindness (Planet of the Blind[11]) to epilepsy (E is for Epilepsy[12]) to amputation (Amputeehee[13]), and an even larger number of disability topics, from being a Deaf mother (A Deaf Mom Shares Her World[14]) to special education (SpeEd-Change[15]) to assisted suicide (Not Dead Yet[16]) to inclusive tourism (Rolling Rains Report[17]).

Peace, a wheelchair user, explains why he decided to blog on disability issues:

> My experience with mainstream media has been overwhelmingly negative. The message the mainstream media wants to present is you're either a hero or a lazy shit and there is no in between. You are either the hero, the supercrip image, who is going to put all those other lazy cripples to shame or you're a lazy bastard and everything is stacked against you and you're going to die or you have some horrific sob story. Any nuance is out of there and that's kind of why I keep that blog going . . . if somebody is doing research about a given subject matter – maybe immigration or the Ashley treatment – they may, if they do an Internet search, come across my blog. And I want to be an advocate and antithesis to what the mainstream media is presenting.[18]

Some disability organizations also see blogging as a crucial component of their advocacy efforts. The policy head of a British disability organization, Leonard Cheshire Disability, sees blogging as a significant information tool. He says, blogging is "a potent new way of both getting our messages out and giving beneficiaries a collective voice."[19] In the U.S., the largest disability organization in New York City, YAI Network, has a blog that lets everyone know about disability in the news and any connection between that news and the YAI Network.[20]

But even with organizations' blogging ventures, in the disability world blogging remains more of an individual pursuit. Robin, a Pennsylvanian with physical disabilities who is a wheelchair user with short-term memory loss, explains powerfully why she blogs:

> While I initially blogged because I wanted to validate my thoughts and ideas about a number of topics, I found that blogging could connect people of like mind and it gave me the opportunity to learn from others. I'm realizing that it also serves another purpose, one that was unexpected. Rereading my blogs helps to keep things current in my mind, it helps to ground me, being able to go back and refresh my memory about how events affected me, the things that have been important to me, and has helped me to analyze how I react to certain triggers or situations. . . . I've also recognized that what I've written is an all encompassing representation of who I am. . . . When people 'knock' blogging as a wasted exercise in self-absorption I wonder if they can imagine the many ways blogging can help the blogger and how many people find commonalities between themselves and others who've faced similar challenges, feel less alone, learn something that helps them on their journey through life?[21]

So blogging continues to offer a powerful way for many people with disabilities to connect with others and get their unique perspective on the world out to the larger society.

Facebook

The social networking site Facebook has emerged as more than just a way to keep up with "friends." It is now a major public relations and promotional tool for individuals, organizations, and events. In March 2010, the social media guide Mashable reported that PR professionals embrace Facebook and other social media, like Twitter, as a way to promote clients, answer questions, get the word out about events, and generally to communicate with others. Social media has become a requirement in the world of political communication as well. It gives politicians a way to be in daily touch with constituents about the issues they want to discuss. Mashable reports on a Missouri senator who is using social media to great effect:

> Claire McCaskill, the junior U.S. senator from Missouri, is one politician that has embraced social media in a big way. On Twitter, @clairecmc has nearly 37,000 followers – making her the second-most popular person in Congress, according to Tweetcongress.org. The senator also has a YouTube channel and a Tumblr blog that she uses to share information with her constituents and to respond to questions. Anamarie Rebori, a spokesperson for Senator McCaskill, told us that the senator actively uses social media. 'While it definitely has changed the way she gets the word out, McCaskill has said that if anything, she is glad she has the opportunity to bring a more personal touch to her communications and get outside the Washington bubble,' Rebori said. Especially for politicians, authenticity is an important part of PR. According to Rebori, McCaskill has been able to utilize social media to communicate authentically. 'People seem to respond best to an authentic touch over Twitter, and that's something that Senator McCaskill has been able to convey in her use of social media,' Rebori said. 'It's really her typing each of those tweets, and people can tell.'[22]

Facebook became the No. 1 social networking site in early 2009, when its 62.4 million users overtook the 60.6 million users who continued to use the social networking site MySpace.[23] Its growth continued to explode, especially among older people, with a 513 percent increase in the number of people 55 and older joining Facebook, as reported in July 2009.[24] By the time Facebook celebrated its sixth birthday in February 2010, it had 400 million users.[25] Tech watchers believe Facebook is here to stay because "it is becoming part of the infrastructure of the Web, every bit as indispensible to our daily wanderings as Google or e-mail. . . . Perhaps one day not long from now, everything on the Web will be a mere extension of Facebook."[26]

And this explosion of Facebook has included many people with disabilities. It is a way to organize disability-rights actions, let others know about disability related news, promote events, or just find like-minded disability rights advocates. It also has the advantage of mitigating some disabilities, like providing an easy communication system for people who are deaf or have speech disabilities. On the other hand, text-heavy social networking sites that require being computer savvy might create barriers for people with intellectual disabilities, serious learning disabilities, or those who have visual impairments (because Facebook pages are uniform templates that make them difficult to manipulate with screen readers). But because Facebook has become ubiquitous, an Auburn student used a Facebook page to petition Facebook to make itself more accessible. With more than 2,500 members, the site states its case: "While the new Facebook may look pretty to some, Facebook has repeatedly ignored accessibility. For the growing number of people with visual impairments as well as learning disabilities using screen readers, screen magnification software, or any other adaptive software or hardware, many parts of Facebook are unusable or horrendous looking. It is time for Facebook to take a stand and make its website useable for all. Please invite all your friends to this group to show your support for this cause."[27]

But even with those potential barriers, Facebook is being embraced by the disability community for a variety of reasons. In September 2009, the disability magazine *New Mobility* published an article about why Facebook matters to the disability community. The author of the article, Jean Dobbs, explains the power of Facebook for people with disabilities:

> Today, the operative verb is 'friend.' In the parlance of Facebook, millions of people friend each other every day – and the more connections made, the fewer degrees of separation between everyone who participates. Under his or her real name, each Facebook user shares life updates with an average of 120 friends, and many exceed that number by hundreds or, in some cases, thousands. What does all this mean for people with disabilities? A lot: Every connection represents an opportunity to break stereotypes, exchange support, and reduce isolation. Facebook also offers a free method of publicizing helpful disability organizations, books, products – and the people behind them. Advocates view it as a powerful tool for social change. Throw in the fact that it's just plain fun, and suddenly you have a lively, integrated community that's been hard to achieve in the physical world.[28]

In addition to allowing people with disabilities to show all their Facebook friends that they are living life to the fullest, they are using it for marketing and discussion of disability issues. Many disabled authors use Facebook to promote their latest book. Author and blogger Gary Presley talks about his memoir, his blog posts, and other freelance writings on Facebook. "As author of *Seven Wheelchairs: A Life beyond Polio* and a frequent blogger, Presley, 67, reveals in discreet increments his unique point of view. 'For me, the personal is professional,' he explains in New Mobility. 'I reveal personal elements in order to speak out about what it means to be a person with a disability in the world. As to the ultimately personal, I never post anything I would not say in public.'"[29]

Many in the disability world from Quickie wheelchairs to *New Mobility* magazine to the Disabilities Network of NYC (DNNYC) have Facebook pages to promote themselves, as well as to give their "fans" information about what they are up to. DNNYC posted this on their Facebook wall March 25, 2010: "Disabilities Network of NYC will be out of the office Thursday and Friday. Headed to Albany to help formulate the New York State Plan for Independent Living, 2011-2013. What would YOU include?"[30]

And Facebook is way to promote disability events to a larger audience:

> The best commercial use of Facebook may be event marketing. Tucson, Ariz., artist Carolyn Stanley Anderson and her colleagues recently drew 250 people to a gallery show, using social networking alone. And she says her Facebook page has been invaluable in promoting her work. 'Part of my art is my story,' says Anderson, 35 and a T12-L1 para. 'If people see my art and they know about my story, it changes how they view my art. For that to happen someone has to meet me and kind of get to know me, and I think Facebook allows that to happen' because interested people can learn about her accident, her role as a mom, and see her story unfold online in real time. Taking the PR potential to its logical conclusion, Anderson thinks Facebook offers the whole disability community a chance to be seen more clearly by the larger culture. 'It allows a visibility that could have tremendous effects in terms of raising the status of people with disabilities,' she says. 'It makes us visible in a way that wasn't available before.'[31]

The *New Mobility* article's larger argument about Facebook is that it can become a way to lessen the social isolation of disabled people. "Those of us who do not drive or who live in relatively small towns or cities find ourselves in a community," Gary Presley, who lives in Springfield, Mo., tells *New Mobility.* And disability activist Laura Hershey explains how it allows for ongoing connections between disability rights advocates from around the world. Hershey, who has spinal muscular atrophy, says "it's not so much about meeting new people as staying connected with longtime fellow advocates: 'When you see people once or twice a year, or even less often, it's hard to keep up with them. Facebook lets us stay in contact, even see each other's photos of home, families, local actions, travels, etc. I find that really fun.'"

Those who study the use of social networking in people's lives have also noticed the benefits of this phenomenon to people who have disabilities or chronic illnesses. In a March 2010 study, the Pew Internet and American Life Project noted this fact. *The New York Times* reported:

> For many people, social networks are a place for idle chatter about what they made for dinner or sharing cute pictures of their pets. But for people living with chronic diseases or disabilities, they play a more vital role. 'It's really literally saved my life, just to be able to connect with other people,' said Sean Fogerty, 50, who has multiple sclerosis, is recovering from brain cancer and spends an hour and a half each night talking with other patients online. People fighting chronic illnesses are less likely than others to have Internet access, but once online they are more likely to blog or participate in online discussions about health problems, according to a report released March 24, 2010 by the Pew Internet and American Life Project and the California HealthCare Foundation.[32]

So Facebook and other social networking sites may become a means by which attitudes toward and interactions with people with disabilities become revolutionized, not just in America, but worldwide.

Disability-specific social networking sites

In addition to the global phenomenon of Facebook, there are a number of disability-specific social networking sites. Denver-based Disaboom, begun in 2007, has the highest profile of this category of sites. The idea of J. Glen House, a doctor who is a quadriplegic, its mission is four-fold – "providing disabled people with contact with their peers for advice and information; harnessing the power of the disability community; including loved ones and people who work in the disability field in the conversation; and allowing people with disabilities to live their lives to their fullest."[33]

Disaboom is a savvy and well-funded venture in terms of marketing and advertising. Its launch was covered by *The New York Times*. Early advertisers on the site were Netflix, Johnson & Johnson, Avis, and Ford Motors. In 2010, advertisers included companies like Intel and GM, vacation spots like the Florida Keys, and the university Shepherds College. According to *The New York Times*, "Disaboom paid DATA Inc., a computer design firm based in Denver, $280,000 to design the site. At the end of June (2007), the company listed $2.2 million in cash." Disaboom also acquired lovebyrd.com, a dating Web site for people with disabilities, and developed a DisaboomJobs site.[34] CNN Money, which profiled the Disaboom founder in September 2008, reported that Disaboom began with experienced financial leadership with J.W. Roth, one of the founders of biotech firm AspenBio and a friend and neighbor of Dr. House, serving as CEO. Roth quickly raised $15 million in funding and targeted major advertisers like Ford and T-Mobile. By April 2008, Disaboom had $1 million in ad sales. By fall of 2008, Disaboom reported it had 72,000 registered users.[35] (The CEO of Disaboom in March 2010 is John Walpuck, former CFO and senior vice president of Nine Systems.)

Andrew J. Imparato, president of the American Association of People With Disabilities (AAPD), which has 180,000 members, saw the benefit of Disaboom early on. Disaboom sponsored a mentoring event for AAPD in an effort to sign up its members, and AAPD hoped that, through Disaboom, disabled people unfamiliar with AAPD would learn about it. Imparato told *The New York Times*, "Disaboom could serve as an important clearinghouse for people with disabilities, organizing them to make their voice resound more clearly with business and government. The disability community to a large degree is trying to get more visibility as a desirable constituency, whether you're talking about customers with money in their pockets, or a talent pool to hire from, or voters. To a large degree, we feel like we're invisible as a market and a political constituency," Imparato said.

By December 2007, Disaboom reported 1 million visitors to the site that month. The site established itself as a place where people with disabilities and their families and friends could find connection with each other. Disaboom founder Dr. House gave an example of these connections to *Advertising Age*: "'I got an e-mail from someone saying, "I have a son who was born without legs. He's 2 years old and on his third set of prostheses, and he's not walking. We've been told he shouldn't get physical therapy,"' Dr. House said. 'Well, that's absolutely wrong! He should be walking by 10 months like any other kid!' He contacted Disaboom's pediatric expert, who found the mom a better clinic for her son. He also directed her to up-to-date information on her son's condition since it sounded like she wasn't getting that from her doctor. Best of all, though, now that she's on the site, she'll be able to find other moms with kids like hers. Moms of kids dealing with other disabilities can chime in. And as the kids grow up, they'll be chatting with each other on Disaboom too."[36]

Another subset of disability social networking sites focus on specific conditions or disabilities. For example, WrongPlanet.net was begun by a young man with Asperger's syndrome, Alex Plank, when he was 17. The site now has registered users from around the world. In an interview in *Northern Virginia* magazine, Plank explained why he started WrongPlanet.net: "At the time, there were no resources that met my needs with a positive message of where people like me fit in the world. I wanted there to be a positive environment to help [those with AS] better understand themselves." Plank, who studied film at George Mason University, says his advice to those newly diagnosed on the autistic spectrum is "get online, and read other people's stories. It's also a good place to make friends."[37]

Other online sites focus on disability groups like military veteran amputees. Two companies announced in November 2009 that they would offer peer support to disabled veterans in a virtual world. ADL Company Inc. (ADL) and Virtual Ability, Inc. (VAI) are being funded by the Telemedicine and Advanced Technology Research Center (TATRC) of the US Army Medical Research and Materiel Command (USAMRMC). "For individuals with disabilities, virtual worlds are a powerful way to connect with others, to access peer support, and to participate in activities that might not otherwise be possible," said Alice Krueger, President of Virtual Ability, Inc., a not-for-profit corporation, in a Business Wire release. "This project will establish the best way to adopt this technology for the unique needs of the military amputee community."

The project is called the Amputee Virtual Environment Support Space (AVESS). "Individuals come into virtual environments as a way to connect with others who have disabilities," said Krueger, whose group has developed an award-winning support environment in Second Life® for individuals with disabilities. "What they discover is that you don't just find a community, you find a place where you can express yourself and feel like you have a shared space. It's powerful. Virtual worlds offer an immediacy and a sense of presence that a Web site can't offer. Amputees have been shown to respond positively to viewing themselves as an avatar in a three-dimensional environment."[38]

And some newer sites are trying for a completely different take on disability. Alexander Kaminsky, who reports that he has bipolar and obsessive compulsive disorder, said he began the Many Worlds Network as a way to empower himself and others:

> I realized in order to empower myself, I must own my diagnosis and become an advocate for what I experienced in my world. I then began cultivating friendships with people in the disability community, solidifying myself as a leader. I no longer wanted to talk about my story, I wanted to explore all worlds beyond what I experienced to learn of the similarities and differences. Thus, I created the Many Worlds Interpretation of Disability to create an architecture for exploring worlds of disability rather than stigmatizing terminology that scares people away from this fascinating landscape. The theory is derived from the Quantum Mechanics theory of the Many Worlds Interpretation. An infinite amount of worlds exist outside our perception, and each is as vital as the next with its own history and experiences. The challenge is to explore these worlds. The only way to do this is through the inhabitants. I thus devised an imaginative framework for a community and network with the Many Worlds Interpretation of Disability as a conduit to the many worlds that exist in all realms of life, disabled or not. I wanted to document and harness the energy of a disability rights movement I saw taking shape through the relationships I was building in the Disability Community.[39]

Kaminsky says he is marrying the social networking revolution to the disability rights movement as a way to create compelling media, video, and community. "With all these conversations from many worlds taking place in one forum, powerful change will be possible," he says.[40]

All kinds of social networking sites about disability allow disabled people to

11

find information and support. As the 2010 Pew study reports, "the sites are used to share information from the front lines (of disability)." Lily Vadakin, 45, who has multiple sclerosis and is the site administrator for Disaboom, told *The New York Times* that "she has discussed with other patients how to combat fatigue by working at home and taking vitamin supplements. 'That's what the community can give you – a real-life perspective.'"[41]

Twitter

Although created in 2006, Twitter really exploded as an information source in 2009. In 2008, 6 percent of U.S. adults used Twitter and in early 2009 that grew to 12 percent of U.S. adults.[42] It was growing by 2,565 percent in early 2009.[43] The social-networking microblogging site is used for everything from personal comments about a TV show someone is watching in real time to public relations for a company or organization to round-the-clock news feeds from major news organizations like CNN, the BBC, or *The New York Times*.

To disability organizations and disability advocates, it has been growing more useful by the minute. The deaf community, especially, has found it to be an accessible communication tool. The Academy Award-winning deaf actress Marlee Matlin is a prominent user of Twitter, with dozens of tweets per day and almost 40,000 followers (as of March 2010). She says she uses it to promote charities she's involved with and especially to push the issue of captioning on the Internet. She began using Twitter, she said, "because in Twitter there were no barriers. You don't have to know how to sign to understand what I'm saying here on Twitter." In addition, Matlin says that Twitter allows her to follow a wide range of disability issues, as well as news about topics that interest her: "It has given me more insight in all the wonderful people who support important causes that I support. (In 2010) hopefully we'll be able to harness the technology like this wonderful stuff with Twitter to make the world EQUAL for all."[44]

In Matlin's work supporting online captioning (she is the spokesperson on the topic for the National Association of the Deaf), she regularly tweets about it to keep the issue alive. In October 2009, when Netflix released a free download of "The Wizard of Oz" without captions, Matlin told her followers as well as the news media about the issue:

> @hulu has captioned more TV shows/movies than anyone else. Kudos for staying on top of it.

@andersoncooper just an FYI. CNN on Demand covers the Helen Keller statue unveiling LIVE and it's not accessible because no closed captions.

The point is that EVERYTHING is moving to Internet & all technology is in place to get it. But access for EVERYONE goes out the window. Why?

20 years ago I fought the fight for captions. And the law was passed 17 yrs ago. Now Im forced to begin again. I'm screaming NOW not later.

More offenders for lack of captions. TIVO on demand. I love TIVO but if I cant watch a movie that EVERYONE else can whats the point?!

They have technology for HD, surround sound, movies on demand . . . and little words that give equal access is beyond them? What the Bleep!?

And Blockbuster on Demand, @Netflix. say "We don't have the technology yet" Or is it "We don't have the commitment to equal access"?

And CNN on Demand. A story about unveiling of the Helen Keller statue in Wash DC. Wanna guess? NOT captioned. And it's about Helen Keller!!

Breaking it down. iTunes. Says they offer captions. But hardly a movie or TV show that's been captioned on TV is captioned on iTunes. Why?

So I just got an eyeful of info. So here's my question. iTunes, Netflix, Blockbuster, CNN on Demand, Hulu. Where are your closed captions?[45]

Tech experts speculate that Twitter is such a revolutionary application that it will become part of the architecture of the Internet, not a passing fad. "The history of the Internet suggests that there have been cool Web sites that go in and out of fashion and then there have been open standards that become plumbing," said Steven Johnson, the author and technology observer who wrote a seminal piece about Twitter for *Time* in June 2009. "Twitter is looking more and more like plumbing, and plumbing is eternal."[46] David Carr, writing in *The New York Times*, says he's come to understand the significance of Twitter: "the real value of the service is listening to a wired collective voice. The service has obvious utility for a journalist, but no matter what business you are in, imagine knowing what the thought leaders in your industry were reading and considering. And beyond following specific individuals, Twitter hash tags allow you to go deep into interests and obsession: #rollerderby, #physics, #puppets #Avatar, to name just a few of many thousands."[47]

Clay Shirky, who wrote *Here Comes Everybody*, a book about social media, explains: "Anything that is useful to both dissidents in Iran and Martha Stewart has a lot going for it; Twitter has more raw capability for users than anything since e-mail. It will be hard to wait out Twitter because it is lightweight, endlessly useful and gets better as more people use it. Brands are using it, institutions are using it, and it is becoming a place where a lot of important conversations are being held."[48] And many of those important conversations are about disability and disability issues.

The mainstream media has taken notice of this phenomenon. The *Star-News* in Wilmington, N.C., wrote about the addition of computer access for social media at an assisted living center. The story interviewed 69-year-old Edsel Odom, who had two strokes in 2003 and uses a wheelchair and clicks a mouse with his thumb. "To type, he uses an infrared device mounted on a baseball cap. Odom uses all types of social media, including Facebook, Twitter and MySpace, and blogs. 'Of all the tools available, I enjoy MySpace the most. You really get a chance to know people there as opposed to the glimpse you get from looking at Facebook,' he said. Social media is about more than just family and friends for Odom. 'I want to share my message with the world!' he said."[49]

Disability organizations and individual disability advocates are using Twitter to get their issues out. Deaf News Today, a blog that collects news and information about the deaf community worldwide, tweets all of its blog posts. As Marlee Matlin mentioned, Twitter is especially accessible to the deaf community because no one need know sign language to get that community's comments about an issue.

There is a process on Twitter in which news and comments can be re-tweeted, and re-tweeting means that a disability topic can get the notice of not just disability topic followers but journalists, who are looking for sources, story ideas, or more information on a topic. Also, important topics receive a hash tag such as #captioning or #HCR (health care reform). After the earthquake in Haiti in January 2010, many tweets about it included #Haiti. Many on Twitter were interested in disability in Haiti, the conditions for the growing number of amputees there, or for those who wanted to donate to groups specifically helping disabled people in Haiti – so they just looked for the Haiti hash tag or searched for "Haiti and disability." One specific helping organization, Portlight Strategies, which serves the disability community in Haiti, gained a profile on Twitter so the Twitterverse knew of a specific organization that aids people with disabilities in Haiti. This was significant because the number of disabled people, especially amputees, has increased by the thousands since the earthquake.[50]

A Minneapolis journalist explains how he uses Twitter in his work. Jason DeRusha, a reporter at WCCO-TV in Minneapolis, uses Twitter daily. He began using it in 2007, after the 35W bridge collapse there. He puts questions on Twitter at the beginning of each day and then his 2,000+ followers give him story angles or just their opinions. For DeRusha, "rather than interviewing random people on the street, he's able to get more targeted feedback from people with relevant life experience. DeRusha's first Twitter success story was in late 2007. He was doing a story on December sniffles caused by allergies to Christmas trees. He used Twitter to find someone who was allergic to Christmas trees, who has to use heavy protective gloves to decorate theirs. He said he would never have found this source without Twitter."[51]

If a journalist is trying to find people connected to specific disabilities, Twitter can aid in that search. For example, Pamela Wilson of Seattle, Wash., tweets as DownSynAdvocacy, so if someone wanted to find information connected to Down syndrome, she would be a person to follow. She is the mother of a son with Down syndrome and diabetes who writes for a Web site about children with special needs.[52]

YouTube

YouTube began April 23, 2005, and started an online revolution by allowing "the little guy" to have control over video creation.[53] No longer was video content a one-way communication delivered only by broadcast stations or cable outlets. Everyone with a digital camera with video capabilities or a digital video camera could make their own videos that could be seen by the world. And with the advent of Facebook and Twitter video applications, the ease of posting video online became as simple as sending an email.

Many disability organizations and disability activists have used YouTube to get their messages out, to post PSAs or to put mini-documentaries online. When disability activists protested Jerry Lewis receiving the humanitarian Academy Award in 2009, an assortment of videos about the protests appeared on YouTube. These videos were created by the protesters, the news media, and independent bloggers. The open nature of YouTube allows for lots of comments about the videos from anyone. For disability activists, this can be an eye-opening experience because many comments take issue with the disability perspective. When entertainment blogger Zennie 62 did a video report about "The Trouble with Jerry" protest, many of the commenters felt the disability protesters were ungrateful: "How ingrateful can one get. Jerry Lewis raised millions so people with a disability can lead productive, normal lives. The money that has been raised also helps these people to survive, it goes to organizations that pay for medical bills, help them to appointments, as well as ADLs [activities of daily living]. Completely in grateful, and unappreciative," wrote rn2000abc. Other like-minded commenters felt Jerry Lewis deserved praise, not protest, and some of the 352 commenters called Lewis "a saint."[54] But some of the disability protesters made their own videos to post to YouTube, like the "Cure Jerry Lewis" video that interviewed Texas disability activist Sarah Watkins.[55]

YouTube videos can be an important way to get the disability rights message out, but it's a hit-or-miss method – a hit if a good disability rights video "goes viral" and a miss if it receives few page views. The entertainment blogger's video about the protest received 12,665 views, whereas the "Cure Jerry Lewis" video received 1,242. Researchers and the advertising world are still trying to understand why one video draws more views than others and why some become international sensations, known as "going viral." The Washington Post wrote in 2009, "four years after the dawn of YouTube and other online video-sharing forums, the question of which of the legions of videos uploaded daily around the planet will become, however briefly, an object of human fascination, is as mysterious as why any two people fall in love. It's also a question increasingly studied as everyone from advertising executives to politicians, and even teenagers in their parents' basements, all try to go viral."[56]

Many disability organizations aren't aiming at "going viral" but are just using YouTube to get their message out in a more visual way. So the American Association of People with Disabilities (AAPD) posts its PSA that appeared in Times Square, and the San Diego-based What's Next? Mentoring Program for young people with disabilities creates an 8-minute video that highlights its successes and goals.[57] And many organizations use YouTube to archive disability issues that make it into the news or entertainment programming such as when "Saturday Night Live" made fun of New York's blind governor David Paterson or when "Family Guy" featured a character with Down syndrome, which drew the ire of Republican VP candidate Sarah Palin but was applauded by most disability activists.

Many people interested in disability issues post videos on issues internationally, which allows everyone to gain access to information rarely covered in the mainstream news media. Len Davis posted a short documentary on disability in Nepal and the stigma that exists there. Called "Challenging the Cultural Stigma of Disability in Nepal," it was created for the Seattle Channel about a Seattle non-profit, The Rose International Fund for Children, which, in addition to assisting people with disabilities in Nepal, helped the Nepalese start an anti-stigma campaign there.[58] Or YouTube videos introduce the world to the British punk band Heavy Load, some of whose members have disabilities. As the band's drummer with Down syndrome says, "We would like to shock the whole world."[59] A documentary about Heavy Load is underway and YouTube gives the filmmakers and the band a way to create buzz.

Other disability documentaries are being released in their entirety on YouTube. "Alicia, Living with Brain Injury" was released as 14 segments on YouTube in August 2009 so everyone around the world has access to this 52-minute documentary by an Australian company, Stella Motion Pictures. Here's how the filmmakers describe "Alicia": "Seven years ago, Alicia was seriously injured in a car accident. It was her brain rather than her body which suffered and this is the story of her long journey of recovery. Through Beth, the main character from Sam Shepard's play *A Lie of the Mind*, Alicia is able to express the common experiences of brain injury, her alienation from society for being different and her lack of inhibitions. Flashbacks, video diary, interviews told with extraordinary honesty by her family, friends, medical practitioners and theatre colleagues; all contribute to unmask the many faces of Alicia."[60]

An older documentary from 1999, "Enable: People with disabilities and computers," which was originally distributed on VHS, found its way to YouTube in 2006. Now anyone has access to the documentary in six short video segments. And the Disability Rights and Education Defense Fund (DREDF) created an award-winning 18-minute documentary about Section 504 protests called "The Power of 504." The documentary "captures the drama and emotions of the historic civil rights demonstration of people with disabilities in 1977, resulting in the signing of the 504 Regulations, the first Federal Civil Rights Law protecting people with disabilities."[61] It's a significant document of U.S. disability history now available worldwide via YouTube.

Disabled individuals can also get their perspectives out via YouTube videos. Amanda Baggs, a non-verbal person with autism, created a series of YouTube videos in 2007 to explain her life with autism and what she considers communication and language. Her statement about herself with the "In My Language" video says, "The first part is in my 'native language,' and then the second part provides a translation, or at least an explanation. This is not a look-at-the-autie gawking freakshow as much as it is a statement about what gets considered thought, intelligence, personhood, language, and communication, and what does not."[62] The video has been used in disability studies classes around the world and in 2010, almost 900,000 people had viewed the video. People who work with those with autism saw it as a way to encourage autistic people to find their own unique means of expression, as evidenced by a commenter on the video: "Thank you so much for making this video. I work with youth that have a range of disabilities, some verbal but still their communication style is often overlooked. I am going to share this with my students and encourage them to make and post their own videos."[63]

YouTube has been a vibrant place for members of the deaf community as well. Because it is all video, deaf people can post their own videos in sign language for other deaf people to enjoy. For instance, a deaf arts group in Michigan has harnessed the video capabilities of the Internet as a way to show many of the creative endeavors of the deaf community. D-PAN: Deaf Professional Arts Network, begun in 2007, states its goal as:

> promoting professional development and access to the entertainment, visual and media arts fields for individuals who are deaf or hard of hearing (and) creating top-quality ASL-centric music videos, making music and music culture more accessible than ever to millions of individuals worldwide who had traditionally been excluded from participation. With the help of talented deaf and hard of hearing performers and technicians along with the countless individuals who have offered their encouragement and support, we showed that it could be done.[64]

So YouTube showed itself to be a powerful medium for deaf people who want to communicate with each other. But until early 2010, much YouTube content was mostly without captions so deaf people were blocked from much of the content that required hearing.

18

However, all that was changed in late 2009 by Ken Harrenstien, a deaf engineer at Google (which owns YouTube) who created a mechanism to easily allow captions to be automatically added to YouTube videos. The move allowed the deaf community as well as non-English speakers[65] to have better access to online video. Harrenstien explained in *The New York Times:*

> A vast majority of clips on YouTube did not have captions and the new Google technology would generate them automatically. YouTube is initially applying the captioning technology only to a few channels, most of them specializing in educational content. They include channels from universities like Stanford, Yale, Duke, Columbia and the Massachusetts Institute of Technology, PBS and National Geographic, and Google itself – its corporate videos will be captioned. The company plans to gradually expand the number of channels that work with the automatic captioning technology. 'Because the tools are not perfect, we want to make sure that we get feedback from the video owners and the viewers before we roll it out for the whole world. Sometimes the auto-captions are good. Sometimes they are not great, but they are better than nothing if you are hearing-impaired or don't know the language.'[66]

Harrenstien says he has long dreamed of a captioned YouTube: "To see it happen is amazing."[67]

The captioning of YouTube will open the door to many opportunities for the deaf community's use of it, as evidenced by deaf actress Marlee Matlin's launch of a Web series, "My Deaf Family," on YouTube March 30, 2010. The Academy Award-winner developed a reality show focused on a CODA (Children of Deaf Adults) family.[68] She wants the show to be similar to the popular "Little People, Big World" on TLC (The Learning Channel). Because the broadcast and cable networks didn't pick up her show, she decided to release the show in short webisodes on YouTube now that it can guarantee the webisodes will be captioned.[69] Matlin says she hopes that if the series[70] is popular on YouTube with thousands of page views, it will entice a network to run it.

Conclusions

Technology has always had both positive and negative ramifications for the disability community. In the case of new technology for medical equipment and communication, technology can be positive. The iTouch from Apple is being used as a less-expensive augmentative communication device for some non-verbal disabled children. A portable media player with Wi-Fi but not cellular capacity like an iPhone, it uses a touch screen so a child with a disability can touch pre-set icons for words and phrases to "speak." A New York 12-year-old with Fragile X syndrome began to easily express his thoughts using an iTouch and was able to have conversations with the 7,000 words and terms available to him with the device.[71]

Even technology that threw up barriers at first has adapted to a variety of disabilities. When cell phones became a necessity for most Americans, they were very helpful to wheelchair users but not the deaf community. Wheelchair users could feel less trapped when confronting architectural barriers because they could call for help. Although initially cell phones seemed useless for the deaf community, the phones began to be used for text messaging as much as for speaking and texting is now part of deaf culture. Joe Shapiro of NPR describes the scene on the Gallaudet campus in 2006: "Even more popular is text messaging. Students walk across campus, often with their heads down, banging out messages on Blackberrys and Sidekicks."[72] TTY machines, teletypewriters that convert phone conversations to text so a deaf person can read an incoming call, were once specialized equipment; now that function comes on everyone's cell phone. And with the ease of video conferencing on computers via Skype or other computer video software, deaf people can communicate via sign language for the cost of a $40 webcam added to their computer.

Technology does not create a barrier-free utopia for people with disabilities, but much of the new technology of the late 20th and early 21st centuries has served to give disabled people more access to American society, if they have the monetary resources to afford the cost of the new technology. But even more importantly, much of the new communication technology, such as methods using the Internet, have given disabled people a way to communicate that does not have to be filtered through mainstream news or entertainment media. With that voice, people with disabilities can tell the world about their own stories and life experiences.

Notes

1. Jennifer Van Grove, "Remarkable Stats on the State of the Internet," Mashable, The Social Media Guide, Feb. 25, 2010, mashable.com/2010/02/26/state-of-internet/

2. J.D. Lasica, "Blogs and journalism need each other," Neiman Reports, 2003, jdlasica.com/ articles/nieman.html.

3. Much of this research is covered in this book and comes from the author's past research: Beth Haller, Bruce Dorries, and Jessica Rahn, "Media Labeling versus the U.S. Disability Community Identity: A Study Of Shifting Cultural Language," *Disability & Society*, Jan. 2006, 21:1; Beth Haller and Sue Ralph, "'Not Worth Keeping Alive?' News Framing of Physician-assisted suicide in the United States and Great Britain," *Journalism Studies*, 2001, 2:3; Beth Haller and Sue Ralph, "Content analysis methodology for studying news and disability: Case studies from the United States and England," *Research in Social Science and Disability*, 2001, 2; Beth Haller, "Content & Character: Disability Publications in the 1990s," *Journal of Magazine & New Media Research*, 2000, 1:3; Beth Haller, "Balancing Acts: Disability, Business, and Government Sources in News Coverage of Disability Legislation." Paper presented at the Association for Education in Journalism and Mass Communication annual meeting, Anaheim, Calif., 1996; Beth Haller, "The Social Construction of Disability: News Coverage of the Americans with Disabilities Act." Paper presented at the International Communication Association annual meeting, Albuquerque, N.M., 1995.

4. Mark 'Rizzn' Hopkins, "A Brief History of the Universe of Blogging," Mashable, The Social Media Guide, Dec. 17, 2007, mashable.com/2007/12/17/a-brief-history-of-the-universe-of-blogging/.

5. Duncan Riley, "A short history of blogging," The Blog Herald, Mar. 6, 2005, www.blogherald. com/ 2005/03/06/a-short-history-of-blogging/.

6. Clive Thompson, "The early years," *New York* magazine, Feb. 12, 2006, nymag.com/news/media/15971/.

7. Andreas Kluth, "The 'death' of blogging," The Hannibal Blog, Nov. 6, 2008, andreaskluth. org/2008/11/06/the-death-of-blogging/.

8. Temple University Disability Studies, "Blogroll (alphabetical)," disstud.blogspot.com/, May 2009.

9. William Peace, Speaker for CUNY "Disability & Embodiment" graduate class, CUNY Graduate Center, March 13, 2010.

10. Autism Street, blog, www.autismstreet.org/weblog/, 2009.

11. Steve Kuusisto, The Planet of the Blind blog. kuusisto.typepad.com/, 2009.

12. Paula Apodaca, E is for Epilepsy blog. epilepsy-paula.blogspot.com/, 2009.

13, Amputeehee, blog, amputeehee.blogspot.com/, 2009.

14. Karen Putz, A Deaf Mom Shares Her World blog, deafmomworld.com/, 2009.

15. I.D. Socol, SpeEdChange, blog, speedchange.blogspot.com/, 2009.

16. Stephen Drake, Not Dead Yet blog, notdeadyetnewscommentary.blogspot.com/, 2009.

17. Scott Rains, The Rolling Rains Report blog, rollingrains.com/, 2009.

18. Peace, op. cit.

19. John Knight, "Blogging is a force to be reckoned with," Third Sector, Apr. 9, 2008, 15.

20. YAI Network, Disability in the News blog, Mar. 26, 2010, www.yai.org/about/newsroom/disability-in-the-news.html.

21. Robin, "Blogging . . . Why?" Disability, "Kodi" & Me blog, Jan. 19, 2010, open.salon.com/blog/disability_kodi_me/2010/01/19/blogging_why.

22. Christina Warren, "How PR pros are using social media for real results, Mashable, The Social Media Guide, March 16, 2010, mashable.com/2010/03/16/public-relations-social-media-results/.

23. Adam Ostrow, "Facebook overtakes MySpace (Again)," Mashable, The Social Media Guide, Feb. 19, 2009, mashable.com/2009/02/19/facebook-bigger-than-myspace-in-us/.

24. Stan Schroeder, "Facebook users are getting older. Much older," Mashable, The Social Media Guide, July 7, 2009, mashable.com/2009/07/07/facebook-users-older/.

25. Barb Dybwad, "Facebook passes 400 million user mark, " Feb. 4, 2010, Mashable, The Social Media Guide, mashable.com/2010/02/04/facebook-400-million/.

26. Farhad Manjoo, Can anyone stop Facebook?" Slate magazine, Dec., 3, 2009, www.slate.com/id/2237376/.

27. "The official petition for a more accessible Facebook," Facebook.com, facebook.com/home.php?#!/group.php?v=wall&ref=ts&gid=2384051749.

28. Jean Dobbs, "Why does Facebook matter?" New Mobility, Sept. 2009, newmobility.com/articleViewIE.cfm?id=11499.

29. Dobbs, op. cit.

30. Disabilities Network of NYC Facebook page, Mar. 25, 2010, facebook.com/profile.php?ref=profile&id=1361690792#!/pages/Disabilities-Network-of-NYC/261969564334?ref=ts.

31. Dobbs, op. cit.

32. Claire Cain Miller, Social networks a lifeline for the chronically ill, The New York Times, Mar. 24, 2010, nytimes.com/2010/03/25/technology/25disable.html.

33. Disaboom, "About us," aboutus.disaboom.com/About-Us.aspx.

34. Andrew Adam Newman, "Web Marketing to a Segment Too Big to Be a Niche," The New York Times, Oct. 30, 2007, p. C9.

35. Chris Taylor, "Opening new worlds: The disability boom," CNN Money, Sept. 15, 2008, money.cnn.com/2008/09/11/smallbusiness/disability_boom.fsb/index.htm?postversion=2008091509.

36. Lenore Skenazy, "Savvy lifestyle site for the disabled is off to running start," Advertising Age, January 28, 2008, p. 16.

37. Tracey Meloni, "Am I on the wrong planet?" Northern Virginia Magazine, Feb. 2009, northernvirginiamag.com/health-and-beauty/health-beauty-features/2009/02/19/aspergers-sydrome.

38. Business Wire, "Can Virtual Worlds Provide Support to Military Amputees? Amputee Virtual Environment Support Space to Research and Establish Best Practices," Nov. 2, 2009, businesswire.com/portal/site/google/?ndmViewId=news_view&newsId=20091102005423&newsLang=en.

39. Alexander Kaminsky, "About," Many Worlds Network, manyworldsnetwork.com/page/about-1.

40. Kaminsky, op. cit.

41. Miller, New York Times, op. cit.

42. Adam Ostrow, "How many people actually use Twitter," Mashable, The Social Media Guide, Apr. 28, 2009, mashable.com/2009/04/28/twitter-active-users/.

43. Adam Ostrow, "The fastest growing social sites," Mashable, The Social Media Guide, Apr. 20, 2009, mashable.com/2009/04/20/the-fastest-growing-social-sites/.

44. The Shorty Awards, "The Shorty interview with Marlee Matlin," Jan. 19, 2010, shortyawards.com/MarleeMatlin#.

45. Beth A. Haller, "Join Marlee Matlin in demanding online captions," Media dis&dat blog, Oct. 21, 2009, media-dis-n-dat.blogspot.com/2009/10/join-marlee-matlin-in-demanding.html.

46. Steven Johnson, "How Twitter will change the way we live," Time, June. 5, 2009, http://www.time.com/business/article/0,8599,1902604,00.html.

47. David Carr, "Why Twitter will endure," The New York Times, Jan. 1, 2010, http://www.nytimes.com/2010/01/03/weekinreview/03carr.html.

48. Carr, op. cit.

49. David Morrison, "Social media opens social world to elderly, disabled," The Star-News, Jan. 26, 2010, starnewsonline.com/article/20100126/ARTICLES/100129756/1177?Title=Social-media-opens-social-world-to-elderly-disabled-&tc=ar.

50. Portlight Strategies, "Disaster Relief, Haiti Earthquake," portlight.org/home.html.

51. Leah Betancourt, "The Journalist's Guide to Twitter," Mashable, The Social Media Guide, May 14, 2009, mashable.com/2009/05/14/twitter-journalism/.

52. DownSynAdvocacy, Profile on Twitter, twitter.com/DownSynAdvocacy.

53. Janko Roettgers, New TeeVee, Jan. 2, 2010, newteevee.com/2010/01/02/the-decade-in-online-video-part-2-time-to-upload/?utm_source=feedburner&utm_medium=feed&utm_campaign=Feed:%20newteevee%20(NewTeeVee)&utm_content=Twitter.

54. Zennie62, "Jerry Lewis Award Protest on Oscar Eve - 2009 Academy Awards," Feb. 22, 2009, YouTube video, youtube.com/watch?v=fKCf1NVk8Lw.

55. MadeB, "Cure Jerry Lewis," Feb. 21, 2009, YouTube video, youtube.com/watch?v=BnooXkJYBDQ&feature=PlayList&p=2DA424F8E2FA3096&index=2.

56. April Witt, "Going viral," The Washington Post, May 31, 2009, washingtonpost.com/wp-srv/special/artsandliving/brandon-hardesty/article.html.

57. William G. Stothers, "What's Next? Mentoring Program," YouTube video, Feb. 12, 2010, youtube.com/watch?v=wIKX8yoXhWQ.

58. Len Davis, "Challenging the Cultural Stigma of Disability in Nepal," YouTube video, Feb. 3, 2010, youtube.com/watch?v=Gc-2B9sMQ8A.

59. Cinelan Films, "Heavy Load in New York," YouTube video, Apr. 29, 2009, youtube.com/watch?v=3OQTwA7Gc8s.

60. Stella Motion Pictures, stellamotion.com.au/Documentaries.html.

61. DREDF, "The Power of 504 (open caption) part 1," YouTube video, Feb. 9, 2009, youtube.com/user/DREDFvideo#p/a/4EEE286B0AA7A774/0/HMC5UuiIQkI.

62. Amanda Baggs, "In My Language," [Video], YouTube, Jan. 14, 2007, youtube.com/watch?v=JnylM1hI2jc.

63. boudica82, "In My Language," [Comment], YouTube, 2009, youtube.com/watch?v=JnylM1hI2jc.

64. D-PAN, "This is D-PAN," 2009, d-pan.org/index.php/this-is-d-pan/who-are.

65. The new Google captioning system will allow users created captions in 51 different languages, so the system is expected to open YouTube videos up to a worldwide market.

66. Miguel Helft, "Google to add captions, improving YouTube videos," *The New York Times*, Nov. 19, 2009, nytimes.com/2009/11/20/technology/internet/20google.html?_r=3&scp=1&sq=google%20captioning&st=cse.

67. Helft, op. cit.

68. Marlee Matlin Official Facebook Page, "Marlee Matlin is looking for a CODA Family for a reality show," [Notes], July 9, 2009, facebook.com/note.php?note_id=122253219953&ref=mf.

69. Marlee Matlin Official Facebook Page, [Wall post], March 25, 2010, facebook.com/note.php?note_id=122253219953&ref=mf#!/pages/Marlee-Matlin-Official/43959439932.

70. Marlee Matlin, "My Deaf Family – Reality Show," YouTube channel, youtube.com/mydeaffamily.

71. Aaron Boyd, "A Twist on a Useful Gadget Gives the Gift of Speech," Hamptons.com, Jan. 15, 2010, hamptons.com/news/top-stories/9775/a-twist-on-a-useful-gadget-gives-the-gift-of.html.

72. Joe Shapiro, "Technology no longer distances deaf culture," NPR, May 1, 2006, npr.org/templates/story/story.php?storyId=5374451.

2.

Researching media images of disability
How content analysis provides a method for assessment

n the field of social science research, content analysis of media has been a useful tool in what has been deemed "unobtrusive research." This means a subject
can be studied with little impact on that subject. This chapter examines content
analysis as a methodology for looking at disability representations in mass media.
It discusses both quantitative and qualitative methods of analysis using newspaper stories and cartoon images. For the quantitative analysis, the chapter looks
at generally what was represented in news stories about disability in major U.S.
news publications in several months of 1998. For the qualitative case analysis, the
chapter looks at newspaper political cartoons with disability imagery.

Content analysis as method

Media researcher Earl Babbie emphasizes how appropriate content analysis
is in mass communication research. The content analysis method can answer
the Lasswellian communications research question: "Who says what to whom,
why, how, and with what effect?"[1] The quantitative analysis in this chapter illustrates what the news media say about disability through the sources they use,
the language they use, the images they use, and with what effect. Content analysis specialist Morris Janowitz explains in general terms that "wherever symbolic
behavior is being scrutinized, the analysis of content is involved."[2] He discusses
how Harold Lasswell helped revolutionize content analysis by imposing quantitative methods upon it. Although Lasswell is seen as the creator of the modern

orm of quantitative content analysis through his propaganda studies, research-er Klaus Krippendorf explains that empirical studies of communication content have been conducted since the 1600s, when the religious leaders worried about the spread of non-religious information through newspapers.[3]

Content analysis of mass media seeks to discover two different types of con-tent: manifest content and latent content.[4] Lasswell believed that content analy-sis should search for both types of content. Manifest content refers to that which is directly observable, the actual attributes of a communication. For example, a manifest content analysis may look at the terminology used about disability in a newspaper story. Latent content encompasses the meanings within communica-tion and requires the researcher to make inferences.[5] For example, what are the implications when a major U.S. newspaper such as *The New York Times* still uses the term "handicapped" in some of its articles about disability issues in the late 1990s?

> . . . for Lasswell, content analysis involved the application of historical, cultural, psychological, and legal frames of reference with various levels of meaning, subtleties, and efforts at explication of ambiguities. In the broadest sense, content analysis is a system for objectifying the process of inference, since the meaning of the symbolic environment can be derived only by a process of inference.[6]

Studying mass media content through content analysis enables researchers to study various aspects of society and media. Researchers can understand the char-acteristics of a particular culture by investigating the content of its mass media. "The basic assumption is that both changes and regularities in media content reliably reflect or report some feature of the social reality of the moment. . . . The purpose of the cultural indicator analysis is often to test propositions about effects from media on society over time, but it is also a method for the study of social change in its own right and for the comparison of different national soci-eties and cultures," according to media researcher Denis McQuail.[7] But as media sociologist Charles Wright says, "Mass media content does not 'speak for itself,' however. Its meaning may not be self-evident. Media content can be classified and analyzed from a variety of perspectives."[8] The qualitative analysis of po-litical cartoons, for example, helps us to understand characteristics of American society's attitudes toward disabled people through this imagery.

In addition to searching for reflections of a culture in the media, content analysis can be used to assess the performance of the media. For example, researchers have investigated the diversity of ideas within mass media by studying the content of news stories or TV shows.[9] The content analysis can show how alternative ideas and minority groups are portrayed, and thereby reflect the access these groups have to the mainstream media. Looking at the sources used in news stories about disability allows for an investigation of how many diverse perspectives about disability issues are, or are not, getting into the media.

The notion of the framing of disability issues and disabled people by news media lends credence to media scholar Doris Graber's view that journalists select the content and frame of the news, thereby constructing reality for those who read, watch, or listen to their stories. But because the journalist and the audience usually are steeped in the same culture, an exchange of meanings can take place.[10] Content analysis works within an understanding that most Western societies are now mass-mediated cultures in which their citizens understand "reality" through personal experience and mass media information. As media scholars Pamela Shoemaker and Stephen Reese explain: "If we assume that the media provide most of the 'reality' that people know outside their own personal experience, then studying media content surely helps us assess what reality it is that they consume."[11]

All these issues must be considered when developing the specific technique used in a content analysis. Denis McQuail's excellent book on media research explains the traditional approach to quantitative content analysis:

> (1) choose a universe or sample of content; (2) establish a category frame of external referents relevant to the purpose of the enquiry (e.g. a set of political parties or countries); (3) choose a 'unit of analysis' from the content (word, sentence, item, story, picture, sequence, etc.); (4) match content to category frame by counting the frequency of the references to items in the category frame, per chosen unit of content; (5) express the result as an overall distribution of the total universe or sample in terms of the frequency of occurrence of the sought-for referents.[12]

Because this method presents a statistical conclusion about a larger universe, it is well-suited to studying how media presentations correlate with other perspectives and with the social and cultural factors in place at a given time. Con-

27

tent analyses have been used to study a wide range of media content, from ads in children's TV programming in the 1950s[13] to gender roles on MTV,[14] to the ideological content of TV news magazines' portrayal of crime.[15] All these analyses reveal the underlying meanings within media texts and their implications within the social culture. Janowitz explains that the content of the mass media can provide two contrasting indicators of social culture: "The contents of the mass media are a reflection of the social organization and value system of the society or group interest involved. Simultaneously, the contents of the mass media are purposive elements of social change, agents for modifying the goals and values of social groups."[16]

The content of the news media allows us to understand the values of the news media in portraying people with disabilities and their concerns. This, in turn, helps assess the societal status of disabled people and whether there are changes in the social culture regarding their issues.

Quantitative content analysis:
What's represented in news stories about disability

To determine what is generally represented about disability in U.S. news media, major newspapers and news magazines in 1998 were analyzed using a 294-question code sheet. Eleven newspapers and news magazines were selected primarily because of their large circulations and their prominence as agenda-setting elite media in the U.S. Although much mass communication research has revealed the effects of mass media in the cultural lives of Americans, it should be remembered that content analysis does not make claims about the effect of news stories on audiences. However, content analysis can show how alternative ideas or minority groups, such as the disability community, are portrayed. This, in turn, reflects the access these groups have to the mainstream media. Content analysis makes judgments about content, not media effects. The analyses in this chapter allow us to look at some journalistic behavior and some political cartoonist behavior, as reflected in media content.

The content analysis of news media provides a gauge of whether the disability perspective is being included on the media agenda. Journalists select the content and frame of the news about disability and reveal societal perspectives on disability. A 1996 media study of diversity also found that news audiences receive information about diversity issues directly from content in the news: "The content is what activates, motivates, interests, and involves its mass audience."[17]

28

The ability of the news media to make people aware and characterize social issues fits with Max McCombs and Don Shaw's famous media theory called "agenda-setting."[18] McCombs and Shaw have shown us that the media not only tell their audiences what to think about but how to think about certain issues.[19] McCombs and Shaw believe the way that journalists frame the news is germane to agenda-setting: "Both the selection of topics for the news agenda and the selection of frames for stories about those topics are powerful agenda setting roles and awesome ethical responsibilities," they say.[20] How the attributes of news stories about disability are played in the news media can potentially sway public opinion about disability issues and toward the cultural representations of people with disabilities in general.

Because people with disabilities still face many architectural, occupational, educational, and communication barriers in the U.S., interpersonal contact between able-bodied and disabled persons is still limited. Therefore, mass media images still provide many of the cultural representations of disability to American society. A 1991 Louis Harris poll showed that Americans surveyed were less likely to feel awkward around people with disabilities after having viewed fictional television and movie presentations about people with disabilities.[21] These surveyed Americans were relying on information about the disability experience obtained from mass media to form their views.

As media scholar Todd Gitlin says, "The mass media are, to say the least, a significant social force in the forming and delimiting of public assumptions, attitudes, and moods – of ideology, in short."[22] So as to understand this ideology about people with disabilities in the news, this quantitative content analysis of general disability issues investigated the traditional print news media. Even though more people get their news from TV or the Internet, most Americans still have favorable impressions of traditional news sources, the Pew Research Center for People and the Press reported in 2009. "While the public has become much more critical of the way news organizations do their jobs, most Americans continue to give favorable ratings to traditional news sources – local TV news, daily newspapers and network television news. Favorable opinions of all three have declined since 1985; nonetheless, majorities continue to express favorable opinions of local TV news (73%), the daily newspaper they are most familiar with (65%), and network TV news (64%)."[23] It should also be remembered that even though most Americans report getting much of their national news from the Internet (42%) or TV (71%) rather than newspapers (33%), many of the stories in the TV or Internet news sources actually originated from reporting by newspapers. The assumption within a content analysis is that many readers receive some of what they perceive to be the "reality" about disability from traditional print sources. The news media sources used in this analysis were *The Wall Street Journal, USA Today, The New York Times, The Los Angeles Times, The Washington Post, Chicago Tribune, The Philadelphia Inquirer, The Baltimore Sun, Time, Newsweek,* and *U.S. News and World Report.*

The print stories in the data set were collected from Lexis-Nexis or the publication's Web archives. The search terms used were "disabled," "disability," "disabilities," and "handicapped." All the stories with these terms were evaluated, and the stories that were not connected to disability issues or people with disabilities were eliminated from the sample. For example, sports stories about an athlete on the "disabled list" and restaurant listings that had a reference to "handicapped accessible" were eliminated. However, stories that had any mention of a person with a disability, even one reference unconnected to the rest of the story, were still included in the sample. The limitation of this search is that it missed stories about individual disabilities if there was no use of one of these terms, such as a story about a blind person that never used the term disability. However, because the focus of this media analysis is disability issues and people with disabilities in general, using the four terms above was the most viable option, although slightly limiting the number of stories in the study.

The sample of news stories analyzed came from October and November 1998 for the newspapers and the entire year of 1998 for the three news magazines, which led to 256 stories being collected and analyzed. The code sheet developed to analyze the articles looked for placement of the stories, kinds of disabilities mentioned, kinds of sources used, disability issues mentioned, and language about disability used. The study does not pretend to give an all-encompassing picture of disability coverage, but by using these two months hoped to show trends in news stories about disability. Three coders analyzed the stories. All were trained in content analysis, and all three had analyzed stories related to disability in the past.

In terms of placement, stories about disability seem to be associated with the local news angle most often. Slightly more than 60 percent of the stories were located in the local Metro section or the neighborhood/suburban section. Only about 14 percent of the stories were in the front national news section. *The Philadelphia Inquirer* had the most suburban section stories at 57 percent of

its stories, most likely due to the collection method. The newspaper had extensive suburban sections for the counties that surround the city and had several
freelancers who seemed to actively cover any disability-related stories in those
counties. However, *The Los Angeles Times* had the largest percentage of disability-
related stories in its Metro section at 69 percent. *The Los Angeles Times* was also
the most likely to use a photo with its stories at 62 percent, and it put 38 percent
of its disability stories on the front of a section. However, a number of these
stories appeared to be "inspirational" features that editors may have selected
for the Metro section to counterbalance the hard news. For example, one story
tells of a deaf woman who found a career in taking care of pets[24] and another
tells of a local guitarist with only one arm.[25] Both are sentimental feature stories and have some pity and an inspirational tone imbedded within them and
give no "news" about any substantive disability issue. On the other hand, *The
Los Angeles Times* also put some substantive disability stories on the front of its
Metro section, such as in-depth look at problems from warehousing children
with disabilities in psychiatric facilities or inappropriate group homes. The story
featured excellent comments from disability experts who explained the problem
of institutionalization.[26] Although it only wrote a small number of stories, *The
Wall Street Journal* put four of its six stories on the front of a section.

Most of the stories were news (48%) rather than feature stories (37.5%), which
means disability issues are being associated with newsworthy information. And
even though many of *The Philadelphia Inquirer's* stories were in suburban sections, a large number were news (53%), rather than feature (39%), stories. Due
to its large number of stories, *The Philadelphia Inquirer* was also the most likely to
mention the Americans with Disabilities Act, with 10 of the 29 total mentions of
the ADA (the study looked at 256 stories from all the publications [N=256]) in
that newspaper. *The Baltimore Sun* also had a high number of news stories, with
11 out of its 20 stories in that category, although many of *The Sun's* news stories
were short reports on grants or new programs, such as a story about the Baltimore
Arc (formerly called the Association for Retarded Citizens) receiving a grant to
provide job training.[27] It is interesting to note that *The Sun* carried slightly more
stories related to disability than did *The Washington Post*, despite the much larger
resources of *The Washington Post* and its agenda-setting place as elite news media.
It may signal problems in the coverage of disability issues if a premier newspaper
is disregarding the issues. The *Chicago Tribune* stories were the most feature-ori-
ented with 50 percent being features. All the stories in the study were of sub-

stantial length, with 67 percent of them longer than six inches, a good sign that some depth is being given to disability-related stories.

The analysis also tried to assess what types of disabilities were mentioned in the stories. As expected, due to the general search terms used, people with disabilities in general accounted for the largest category at 54 percent. However, the more interesting finding is the high number of disabilities mentioned that related to cognitive impairment. Learning disabilities were the No. 2 most mentioned disability at 14 percent, with mental retardation (12%), mental illness (9.3%), and emotional disabilities (6%) all in the Top 10. These findings are surprising and very interesting because they seem to indicate that disability in these print stories is being associated with education and children's issues. A number of the stories reported on school districts' special education programs in both positive and negative ways. For example, a *Baltimore Sun* story called a county's special education program "bloated" because it constitutes a high percentage of the budget.[28] However, the story did balance that perspective by explaining that many students may be wrongly labeled as having learning disabilities, thus overburdening the program. Another education-and-disability related issue that appeared and will probably take on greater prominence in the future is children with disabilities who need medical services while in school. A *Chicago Tribune* story reported on a school district in Illinois mandating that young children be in charge of their own prescription medication.[29]

The analysis revealed a trend in the coverage of education and children-related news by the topics covered in the stories. Children with disabilities was the No. 1 topic covered in 23.3 percent of the stories. In addition, inclusive education issues (17%) and general education issues (10.5%) both were in the top ten issues covered in the print stories. Other topics covered more often were: government funding for disability programs (19%), health care access and costs (12%), attitudinal barriers (11%), and access to jobs (10%).

In terms of language use, the news media seemed to understand that the term "handicapped" is no longer an acceptable term. "People with disabilities," the less stigmatizing "people first" language, was used most often in the stories (25%). ("The disabled" was used 15 percent of the time and "handicapped" was used in 10 percent of the stories.) Interestingly, *The New York Times*, which, it could be argued, has the most agenda-setting function of all the print media, was the most likely still to use the term "handicapped," but it contained only five references within the total 25 uses of the term fund by the study.

One criticism of quantitative content analysis is that it just counts aspects of news articles and takes no notice of context. However, percentages from content analysis reveal significant trends and allow us to understand media "behavior" toward disability topics. The numeric data from this content analysis, for example, revealed an unexpected finding that deserves much more study: There was a conspicuous link between disability issues, education, and children in major news stories. Several common-sense explanations may contribute to this. First, the analysis looked at stories from October and November, when all U.S. schools are in session. Second, mandatory public education is a prominent feature of American society and has been for many decades, and most print news sources, no matter how large or small, traditionally cover education and schools as part of their geographic community. Third, inclusive education for children with disabilities has been a major focus for local disability activists and parents of children with disabilities since the Individuals with Disabilities Education Act (IDEA) became law in 1975. Revealing that the print media are finally covering education issues related to disability was a major finding from this analysis.

The content analysis also considered the sources within the news stories and showed that often journalists write stories that have no person with a disability as a source (36%). Print journalists are much more likely to use people with disabilities as examples than sources in their news stories. People with disabilities were much more likely to be sources in feature stories (48%), rather than in news stories (17%), which means they may not have been used as sources on more hard-hitting issues. This has implications for the message that may be getting across to the general public: that people with disabilities can't speak for themselves. This is obviously untrue, but that is the impression that might be left in the minds of readers.

Nevertheless, people with disabilities and local disability organizations did have a "voice" in the newspaper and news magazine stories. People with disabilities (24%) or their families (24%) were most often sources in the stories, which is a very good sign. Local disability organizations also were sources in 10 percent of the stories. The disability groups that were largely missing from the coverage were national disability organizations, which was a somewhat unexpected finding, because some of the newspapers and news magazines used in this analysis are the largest in the U.S. and many consider themselves to be "national" sources. The journalistic practice of localizing stories may have accounted for this lack of national disability sources.

One thing that findings from content analyses can do is guide disability organizations in developing strategies for better media relations. With the obvious media and public interest in education issues, disability and education spokespeople could work together to get correct information about these issues into the news. As found previously in the study of news coverage of the ADA, in which business sources countered the disability rights narrative,[30] other groups may work against laws preventing discrimination against people with disabilities, and their "side" of the story may be given equal credence. For example, people who are against inclusive education – even schools and parents – may actively seek to turn the news discourse into one about inclusive education being "bad." This content analysis of print media suggests that disability organizations must be pro-active in influencing the news agenda on this and other topics about disability issues.

Qualitative content analysis: Political cartoons

Qualitative assessment adds richness and is a context-based content analysis. It helps reveal the media frames and themes that are being used to characterize disabled people. This qualitative assessment – a study of political cartoons in U.S. newspapers – looks at the disability themes long found in these cartoons. This qualitative content analysis allows us to see the kinds of visual metaphors that are used historically and in specific cartoon representations of an ongoing category of disabled person – veterans disabled by war.

Media scholars Clifford Christians and James Carey say that one mission of qualitative studies is to better understand the interpretations of meaning that take place in media texts. The goal is to find out "what are the interpretations of meaning and value created in the media and what is their relation to the rest of life?"[31] As qualitative media researcher David Altheide says, this type of analysis documents and illuminates the communication of meaning between the media text and a culture.[32] This is crucial with regards to news about disabled people because the U.S. is trying to shift to become a more inclusive society. Christians's and Carey's notion is that the qualitative researcher should assess verbal, non-verbal, and graphic symbols, so the symbols about disability within political cartoons make an apt area of study. As Altheide explains, the researcher using the qualitative approach is more reflexive and oriented toward narrative description, and cartoons lend themselves to this in-depth delineation. Cartoons also contain a high level of emotional symbolism, according to a political psychology study: "Themes of shame, indulgence, and fear are prominent in the cartoons' emotional symbolism."[33] It could be argued that disability imagery in political cartoons reflects these themes, especially non-disabled people's fear of disability.

In terms of media content, events featuring disability in cartoons illustrate the role of media in framing social events in a culture and therefore potentially redefining them. As media researcher Klaus Bruhn Jensen says of how qualitative studies can be used in mass communication research: "Qualitative approaches examine meaning production as a process which is contextualized and inextricably integrated with wider social and cultural practices."[34]

Disability imagery has long filled American newspapers in the form of political cartoons, and one category of imagery in these cartoons – soldiers disabled by war – combines both realistic images of actual war-related disabilities and metaphorical images used by cartoonists to criticize wars and other societal problems. These images occur in political cartoons every time the U.S. participates in a war, and unpopular wars of recent decades are particularly rich in imagery – the Vietnam War, the Iraq war, and the Walter Reed Military Hospital scandal.

Political cartoons in general are an excellent source of disability imagery because many focus on exaggeration and satire to convey messages in broad themes.[35] For centuries, metaphors about persons with disabilities have been embedded in language, literature and the arts.[36] Common linguistic metaphors such as "to be blind to," "lame duck," or "crippled by fear" not only express ideas, they shape them, and thus they have shaped attitudes toward disability. Cartoonists translate linguistic metaphors into visual and symbolic ones.[37] This qualitative analysis of cartoons featuring disabled veterans or disability metaphors in general illustrates that both realistic images and metaphorical imagery have long been used to give disability negative connotations.

In specifically looking at photographic images, Knoll developed 83 categories for use in assessing photos of disabled people in a qualitative way.[38] Based on Knoll's criteria, one might look for whether the person with a disability is shown as helpless in photographs or whether the people with disabilities are being shown as victims or pitiable. One of Knoll's interpretive categories tries to assess whether visual images of people with disabilities are portraying them as childlike or as children. These categories can be useful in analyzing realistic imagery in political cartoons.

The metaphoric imagery of disability found in political cartoons illuminates the long history of disability imagery in American society. Disability historians Paul Longmore and Lauri Umansky explain: "Unraveling the underlying meanings of disability's ubiquity as an organizing concept or symbolic structure promises to become as much a goal of disability history in the future as charting the specific pasts of people with disabilities."[39] These ubiquitous disability images have long fulfilled a symbolic role in political cartoons. They are basically the visual version of linguistic metaphors about disability. In the context of political cartoons' placement in newspapers and magazines, communication theory models discuss how these cartoons are generally "read" by audiences.

Communication scholar James Carey put forth the theory that communication functions within two models: the transmission model, in which information moves in a linear fashion from a source to an audience, and the ritual model, which is directed, "not toward the extension of messages in space but toward the maintenance of society in time; not the act of imparting information but the representation of shared beliefs."[40] Newspaper reading, his overarching example, can be understood according to both models. Readers go to a newspaper seeking information; on the other hand, readers use newspapers as an affirmation of a "reality" that is constructed by the narratives about the world in the news. A ritual view of communication will "view reading a newspaper less as sending or gaining information and more as attending a mass, a situation in which nothing new is learned but in which a particular view of the world is portrayed and confirmed."[41]

News audiences reading political cartoons is a good example of the ritual model, according Ruth Palmer, who studied Cuban-American identity in political cartoons.[42] The intent of a cartoon is not to convey new information; on the contrary, it relies on a reader's understanding of the topic being satirized and of general cultural metaphors such as those about disability: e.g., "justice is blind" is a popular cartoon image about the justice system. Looking at a political cartoon on the editorial page of a newspaper, readers know to read it as satire. Within the ritual view of communication, these cartoons also project and confirm the social order within the cultural world. They frame and reinforcement a specific view of the world. But in a political cartoon, these frames are exaggerated and twisted to comment on society. As cartoonist David Horsey has noted, political cartoonists deliberately hold up a kind of "fun house mirror" to the world: They depict a distorted, exaggerated, often grotesque view of "reality,"[43] and to symbolize that "grotesqueness" or "societal dysfunction," they many times use disability imagery.

Retired education professor Art Shapiro dedicated his academic life to trying to change negative attitudes toward people with disabilities, especially among schoolchildren.[44] His belief that some of these negative attitudes came from the disability metaphors in cartoon imagery led him to collect more than 700 political cartoons from Colonial times to 2009 that contained disability themes. The qualitative analysis of disability metaphors in political cartoons is based on his collection. To narrow the analysis of such a large collection, the study looked at cartoons of disabled veterans from the Civil War to present (N=149) so as to better understand how these cartoons have contributed to cultural representations of people with disabilities. The belief behind this qualitative analysis is that these images, as in the Carey ritual view of communication, have helped reinforce and confirm a particular view of disability throughout U.S. history.

Descriptive analysis of five cartoons featuring disabled soldiers/veterans

Cartoon 1: "Doctor's waiting room is filling up" *(by Jay N. "Ding" Darling, October 17, 1915).* This cartoon comes from a famous American cartoonist of the early 20th century named Ding Darling. His cartoons are a particularly excellent resource when looking for disability imagery because the foundation set up after his death and the University of Iowa Libraries completed a project in 1999 to digitize 12,000 of his cartoons that are now in a searchable database online.[45]

This cartoon comes from before the U.S. entered World War I, at a time when the U.S. government was in much turmoil about what role it should play in world affairs. The cartoon has an overall "medical" theme, depicting eight figures in a doctor's waiting room. The doctor, according to the label on the door, is "Doctor Congress." The figure first in line at the door is an emaciated figure in a wheelchair labeled "U.S. Treasury deficit"; behind him is an older woman with glasses and bonnet and frilly frock labeled "democracy." Next in line is a man with a crutch, a peg leg, his arm in a sling, and a bandage wrapped around his head. He is labeled "U.S. Merchant Marine." His arm sling is labeled the "La Follette Seaman's Bill." At the end of the line is Uncle Sam, the symbol of America, with his striped suit, top hat, and goatee. He is labeled "Preparedness" and is holding two screaming children, labeled "U.S. Navy" and "U.S. Army." Seated in chairs in the left corner of the cartoon are two older women, one labeled "Suffrage" and one "Tariff." Suffrage says: "I've been coming here year after year but it never does me any good." To which Tariff replies: "That's nothing. I've been coming 30 years and keep getting worse."

In this cartoon, disability is used as a metaphor for weakness and problems, as symbolized by the U.S. treasury deficit and the multiple disabilities of the Merchant Marines. Although this cartoon doesn't explicitly focus on disabled soldiers, it is metaphorically showing merchant marines as "disabled" because the La Follette Seaman's Bill hadn't passed yet. The legislation took two years to pass; when it did, it gave better living and working conditions to seamen serving in the U. S. Merchant Marine.

Cartoon 2: "They have paid your dues. Your installment is now due" (*by Ding Darling, April 21, 1919*). In this Ding Darling cartoon from 1919, three disabled soldiers in uniform, one blind with a cane, one with an arm amputation, and one on crutches with a leg amputation, stand before a sign that says "The victory has been bought but only partly paid for." Two gentlemen in business suits stand to the left of the sign and one who is looking at the sign says, "Gosh, I don't see how I can afford it." The other gentleman who is looking at the disabled vets says, "I'll dare you to look at where I'm looking and repeat that."

The cartoon appears to be a plea to get Americans to continue to buy WWI Victory Bonds or to ready the American public for the higher taxes needed to pay off the U.S. war debt. World War I cost the U.S. government more than $30 billion (by way of comparison, total federal expenditures in 1913 were only $970 million). The disabled soldiers in this cartoon serve to invoke a kind of "guilt trip" on the American public so they will understand and not complain about the financial cost of war when faced with the actual physical cost of war on men who returned home with significant disabilities.

Cartoon 3: "Don't Look Back" (*by Jeff Danziger of* The Los Angeles Times, *April 30, 1999*). This cartoon uses images of disabled veterans of past wars to talk about misinformation given to modern-day soldiers. Two disabled soldiers – one who appears to be from the Vietnam war is in a wheelchair and is missing a leg, and one who appears to be begging is a Persian Gulf War veteran in desert fatigues – sit before five signs that say: "1. Notice. There is no such thing as Post Traumatic Stress Syndrome. Pentagon." "2. Notice. Agent Orange is a figment of your imagination. Pentagon." "3. Viet vets are crazy. Not our fault. Pentagon." "4. Notice. There is no such thing as the Gulf War syndrome. Pentagon." "5. Notice. Your benefits have been reduced. War is hell. Pentagon." The cartoon's title,

"Don't Look Back," becomes clear as a modern-day soldier in the right side of the cartoon does just that with a scared look on his face.

This cartoon is reportage rather than metaphor, as it critiques the poor treatment of disabled veterans by the Pentagon. The Pentagon has had a history of denying the effect of war on soldiers, as in the lack of acknowledgement of the long-term effects of PTSD, the cancer-causing effect of Agent Orange (which has recently been shown to affect the offspring of exposed soldiers),[46] and the refusal to believe that Gulf War Syndrome caused grave health problems. The cartoon attacks the Pentagon for its continued recruitment of soldiers when it hasn't done right by the soldiers of past wars.

Cartoon 4: "Double Amputee" *(by Corky Trinidad, the* Honolulu Star-Bulletin, *February 27, 2007).* It depicts an African-American veteran in a wheelchair with both his legs amputated. One knee is labeled "Iraq war" and the other is labeled "Cuts in vets care funding." This cartoon combines realism and metaphor, because it uses the missing legs of what could be a real disabled veteran to symbolize the double brutality vets face from both the war and the fact that funding for veterans benefits has been decreased.

It should be noted that February 2007 is when the Walter Reed Army Medical Center scandal broke, as reported on by *The Washington Post. The Post* won a 2008 Pulitzer Prize for its reporting on it.[47] Dozens of cartoonists took on the subject of Walter Reed Army Medical Center when the media reported on the neglect of wounded soldiers there and the Center's disgusting conditions. *The Post* described Walter Reed as rat- and cockroach-infested, with stained carpets, cheap mattresses, black mold, and no heat or water.

Cartoon 5. "Rehab" *(by Dana Summers in the* Orlando Sentinel, *2007).* This cartoon combines reportage on the Walter Reed scandal in 2007 with a critique of the wrong-headed priorities of the U. S. health care system. The top panel labeled "For Britney" shows a bald singer Britney Spears sitting in a nice room before a doctor who says, "Don't worry, we have a state-of-the-art facility here to help you recover." The bottom panel, labeled "for our soldiers" shows a soldier in a grungy room with a sign that says "Walter Reed" and a rat sitting on a table looking at the veteran's predicament. He is missing a leg and has a bandage on his head and arm; even his one crutch is bandaged. He is wobbling and trying not to fall over on his one crutch. The doctor says, "I requisitioned another crutch, but it could take months."

This cartoon contrasts the public's apathy over the Walter Reed scandal with the over-zealously covered, but not really important, story of singer Britney Spears's possible mental breakdown, which seemed to be indicated when she abruptly shaved her head. The cartoonist also is commenting on the priorities of America and its medical system, when an entertainer receives top-of-the-line health care and soldiers who have been disabled by war receive sub-standard care.

Conclusions and discussion

The analysis of media content about disabled people is crucial in understanding their changing status in various societies. Because of the stigma heaped upon them in the past and the architectural, occupational, educational, communication, and attitudinal barriers still in place for many disabled people, many people in Western cultures get their information about people with disabilities and their issues primarily from mass media sources.

Content analysis allows us to assess if the disability rights perspective is making its way into U.S. society. This perspective contrasts with the reigning stigmatizing view of people with disabilities, which has adopted a medical or social welfare perspective in which disability is seen as a physical problem alone residing within individuals.[48] The disability rights perspective views disability as a phenomenon created by society, which has yet to modify its architectural, occupational, educational, communication, and attitudinal environments to accommodate people who are physically different.[49] In the rights perspective, physical difference is acknowledged, and even celebrated as an ethnicity might be by some, but the focus is away from the disabled individual as the problem and on society's structures instead.

In terms of content analysis methodology as it relates to disability, the pioneer in applying structured analytical processes to assessing news representations of disability was John Clogston. He created useful models based on the findings of past studies of minority group and deviance theories, which can be applied by researchers looking at media images of people with disabilities.[50] In his content analysis of 13 newspapers and three newsmagazines,[51] he created two categorizations of media portrayal of disabled persons: traditional and progressive. A traditional disability category presents a disabled person as malfunctioning in a medical or economic way. The progressive category views people as disabled by society, not a physical attribute.

Clogston illustrated with these models that researchers can understand, by studying media content, whether disabled people were still being presented in stigmatizing, traditional ways, or whether they were being presented in a more progressive, disability rights manner. These findings reflect the status of disabled people in society in general because, as Paul Higgins says, we as a society "make disability" through our language, media, and other public and visible ways.[52] Media depictions help us understand the media's role in "constructing" people with disabilities as different and their role in framing many types of people who may not fit with "mainstream" constructions. These media images affect society as a whole, but they also have implications for the self-concept of people with disabilities themselves.

Disability studies pioneer Irv Zola said societies give people with disabilities a dual message through the media: On the one hand, stories about the successes of people with disabilities illustrate that they can live full, happy, goal-oriented lives. On the other hand, the message of success sets up expectations that all disabled people must try to meet. This message "states that if a Franklin Delano Roosevelt or a Wilma Rudolph could OVERCOME their handicap, so could and should all the disabled. And if we fail, it is our problem, our personality, our weakness."[53] Higgins adds that in U.S. culture "we present disability as primarily an internal condition that estranges disabled people from others."[54]

It seems clear that mass media content – everything from a newspaper story to a political cartoon to an ongoing disabled character on a popular TV show – plays a crucial role in the societal perception of disabled persons. The information in newspapers, whether correct or not, reaches millions of people each day in print form and then has a second life on the Internet as the information lands in blogs or news sites. These news stories act as significant agents in socially constructing images of people with disabilities and disability issues in many cultures. News stories filter out into public consciousness and are still typically viewed as representations of "reality." Within the ritual view of communication, James Carey calls news stories *culturally constructed narratives*. Within this framework, news still has the power to inform, but media scholars Elizabeth Bird and Robert Dardenne explain that the information audiences receive is not facts and figures but a larger symbolic system of news. As a method of communication, news can take on qualities like myth. Both convey culture. Therefore, journalists are transmitters of the stories of a culture. "The journalist-storyteller is indeed using culturally embedded story values, taking them from the culture and re-presenting them to the culture. . . ."[55]

The cultural messages that journalists and cartoonists present in this media content reflect their own misconceptions about and fear of disabled people. Writer Laura Rensom Mitchell asserts that the press has a history of missing stories related to disabled persons. And when journalists do notice that they exist, they cover them as inspirational "supercrips" or as "helpless victims." She says:

> The fact is that the press misses the boat largely because of a narrow view that pigeonholes people with disabilities and makes subconscious assumptions about who we are and what we do. . . . Insensitivity and stubborn ignorance characterize much press coverage of disability-related stories. The insensitivity is somewhat understandable, since most journalists have had little direct contact with those whom they might recognize as disabled. Just as in the case of racial and ethnic minorities, stereotypes rush in to fill the void.[56]

Martin Krossel explains the remedy needed for most news stories about disability: "Hard-nosed reporting must replace cheap sentimentality and the creation of 'handicapped heroes.'"[57] These actions by journalists in creating media content help perpetuate the societal myths about disabled people already in place. In criticizing a Pulitzer Prize-winning story in *The Baltimore Sun* about a blind boy, Anne Peters explains that in playing on readers' emotions about a disability, reporters are also drawing out all the myths as well.[58]

As we have seen in this chapter's case studies on news and political cartoons, the media continue to present some content filled with pity, inspiration, and downright ignorance. There are some glimmers of hope in media content, however. Some of the articles in the quantitative study did have people with disabilities as sources. In the qualitative study, some modern cartoonists used their political cartoons to "report" on the problems faced by disabled veterans. However, many in the news media still present many stories about disabled people and their issues within a framework similar to Clogston's "traditional" categories – meaning that it was reported on as a medical or social welfare issue, or presented people as "supercrips."

As America moves forward in an online media environment, and as society becomes more inclusive of people with disabilities, these case studies illustrate that media still need to break free of the cultural stereotypes about disabled people they have long perpetuated. Some news stories are still similar to those found by disability studies scholar Douglas Biklen more than 20 years ago: When covering disability, he wrote that reporters "typically cast in terms of tragedy, of charity and its attendant emotion, pity, or of struggle and accomplishment."[59] Biklen found that the themes of news stories had become predictable. They focused on the angles of inspiration and courage.

Kenneth Jernigan, the longtime president of the National Federation of the Blind, succinctly explained how a journalist creates a news story within the haze of negative stereotypes and misconceptions about people with disabilities:

> A reporter. . . came to one of our meetings and said, 'I'd like to get pictures of blind persons bowling and of some of the members with their dogs.' I tried to explain to him that such a story would be a distortion – that we were there to discuss refusal by employers to let us work, refusal by airlines to let us ride, refusal by hotels to let us stay, refusal by society to let us in, and refusal by social service agencies to let us out. He said he was glad I had told him and that it had been very helpful and enlightening. Then he added, 'Now, can I see the dogs and the bowlers? I'm in quite a rush.'[60]

Media content gives us a blueprint of the cultural codes in societies because all facets of the mass media are created by humans, people with conscious and unconscious perceptions about people with disabilities. Their interaction with disabled persons may be impaired by a dominant social order that views disabled persons as different or deviant. This chapter's case studies illustrate that sometimes journalists, editors, and cartoonists, plying their trade in this culture, assimilate these inaccurate cultural beliefs and present them back to society as news "facts."

Notes

1. Earl Babbie, *The Practice of Social Research*. Belmont, Calif.: Wadsworth, 1989, p. 294.

2. Morris Janowitz, "Harold Lasswell's contribution to content analysis," *Public Opinion Quarterly*, Winter 1968, p. 647.

3. Klaus Krippendorf, *Content Analysis*. Newbury Park, Calif.: Sage, 1980.

4. Janowitz, op. cit.

5. Babbie, op. cit.

6. Janowitz, op. cit., p. 648.

7. Denis McQuail, *Mass Communication Theory.* London: Sage, 1989, p. 178.

8. Charles R. Wright, *Mass Communication: A Sociological Perspective.* N.Y.: Random House, 1986, p. 125.

9. McQuail, op. cit.

10. Doris Graber, "Content and meaning," *American Behavioral Scientist,* 1989, 33:2, pp. 144-152.

11. Pamela J. Shoemaker and Steven D. Reese, *Mediating the Message, Theories of Influences on Mass Media Content.* N.Y.: Longman, 1996, p. 28.

12. McQuail, op. cit., p. 183.

13. Alison Alexander, Louise M. Benjamin, Keisha Hoerrner, and Darrell Roe, "'We'll be back in a moment:' A content analysis of advertisements in children's television in the 1950s," *Journal of Advertising,* 1998, 27:3, pp. 1-8.

14. Joe Gow, "Reconsidering gender roles on MTV: Depictions in the most popular music videos of the early 1990s," *Communication Reports,* 1996, 9:2, pp. 152-63.

15. Maria Elizabeth Grabe, "Television news magazine crime stories: A functionalist perspective," *Critical Studies in Mass Communication,* 1999, 16:2, pp. 155-171.

16. Janowitz, op. cit., p. 648.

17. Paul S. Voakes, Jack Kapfer, D. Kurpius, and David Shano-yeon Chern, "Diversity in the news: A conceptual and methodological framework," *Journalism and Mass Communication Quarterly,* 1996, pp. 582-593.

18. Maxwell McCombs and Donald Shaw, "The agenda-setting function of the press," *Public Opinion Quarterly,* 1972, 36, pp. 176-187.

19. Maxwell McCombs and Donald Shaw, "The evolution of agenda-setting research," *Journal of Communication,* 1993, 43:2, pp. 58-67.

20. Maxwell McCombs, "Explorers and surveyors: Expanding strategies for agenda-setting research," *Journalism Quarterly,* 1992, 69:4, 813.

21. Louis Harris and Associates, Inc. *Public Attitudes Toward People With Disabilities.* N.Y.: National Organization on Disability, 1991.

22. Todd Gitlin, *The whole world is watching.* Berkeley: University of California Press, 1980, p. 9.

23. The Pew Research Center for the People and the Press, "Press Accuracy Rating Hits Two Decade Low, Public Evaluations of the News Media: 1985-2009," Sept. 19, 2009, people-press.org/report/543/.

24. John M. Glionna, "Woman's deafness proves no barrier to listening," *The Los Angeles Times,* Oct. 6, 1998, p. B2.

25. James Ricci, "Guitarist uniquely strums to the rhythm of his heart," *The Los Angeles Times,* Oct. 17, 1998, p. B1.

26. James Rainey, "County policy on troubled children faces court test," *The Los Angeles Times*, Oct. 19, 1998, B1.

27. "Three nonprofits get training, job grants," *The Baltimore Sun*, Oct. 21, 1998, p. 1D.

28. Kris Antonelli, "Auditors say special education misused," *The Baltimore Sun*, Oct. 23, 1998, p. 3B.

29. J. Manier, "Medicine in kids' hands," *Chicago Tribune*, Nov. 22, 1998, p. SW1.

30. Beth Haller, *Disability Rights on the Public Agenda: News Media Coverage of the Americans with Disabilities Act.* Unpublished doctoral dissertation, Temple University, Philadelphia, Pa., 1995.

31. Clifford Christians and James Carey, "The logic and aims of qualitative research," in G.H. Stempel and B.H. Westley, eds., *Research methods in mass communication.* Englewood Cliffs, N.J.: Prentice-Hall, 1981, p. 347.

32. David L. Altheide, *Qualitative Media Analysis.* Thousand Oaks, Calif.: Sage, 1996.

33. Ted Goertzel, "The Gulf War as a Mental Disorder? A Statistical Test of DeMause's Hypothesis," *Political Psychology*, 1993, 14, pp. 711-723.

34. Klaus B. Jensen, "Introduction: The qualitative turn," in K.B. Jensen and N.W. Jankowski, eds., *A Handbook of Qualitative Research Methods for Mass Communication Research.* London: Routledge, 1991, p. 4.

35. Randall Harrison, *The Cartoon: Communication to the Quick.* Beverly Hills, Calif.: Sage, 1981.

36. Carrie Sandahl, "Ahhhh Freak Out! Metaphors of Disability and Femaleness in Performance," *Theatre Topics*, March 1999, 9:11, pp. 11-30.

37. Roger A. Fischer, "Political Cartoon Symbols and the Divergence of Popular and Traditional Cultures in the United States," in Ray B. Browne, M.W. Fishwick, and K.O. Browne. eds., *Dominant Symbols in Popular Culture.* Bowling Green, Ohio: Bowling Green State University Popular Press, 1990.

38. James A. Knoll, *Through a glass, darkly: The photographic image of people with a disability.* Unpublished doctoral dissertation, Syracuse University, 1987.

39. Paul Longmore and Lauri Umansky, "Introduction: Disability History: From the Margins to the Mainstream," *The New Disability History: American Perspectives.* N.Y.: NYU Press, 2000.

40. James Carey, *Communication as Culture.* N.Y.: Routledge, 1992, p. 18.

41. Carey, op. cit., p. 20.

42. Ruth Palmer, "What's in a Cartoon? Circulation, Satire, and Cuban-American Identity." Paper presented at the American Journalism Historians Association – AEJMC History Division joint conference, New York, N.Y., March 20, 2008.

43. Debra Gersh Hernandez, "Cartoonists confront political correctness," *Editor & Publisher*, Aug. 6, 1994, 127:32, pp. 14-15.

44. Arthur Shapiro, *Everybody Belongs: Changing Negative Attitudes Toward Classmates With Disabilities.* N.Y.: RoutledgeFalmer, 2000.

45. Iowa Library Archives, "The editorial cartoons of J.N. 'Ding' Darling," 2007, digital.lib.uiowa. edu/ding/

46. Tim Jones, "Agent Orange's lethal legacy: The next generation," *Chicago Tribune*, Dec. 6, 2009, chicagotribune.com/health/agentorange/chi-agent-orange2-sidebar-dec06,0,3886506.story.

47. Dana Priest & Anne Hull, "Soldiers Face Neglect, Frustration at Army's Top Medical Facility," *The Washington Post*, Feb. 18, 2007, washingtonpost.com/wp-dyn/content/article/2007/02/17/ AR2007021701172.html.

48. Richard K. Scotch, "Disability as the basis for a social movement: Advocacy and politics of definition," *Journal of Social Issues*, 1988, 44:1, pp. 159-172.

49. Frank Bowe, *Handicapping America*. N.Y.: Harper & Row, 1978.

50. John S. Clogston, "Changes in coverage patterns of disability issues in three major American newspapers, 1976-1991." Paper presented at the Annual Meeting of the Association for the Education in Journalism and Mass Communication, Kansas City, Mo., August 1993; John S. Clogston, "Media models," Personal communication, Mar. 8, 1993; John S. Clogston, "Fifty years of disability coverage in *The New York Times*, 1941-1991." Paper presented at the Annual Meeting of the Association for the Education in Journalism and Mass Communication, Montreal, Canada, Aug. 1992; John S. Clogston, "Coverage of persons with disabilities in prestige and high circulation dailies." Paper presented at the Annual Meeting of the Association for the Education in Journalism and Mass Communication, Montreal, Canada, Aug. 1992; John S. Clogston, "Journalists' attitudes toward persons with disabilities: A survey of reporters at prestige and high circulation dailies." Paper presented at the spring conference on Women, Minorities, and the Mass Media, Association for the Education in Journalism and Mass Communication, Atlanta, Ga., Mar. 1992; John S. Clogston, *Reporters' attitudes toward and newspaper coverage of persons with disabilities*. Unpublished doctoral dissertation at Michigan State University, 1991; John S. Clogston, "Perceptions of disability in *The New York Times*." Paper presented at the annual meeting of the Society for Disability Studies, Washington, D.C., June 1990; John S. Clogston, "A theoretical framework for studying media portrayal of persons with disabilities." Paper presented at the Annual Meeting of the Association for the Education in Journalism and Mass Communication, Aug. 1989.

51. John S. Clogston, *Disability Coverage in 16 Newspapers*. Louisville: Advocado Press, 1990.

52. Paul C. Higgins, *Making Disability: Exploring the Social Transformation of Human Variation*. Springfield: Ill.: Charles C. Thomas Publisher, 1992.

53. Irving K. Zola "Communication barriers between 'the able-bodied' and 'the handicapped,'" in R.P. Marinelli and A.E. Dell Orto, eds., *The Psychological and Social Impact of Disability*. N.Y.: Springer, 1991, p. 161.

54. Higgins, op. cit., 19.

55. S. Elizabeth Bird and Robert W. Dardenne, "Myth, chronicle, and story," in James W. Carey, ed., *Media, Myths, and Narratives*. Newbury Park, Calif.: Sage, 1988, p. 80.

56. Laura R. Mitchell, "Beyond the Supercrip syndrome," *Quill*, 1989, pp. 18-19.

57. Martin Krossel, "Handicapped heroes and the knee-jerk press," *Columbia Journalism Review*, 1988, pp. 46-47.

58. Anne Peters, "Heart-wrencher wins journalism's top prize," *The Disability Rag,* August 1985, pp. 45-47.

59. Douglas Biklen, "Framed: Print journalism's treatment of disability issues," in A. Gartner and T. Joe, eds., *Images of the Disabled, Disabling Images.* New York: Praeger, 1987, p. 81.

60. Biklen, op. cit., p. 82.

3.

Changing disability terminology in the news

This chapter looks at the terms the media use to refer to people with disabilities.

Language has always had power to define cultural groups. The words used to refer to a group of people are important: they have ramifications for self-perception, but they also play a large role in shaping what the general public believes about the group. Activists and scholars in the U.S. disability rights movement have for the last several decades been calling for what they term "appropriate language" because, like other social groups before them, they contend that what they are called is intrinsic to their identity as people with disabilities. They insist that they, not others, should define these terms. The language used in stories about disability, they say, helps shape what the public understands about the disability condition. Both activists and theorists say that the way media cover disability, and the language used by journalists as they do this, is central to how people with disabilities view themselves, as well as being central to how the public perceives people with disabilities.

The passage of the Americans with Disabilities Act (ADA) in 1990 – a law primarily crafted by disability rights activists – tried to bring about significant change in the U.S. by eliminating many societal barriers that people with disabilities faced.[1] In many ways, the law was also an effort to shift society's perceptions about disability. Its passage ushered in a new era in America for framing disability via the media.

Yet more has changed in U.S. society than just the law. Preeminent disability studies scholar Paul Longmore says that since passage of the ADA, the disability rights movement has moved into "The Second Phase." Phase One, he says, focused on shifting people with disabilities into the mainstream by outlawing discrimination and mandating access – it argued for social inclusion. The disability rights movement's more recent work, in the Second Phase, has been aimed at strengthening disability culture through self-definition. Both activists and theorists consider media coverage and the language used by journalists to represent disability issues to be central to this self-definition process.[2]

Numerous studies have assessed aspects of media coverage of disability issues other than language and terminology.[3] This chapter seeks to assess the impact of the disability rights movement's efforts to change the media's use of language to refer to disability. The following pages examine news stories' terminology to see whether the efforts of the disability rights movement to change society's attitudes and behaviors toward disability is succeeding.

Language, framing, and disability identity

The concept of framing gives a useful perspective for this study because it "offers a way to describe the power of a communicating text," according to media researcher Robert Entman. Media texts contain frames, "which are manifested by the presence or absence of certain keywords, stock phrases, stereotypical images, sources of information, and sentences that provide thematically reinforcing clusters of facts or judgments."[4] Through their selection of certain words over others, the media make certain terms more salient or memorable for their audiences. This chapter looks at one small, but powerful, element of media framing of people with disabilities – how they are referred to as a social group.

Language about groups engaged in a social movement has always been a site of contested terrain.[5] As society changes, certain terminology falls out of favor, such as the continuum in the U.S. from "colored" to Blacks to African Americans. The dominant culture, or majority, generally resists these language shifts, often derogatorily labeling them as "just political correctness," according to R. Reiser in the *Disability Tribune*.[6] Often the media have been sluggish in assimilating new terms. Accordingly, activists for social movements have had to push their language changes into media frames, usually with only moderate success.

For decades, both overt and implied references to people with disabilities have concerned disabilities studies scholars and the disability rights movement because they are so integral to disability culture and identity. Disability policy consultant June Isaacson-Kailes explains: "A significant element in the struggle for basic human rights is what people call themselves. . . . Disability culture is the commonality of the experience of living with a disability, and language is one of the keys to acknowledging this culture."[7] British disability studies scholar Mairian Corker explained "that the process of defining is bound up in 'matters of identity' and therefore with action, political and otherwise, which is taken."[8]

Since the 1980s, the disability rights movement has been trying to move from the term "handicapped," which many feel associates people with disabilities with cap-in-hand beggars[9] (although recent research reports that derivation of the word is inaccurate[10]), to "people with disabilities," which is known as "people-first" terminology. The passage of the ADA tried to push out the term "handicapped"; activists were involved in writing the legislation and made sure it included the "people-first" terminology. As political science professor Art Blaser notes: "With the term 'disability,' we have a major advantage because it's been used for decades, and was used by an almost unanimous Congress in passing the Americans with Disabilities Act."[11] The preferred disability terminology was a way that activists infused some disability culture into the ADA.

Disability culture as an outgrowth of identity is imbedded with political activism. Since the 1960s, U.S. disability rights activists have advocated for a "frame" in which society views them and their issues as a legitimate minority group that faces societal barriers and discrimination, according to historians of the disability rights movement Doris Fleischer and Frieda Zames.[12] Journalist Joseph Shapiro in his 1993 book, *No Pity. People With Disabilities Forging a New Civil Rights Movement*, explained that the 20th-century history of the U.S. disability rights movement had an emphasis on activists coming together to push for federal legislation such as the Rehabilitation Act in the 1970s, which was a precursor to the ADA.[13] And C. J. Johnstone argues that formalized education and the recent growth of disability studies college programs forged modern disability identity. He argues that disability identity is becoming a formalized part of U.S. society:

> The common voice and other empowering identities for people with disabilities are emergently receiving support by formalized structures. These structures publicize and communicate the notion of disability identity to the larger population. Messages such as: people come be-

fore disability, disability as a social and political issue, and promotion of disability culture are found in formal education, organizations and communications. . . . Publications have institutionalized the disabled identity into mainstream society. Narrative accounts of disability have brought the reality and complexity of disability to a wide readership, some with no previous experience with the notion of identity.[14]

The narrative accounts to which Johnstone refers are personal accounts within memoirs and other books about personal stories, rather than the mass media.

Media reports, too, prefer these personal stories that are fashioned into narratives of "overcoming the odds" or exceptional accomplishments, according to disability studies scholar Rosemarie Garland-Thomson;[15] however, in the media's hands, these narratives serve to undermine disability identity with their syrupy messages infused with pity. Therein lays the tension between the internal pride, identity, and culture of the disability rights movement and the misinterpretation by the wider society, represented by the media, that active people with disabilities are "inspirational" or are "superior" in the face of "tragedy." The disability rights movement is trying to move forward a serious political agenda, but the media focus on blind people who go bowling or a teen with a severe facial disfigurement who copes with life gracefully.[16]

These issues underpin the discussions of disability terminology, the terms preferred by the disability rights movement, and what is actually used by the news media. For decades, publications intended primarily for the disability community have noted that much media coverage of disability issues often does not include language that reflects current usage within the community.[17] The disability rights magazine *The Disability Rag's* editor Mary Johnson noted that, after the ADA passed, media coverage continued a seeming lack of awareness and context when addressing disability issues.[18]

Some disability activists criticize the disability rights movement for the "media problem," saying it stems from lack of a single, national voice for the movement, lack of training in conveying the importance of language choice to the media, as well as lack of framing issues in ways that emphasize people-first and other standards for addressing disability issues.[19] However, many in the disability community say they are hampered by the negative associations that already exist inherently in the words "disabled" and "disability." As activist Bill Bolt argued in *Ragged Edge* (formerly *The Disability Rag)*: "The name that we've insisted on for ourselves – the word 'disabled' – sends journalists into a tailspin. If we are 'disabled,' that is, 'without abilities,' then what is this demand for equal employment, journalists likely think. On the other hand, if we can work with only minimal special arrangements, then why do we need all kinds of government funds to live on?"[20]

U.S. disability studies scholar Simi Linton in her book *Claiming Disability* also notes the problematic nature of the prefix "dis," which connotes separation or taking apart. It has numerous denotative meanings: "absence of, as in disinterest; opposite of, as in disfavor; undo, do the opposite of, as disarrange; and deprive of, as in disenfranchise. The Latin root *dis* means apart, asunder. Therefore, to use the verb disable, means in part to deprive of capability or effectiveness. The prefix creates a barrier, cleaving in two, ability and its absence, its opposite. Disability is the 'not' condition, the repudiation of ability."[21]

Yet disability activists and scholars also counter that any new terms promoted by the movement, regardless of journalists' practices and intentions, would soon be stigmatized by the larger culture; therefore, efforts should concentrate on improving perceptions of people with disabilities. Over time such efforts might erase the stigma associated with "disabled" and similar terms. "Old habits die hard, in part because they are reinforced by the media," notes Blaser, adding, "But they do die."[22] He disagrees with those who consider negativity inherent in the words "disabled" and "disability" and public perception of the terms as unalterable. Decades of work by the movement has been changing the meaning of disability, much as African Americans transformed the term "black" and the gay and lesbian movements altered "queer." Blaser says the disability community is fighting the same fight as these other social groups: "I'm not convinced that our task in changing language is more difficult than Malcolm X's was, or unusually difficult when compared with other groups'. But I'll really be surprised if it's not still being fought by my children's grandchildren."[23]

Some rhetorical and linguistic theorists agree with Blaser. Although disability has long been equated with tragedy, suffering, and weakness in the minds of many in the general public, the disability rights movement will continue to battle for a new understanding of the word over many years or decades to come. British disability studies scholar Jenny Corbett maintains that language, as a primary source of power and control, must be contested – words, e.g., disabled, must be won by the "voice of enlightened modernity" in debates about political correctness, so that old usages are redefined. Language that retains a metaphorical suffering, pathos, and dependency needs to be challenged.[24] For example, by reclaiming the word "crip," disabled activists take the image in their identity that scares outsiders and make it a source of militant pride.

In the same vein, Linton maintains that wrestling for control of language and attempting to reassign the meaning of terminology used to describe disability and disabled people is vital to show how language reinforces the dominant culture's views of disability. She argues that since roughly 1980 people with disabilities themselves have gained more control over definitional issues, including within the news media. "Less subtle, idiomatic terms for people with disabilities, such as: 'cripple,' 'vegetable,' 'dumb,' 'deformed,' 'retard,' and 'gimp' have generally been expunged from public conversation though they appear in discourse. . . . Cripple as a descriptor of disabled people is considered impolite, but the word had retained its metaphoric vitality, as in 'the exposé in the newspaper crippled the politician's campaign.'"[25]

However, U.S.-based Israeli disability studies scholar Liat Ben-Moshe believes even the metaphoric use of disability terms stigmatize people with disabilities: "When we use terms like 'retarded,' 'lame,' or 'blind' – even if we are referring to acts or ideas and not to people at all – we perpetuate the stigma associated with disability. By using a label, which is commonly associated with disabled people to denote deficiency, a lack, or an ill-conceived notion, we reproduce the oppression of people with disabilities."[26]

Other types of negative terminology that remain in the media reinforce a "sick role" or the medicalization of the disability identity. The news media sometimes refer to people who had contracted polio earlier in life as having been "stricken" with polio. People with AIDS are sometimes referred to as "AIDS sufferers," "suffering from" AIDS, "AIDS patients," or "victims of" AIDS. Activist Jo Bower explains how dislike of this language has been a bond between many people with different disabilities. "All of us have rejected the terms 'victim' and 'patient' to describe our relationship to our conditions and instead have chosen terms with dignity, which underline our personhood primarily and our condition second, as in people with HIV or people with disabilities."[27] Linton adds that phrases found in media writing, such as, "the man is a victim of cerebral palsy," make the condition an agent that acts upon a helpless victim. Use of "victim" implies criminal action while also giving life, power, and intention to the condition while rendering the person passive and helpless. Problematic assumptions also apply to terms such as "suffering from" or "afflicted with." If the person's condition is germane to the story, language such as "he has cerebral palsy," serves as a better descriptor because it doesn't impose extraneous meanings while more accurately reporting the facts.

With regard to the stereotyping phrases "wheelchair-bound" or "confined to a wheelchair," Linton notes these common descriptions in the print media grant more power to the chair than the person. To report instead that someone uses a wheelchair "not only indicates the active nature of the user and the positive way that wheelchairs increase mobility and activity but recognizes that people get in and out of wheelchairs for different activities: driving a car, going swimming, sitting on the couch, or occasionally, for making love."[28]

Susan Peters believes such socio-linguistic changes that aim to empower people with disabilities will result in the most positive consequences. Media framing through negative terminology can even prove detrimental to the self-images of people with disabilities. Such practices result in significant negative consequences and barriers to productive living. Many disabled people (particularly youth) internalize labels and language used to inculcate them as passive recipients of state welfare, Peters says. "They develop a false consciousness as they internalize the oppressors' image conveyed through language. This cultural invasion leads many disabled people to a silent world of passive acceptance where they adapt to the status quo. . . ."[29] Corker reaches similar conclusions, but optimistically notes that around the world disabled people have been using language to create a "new disability discourse," and that issues of linguistic and cultural difference go well beyond the "'nice' words and the 'nasty' words relating to disability that are in cultural circulation."[30] To effectively produce socio-cultural change, the U.S. disability rights movement continues to directly engage media and other powerful institutions by calling attention to the linguistic frames used to characterize disability.

The significance of the ADA as an agent of change

The first director of the National Council on Disability recalled what he said was the most important media event in the U.S. disability rights movement – the international Cable News Network (CNN)'s decision to carry the signing of the Americans with Disabilities Act live on TV. He said this one media event may have even been the most significant aspect of the ADA because "laws are as much perception as reality."[31] This one event thrust disability rights before the eyes of a huge TV audience and in turn, got journalists thinking about disability issues as a legitimate news story.

This chapter about disability terminology looks at a time frame after the passage of the ADA because, as strong disability rights legislation, it had the potential to shift U.S. society to be more barrier-free. Linguistically, the ADA helped create a message about people with disabilities that contrasted with narrow stereotypes and misleading myths of the past. The disability rights movement had long been battling a medical or social welfare representation, which the media often reinforced, that viewed disability as a physical problem alone, residing within an individual.[32] Activists have long pushed for the disability rights model of representation, which acknowledges physical differences while shifting the focus from the disabled individual as "the problem" to societies that have yet to modify their architectural, occupational, educational, communication, and attitudinal environments to accommodate everyone.

One of the greatest accomplishments of activists in getting the ADA passed was maintaining the narrative of civil rights and minority group politics in the law.[33] The disability community established a strong narrative for the ADA: "That its protections were an issue of civil rights rather than a charitable obligation or some other rationale."[34] The ADA was "civil rights regardless of cost."[35] With that narrative secure in the legislative language, government sources and disability-related sources gave the news media the same information. For decades, disability had been defined and framed by government through legislation on war veterans, rehabilitation, education, and social security,[36] but this time the disability rights movement had the rhetorical power to craft the ADA. As Richard Scotch explains: "The disability rights movement is one in which the way an issue was framed had serious effects on both movement participation and the ability of the movement to influence public policies."[37]

Previous research I have done has argued that the ADA and the U.S. news media's coverage of it in the early years helped place the disability rights model before the broader public. Disability rights activists helped construct the wording of the ADA, and with those words flowing through the U.S. government to the media, a more rights-oriented frame of disability was presented to the public. Therefore, in one sweeping legislative action, the disability rights perspective was forced onto the media radar and the public agenda of the U.S., possibly shifting the media frames about people with disabilities.[38]

⊷═◑ ◐═⊷

Mass media may be even more significant in presenting people with disabilities and their issues. Many Americans have less interpersonal contact with people with disabilities because of barriers that still exist in society. Much of society is exposed to views of disability almost exclusively through mass media.[39]

The media's coverage of the ADA probably promoted an awareness of the preferred terminology with which to refer to people with disabilities because the news media parroted the government's "people-first" language in the coverage.[40] Past media research has confirmed that most journalists give high credibility to government information.[41] After the ADA, some local or state governments embraced "people-first" language. Pennsylvania Governor Robert P. Casey in 1992 mandated "people-first" language in an executive order barring discrimination based on disability in state government.[42] (Examples of people-first language are saying "a professor with a disability" rather than "a handicapped professor," saying "uses a wheelchair" not "confined to a wheelchair," or "non-disabled" not "normal."[43])

Did this disability rights wording carefully crafted for the ADA, influence how two elite members of the U.S. news media – *The New York Times* and *The Washington Post* – refer to people with disabilities? A content trend analysis of two major U.S. newspapers looked at disability terminology use over a 10-year period. *The New York Times* and *The Washington Post* were selected primarily because of their large circulations and their prominence as agenda-setting, elite media in the U.S.. Although content analysis makes judgments about content, not media effects, the assumption is that elite media act as opinion leaders about disability information and disability terminology in their stories. Most Americans say they use elite news media for information and these media are extremely important to them, according to a poll. Although Americans still tend to use more network TV news as sources of information, they are more likely to value the information from newspapers.[44]

Print stories found via the Lexis-Nexis newspaper database were searched for the following terms: "disabled," "disability," "disabilities," "handicapped," "cripple," and "crippled" in the two newspapers during October and November 1990, 1995, and 2000.[45] October and November were selected because October is Disability Awareness Month and during November most activities in American life continue to occur, such as school and government meetings. The total number of stories in both papers per year were 140 in 1990, 224 in 1995, and 186 in 2000. The analysis of the terminology looked at the ways in which the terms were used, such as "the disabled," "disabled person/people," disability as a noun, "people with disabilities," "handicapped," "cripple," or "crippled." A separate analysis looked at three other terms specifically: "confined to a wheelchair," "wheelchair-bound," and "wheelchair user." The analysis of these terms covered the entire years of 1990, 1995, and 2000, so the findings on those terms were the universe of uses for those years rather than samples.

A significant finding from this trend analysis is that these two U.S. agenda-setting newspapers seem to be learning to eliminate the term "handicapped." *The New York Times* used the term 38 times in 1990 and by 2000 that had dropped to 26 uses; *The Washington Post* used the term 32 times in 1990 and by 2000 that had dropped to 17 uses. This change possibly illustrates the inroads the disability rights movement was making in educating news media about preferred terminology. In addition, because 1990 saw the passage of the ADA, many in the media were only beginning to become aware of disability terminology changes. Two 1990 *New York Times* stories in preparation for ski season used phrases such as ski "clinics for the handicapped"[46] and "expanded handicapped skiers' program,"[47] whereas in 2000, a *New York Times* story that had several references to "handicapped children" was headlined "Parents make toys for disabled children."[48] So there seemed to be a transition occurring in the news media to replace the term "handicapped" with "disabled" in some instances. In addition, both newspapers appear to understand that the term "crippled" is no longer appropriate, although *The Washington Post* used the term occasionally.

Another positive finding is the increased use of the "people-first" terms "person with a disability" or "people with disabilities." In *The Washington Post*, this term increased from 19 references in 1990 to 45 in 2000. Part of this increase is probably due to prevalent use of "people-first" terminology among government and disability organizations, and the media are using verbatim references to terms given to them by these groups. For example, a *Washington Post* education story uses the phrase "students with disabilities," which is probably how the Council for Exceptional Children's report, the source of the story, referred to them.[49]

However, general disability terminology that is not preferred by the disability community also had increases over the years. Use of the term "the disabled" increased in both newspapers, especially in 1995. The reason this noun phrase is not preferred is that these nouns created from adjectives define people with disabilities in terms of their disabilities, rather than as people first.[50] This type of language subjugates people and presents them only in terms of their disability, rather than as multidimensional people. Not surprisingly, researcher Karen Dajani confirmed that the now defunct Disability News Service rarely used "the disabled," but that The Associated Press used the term more often than "people with disabilities" or "disabled people" over a six-month period.[51]

However, most media do not know or understand this problem with the term "the disabled." "The disabled" fits with the norms of journalism because it is shorter than "people with disabilities" in space-sensitive newspapers. Also, many times the newspapers used "the disabled" in combination with other groups, such as the phrase "housing for the homeless, the disabled and people with mental problems" from *The New York Times*.[52] These uses of the terms illustrate another problem in how "the disabled" is used – it seems to be partnered with powerless societal groups. In fact, the majority of U.S. people with disabilities between the ages of 21 and 64 (57%) are employed; therefore, it is inappropriate to identify them as poor or homeless.[53]

The most problematic terminology use found in the two newspapers was the continued and increased use of "wheelchair-bound" and "confined to a wheelchair." *The Associated Press Stylebook*, the "bible" on language use for print journalists, tells journalists not to write about a person's disability unless it is pertinent to the story.[54] The *Stylebook* admonishes writers not to use the terms "confined to a wheelchair" or "wheelchair-bound" because "people use wheelchairs for independent mobility."[55] Therefore, in using incorrect language about disability, the journalists have rejected some of the rules of their profession. Imbedded cultural beliefs seemed to overtake the professional norms of journalists. After the death of Christopher Reeve in October 2004, *The Washington Post* still used "wheelchair bound" in an editorial about stem cell research and Reeve, and in a story about the arrest of an elderly protestor.[56]

The Washington Post was found to be a prevalent user of the term "wheelchair-bound," with use of the term increasing from nine instances in 1990 to 21 instances in 2000. Although this is a small number for the entire year, the term is never supposed to be used at all. The term is typically used as an adjective to describe someone, such as "her wheelchair-bound sister"[57] or "two wheelchair-bound New Yorkers."[58] The use of "confined to a wheelchair" assigns blame to a disease or medical condition that caused the "confinement." For example, *The New York Times* called "Carol Rosenwald, frail and confined to a wheelchair by multiple sclerosis."[59]

As language use, both terms are incorrectly applied, according to any dictionary, because "confined" means "to keep shut up, as in a prison" and "bound" means "tied,"[60] and everyone who uses a wheelchair leaves the chair for activities such as sleeping. When journalists use these terms, they misrepresent disability, as well as showing their misunderstanding of the disability experience. Wheelchairs are not binding or confining but actually increase mobility, speed, and ability. For many people, wheelchairs increase their personal freedom.[61]

A number of disability studies scholars argue that this inappropriate language use reflects the fears of non-disabled people about disability. Human fears of an "imperfect body" that might need to use a wheelchair are great. Feminist disability studies scholar Susan Wendell says that it is more than just fear of physical difference at work here. "Suffering caused by the body, and the inability to control the body, are despised, pitied, and above all, feared. This fear, experienced individually, is also deeply imbedded in our culture."[62] One study showed that 29 percent of Americans surveyed felt wheelchair use was a tragedy.[63] Journalists are inculcated with these same cultural fears.

Even in light of these cultural fears, this analysis of terminology in *The Washington Post* and *The New York Times* does provide some evidence that journalists are learning to integrate new, more favorable terms into their stories. Both newspapers are using the term "wheelchair user" more often. The use of the term more than doubled in *The Washington Post* and more than tripled in *The New York Times*. Considering that entire years of stories were analyzed, there is not much use of the term, but the fact that "wheelchair user" grew in prevalence in 1995 and 2000 means two major newspapers are aware it exists.

Conclusions

As with other oppressed groups in society, language is a site of struggle. And for people with disabilities, issues of identity are tied to media labeling. Even the slight improvement of disability terminology in the news media, i.e., less use of "handicapped" and more use of "wheelchair user," serves to illustrate the growing political influence and identity of the U.S. disability rights movement. Susan Scheer, formerly a deputy director in New York's Mayor Office for People with Disabilities, explains that the growth of an educated, professional class of disability rights advocates has meant a more sophisticated approach to changing media coverage of disability issues:

Litigating cases and lobbying elected officials were the traditional techniques that the community used in the past. But now these techniques are used in combination with establishing connections with television, radio, and newspaper reporters and educating them. The language in the news accounts and editorials, although far from perfect, is much improved; for example, 'wheelchair user' is finally beginning to replace 'wheelchair bound.' Also, stories have more balance, and the result is that the public is beginning to understand disability issues.[64]

Although Scheer's comments are slightly more optimistic than this analysis found, many who follow media reporting are seeing that American journalism has a better understanding of disability topics. The hope is that deep within media practices, changes are percolating – changes that will begin to see people with disabilities and their issues in the same way as they see other social, cultural, and civil rights issues. This analysis offers no definitive proof that the media are beginning to understand disability rights and disability terminology, but the trends found do indicate that their labeling of people with disabilities has improved. For example, if the trends found by this chapter continue, the word "handicapped" may no longer appear in U.S. news media within the next few decades.

Studies such as this one, which track media labeling of people with disabilities, help us understand how far the U.S. news media have come and how far they must go to reach a higher level of disability understanding. Changes in disability language use within the media can signal a new paradigm in the way people with disabilities and their issues will be framed in the future.

Notes

1. This is a reprint of Beth Haller, Bruce Dorries, and Jessica Rahn, "Media labeling versus the U.S. disability community identity: A study of shifting cultural language," *Disability & Society*, 21:1, Jan. 2006. As this chapter is about disability terminology in the U.S. media, the preferred term in the U.S., "people with disabilities," will be used. It is understood that other English-speaking countries have other preferred terms, such as "disabled people" in the U.K.

2. Paul Longmore, "The Second Phase," *The Disability Rag & Resource*, 1995, pp. 4-11.

3. See John Clogston, *Reporters' attitudes toward and newspaper coverage of persons with disabilities.* Ph.D. dissertation., Michigan State University, 1991; John Clogston, *Disability Coverage in 16 Newspapers.* (Louisville: Advocado Press, 1990); John Clogston, "A theoretical framework for studying

media portrayal of persons with disabilities." Paper presented at the annual meeting of AEJMC, Washington, D.C., 1989; Beth Haller, "Confusing disability and tragedy," *The Baltimore Sun*, Apr. 29, 2001; Beth Haller, "If They limp, they lead? News representations and the hierarchy of disability images," *Handbook of Communication and People with Disabilities*, Dawn Braithwaite and Teri Thompson (eds.). Mahwah, N.J.: Lawrence Erlbaum, 2000; Beth Haller, "How the news frames disability: Print media coverage of the Americans with Disabilities Act," *Research in Social Science and Disability*, JAI Press, 1, 1999; Beth Haller, *News Coverage of Disability Issues: A Final Report for the Center for an Accessible Society*. San Diego: Center for an Accessible Society, July 1999, part of Grant No. H133A980045 from the National Institute on Disability and Rehabilitation Research; Beth Haller, *Disability rights on the public agenda: News media coverage of the Americans with Disabilities Act.* Unpublished doctoral dissertation. Temple University, Philadelphia, Pa., 1995; Beth Haller, "Paternalism and Protest: Coverage of Deaf Persons in *The Washington Post* and *New York Times*," *Mass Comm Review*, 1993, 20:3/4; Sharon Barnartt, Kay Schriner, and Richard Scotch, "Advocacy and political action," in G.L. Albrecht, K.D. Seelman, and M. Bury, eds., *Handbook of Disability Studies*. Thousand Oaks, Calif.: Sage, 2001, pp. 430-449; Guy Cumberbatch and R. Negrine, *Images of Disability on Television*. London: Routledge, 1991; and Mary Johnson, *Make Them Go Away: Clint Eastwood, Christopher Reeve & the Case Against Disability Rights*. Louisville, Ky.: Avocado Press, 2000.

4. Robert M. Entman, "Framing: Toward clarification of a fractured paradigm," *Journal of Communication*, 1993, 43:4, pp. 51-58.

5. See Charles J. Stewart, Craig Allen Smith, and Robert E. Denton, *Persuasion and Social Movements* (3rd ed.). Prospect Heights, Il.: Waveland, 1994; Tom W. Smith, "Changing Racial Labels: From 'Colored' to 'Negro' to 'Black' to 'African American.'" *Public Opinion Quarterly*, 1992, 56, pp. 496-514; Irving Lewis Allen, *Unkind Words: Ethnic Labeling from Redskin to WASP*. N.Y.: Bergin and Garvey, 1990.

6. R. Reiser, "Does Language Matter?" *Disability Tribune*, Oct. 2001. Accessed July 11, 2005 at daa. org.uk/e_tribune/e_2001_10.htm.

7. June Isaacson-Kailes, "Language is more than a trivial concern," *The Disability Rag & Resource*, July 1986, p. 5.

8. Mairian Corker, "New disability discourse, the principle of optimization and social change," Corker, M. and French, S. (eds), *Disability Discourse*. Philadelphia: Open University Press, 1999, p. 225.

9. Colin Barnes, *Disabling Imagery and the Media: An Exploration of the Principles for Media Representations of Disabled People*. Derby, U.K.: The British Council of Disabled People, 1992.

10. Melanie Crowley and Mike Crowley, "Spotlight on handicap," Take our word for it, 66, 1999, takeourword.com/Issue066.html.

11. Art Blaser, "Changing the meaning of 'disability,'" *Ragged Edge*, 2002, pp. 25-26.

12. Doris Fleischer and Frieda Zames, *The Disability Rights Movement: From Charity to Confrontation*. Philadelphia: Temple University Press, 2001.

13. Joseph Shapiro, *No Pity. People with Disabilities Forging a New Civil Rights Movement*. N.Y.: Times Books/Random House, 1993.

14. C. J. Johnstone, "Disability and identity: Personal constructions and formalized supports," *Disability Studies Quarterly*, 24:4, Fall 2004, dsq-sds.org/_articles_html/2004/fall/dsq_fall04_johnstone.html.

15. Rosemarie Garland-Thomson, "Seeing the disabled: Popular rhetorics of popular photography," Paul K. Longmore and Lauri Umanski, eds. *The New Disability History: American Perspectives*. N.Y.: New York University Press, 2001.

16. Haller, op. cit., April 29, 2001.

17. Arnold Birenbaum, "Once again, for the first time, people with disabilities are recruited into the workforce," *Ragged Edge*, July/Aug. 2000, raggededgemagazine.com/0700/0700medge1.htm.

18. Mary Johnson, *Make Them Go Away*. Louisville, Ky.: Advocado Press, 2003, p. 17.

19. "What we say, What they hear," *Ragged Edge*, July/Aug. 1999, pp. 19-23.

20. Bill Bolt, "The media don't 'get it' because we don't know what 'it' is," *Ragged Edge*, July/Aug. 1999, p. 24.

21. Simi Linton, *Claiming Disability*. N.Y.: New York University Press, 1998, p. 30.

22. Blaser, op. cit., p. 25.

23. Blaser, op. cit., p. 26.

24. Jenny Corbett, *Bad-mouthing: The Language of Special Needs*. Bristol: Falmer Press, 1996.

25. Linton, op. cit., p. 16.

26. Liat Ben-Moshe, "'Lame idea:' Disabling language in the classroom," *Building Pedagogical Curb Cuts: Incorporating Disability into the University Classroom and Curriculum*. Syracuse, N.Y.: Syracuse University Press, 2005, pp. 107-115.

27. Jo Bower, "HIV and Disability," *The Disability Rag & Resource*, 15:2, Mar./Apr. 1994, pp. 8-14.

28. Linton, op. cit., p. 27.

29. Susan Peters, "Transforming disability identity through critical literacy and the cultural politics of language," Corker, M. and French, S., eds, *Disability Discourse*. Philadelphia: Open University Press, 1999, p. 103.

30. Corker, 1999, op. cit., p. 193.

31. Fleischer and Zames, op. cit., 210.

32. Richard K. Scotch, "Disability as the basis for a social movement: Advocacy and politics of definition," *Journal of Social Issues*, 44:1, 1988, pp. 159-172.

33. Sara D. Watson, "A study in legislative strategy," *Implementing the Americans with Disabilities Act*. Baltimore: Paul H. Brookes, 1993.

34. Watson, op. cit., p. 29.

35. Watson, op. cit., p. 30.

36. Claire Liachowitz, *Disability as Social Construct*. Philadelphia: University of Pennsylvania Press, 1988.

37. Scotch, op. cit., p. 168.

38. Haller, 1995, 1999, 2000, op. cit.

39. Louis Harris and Associates, Inc. *Public attitudes toward people with disabilities.* National poll conducted for National Organization on Disability. New York, N.Y., 1991.

40. Haller, 1995, op. cit.

41. Clarice Olien, Phillip Tichenor, and George Donohue, "Media and protest," in L. Grunig, ed., *Monographs in Environmental Education and Environmental Studies.* Troy, Ohio: North American Association for Environmental Education, 1989.

42. Robert P. Casey, Commonwealth of Pennsylvania Governor's Office executive order. Harrisburg, Pa., July 22, 1992, pp. 1-2.

43. Temple University Institute on Disabilities. *People First: A Language Guide.* 1992 (Brochure available from [IOD/UAP, Ritter Annex, Temple University, Philadelphia, Pa. 19122]).

44. Joe Schwartz, "Local news matters," *American Demographics,* July 1996, p. 18.

45. All the stories with these terms were evaluated. The unit of analysis was an individual newspaper story, not the terms, so one story might contain several different terms. Also, any stories that used metaphorical disability terms that were not connected to disability issues or people with disabilities were eliminated from the sample. Restaurant listings referring to "handicapped accessible" facilities were eliminated. Also, any story in which the only use of the disability term was in an organization's name, such as the President's Committee on the Employment of People with Disabilities, was eliminated because the use of the term reflected no decision-making on the part of the newspaper. However, stories that had any disability term, even one reference unconnected to the rest of the story, were still included in the sample. The limitation of this search is that it missed stories about individual disabilities if there was no use of one of these terms, such as a story about a blind person that never used the term disability. However, because the focus of this study is specifically disability terminology, using the six terms above was the most viable option.

46. Janet Nelson, "Winter in the snow; Breckenridge's wealth of choices," *The New York Times,* Nov. 11, 1990, Section 5, p. 15.

47. Stanley Carr, "Winter in the snow; stretching dollars on the slopes," *The New York Times,* Nov. 11, 1990, Section 5, p. 8.

48. Elsa Brenner, "Parents make toys for disabled children," *The New York Times,* Nov. 26, 2000, Section 14WC, p. 22.

49. "Extra credit," *The Washington Post,* Nov. 7, 2000, p. A18.

50. Longmore, op. cit.

51. Karen F. Dajani, "What's in a name? Terms used to refer to people with disabilities," *Disability Studies Quarterly,* 21:3, Summer 2001, pp. 196-209.

52. Elsa Brenner, "Unease persists over housing mandates," *The New York Times,* Oct. 15, 1995, Section 13WC, p. 1.

53. U.S. Census. (2002) 12th Anniversary of Americans With Disabilities Act (July 26). Press Release census.gov/Press-Release/www/2002/cb02ff11.html.

54. Norm Goldstein, ed., *The Associated Press Stylebook and Briefing on Media Law.* Cambridge, Mass.: Perseus, 2002.

55. Goldstein, op. cit., pp. 74-75.

56. Brewster Thackeray, "Wheelchair users not bound," *The Washington Post* (letter to the editor), Oct. 30, 2004, p. A17.

57. Michael Toscano, "Music rocks into town," *The Washington Post*, Dec. 21, 2000, p. M24.

58. Howard Kurtz, "In the Senate race, what's past is present," *The Washington Post*, Oct. 20, 2000, p. A8.

59. Bill Ryan, "Snapshots of their lives," *The New York Times*, Dec. 31, 2000, Section 14CN, p. 1.

60. *Webster's New World Dictionary of the American Language.* N.Y.: Webster's New World, 1998.

61. Isaacson-Kailes, 1986, op. cit.

62. Susan Wendell, "Toward a feminist theory of disability," *Hypatia*, 1989, 4:2, pp. 104-124.

63. Jeanne Patterson and Barbara Witten, "Myths concerning persons with disabilities," *Journal of Applied Rehabilitation Counseling*, 1986, 18:5, pp. 42-44.

64. Fleischer and Zames, op. cit., p. 208.

4.

Not worth keeping alive?

New York Times narratives about assisted suicide

N ews content is shaped by dominant societal beliefs about disability, and
news framing of assisted suicide presents narratives that ignore or devalue
disability issues. Unfortunately, these news frames are imbued with the
power of the dominant able-bodied culture, which many times defines and classifies disabled people with negative messages. Disability studies scholars call
these dominant beliefs that ignore or stereotype disabled people negatively
"ableism."[1] A particularly heinous narrative frame presents disabled people as
"better off dead" because of their perceived inferiority to able-bodied people
and as "defective" or as having a worthless status, disability studies scholar Joy
Weeber says.[2] Ableism creates a societal meta-narrative in which "society perceives disabled persons to be damaged, defective, and less socially marketable
than non-disabled persons,"[3] according to narrative scholar Marilynn Phillips.
Therefore, disabled people are judged to be "not worth keeping alive."

These beliefs have historical roots. Euthanasia programs directed at disabled
people have been around for quite some time. Some U.S. policies regarding
eugenics and the euthanasia of disabled people were a model for the Nazis'
elimination program of Jews, gypsies, disabled people and other groups they
felt were *die Vernichtung lebenswerten Leben* (lives not worthy of living), according to historian Hugh Gallagher.[4]

In response to the culture of ableism, the disability rights movement in
America has created an oppositional frame to these mainstream media presen-

tations that they say lead to the oppression of people with disabilities. Disability rights activist and editor William Stothers argues that mainstream coverage misrepresents the assisted suicide issue, excludes disabled activists from the debate, and frames a societal message of "disability as a fate worse than death."[5] Consequently, it is important to examine U.S. disability organizations such as Not Dead Yet and disability activist publications to find narratives that try to counter cultural stereotypes of disability in the news media.

This chapter relied on a qualitative content analysis to understand the news narratives in the framing of a major issue for disabled people in the late 20th century – assisted suicide. It should be noted that due to the strength of dominant cultural beliefs about disabled people, many people in the U.S. rarely view assisted suicide as a disability issue.[6] However, this chapter's analysis relies on the disability rights framework, which contrasts with a dominant view of disabled people as medical or social welfare problems. In an ableist perspective, disability is seen as a physical problem alone, residing within individuals, according to disability studies scholar Richard Scotch.[7] In contrast, the disability rights framework views disability as a phenomenon created by external factors, such as architectural, occupational, educational, communication, and attitudinal environments that fail to accommodate people who are physically different.[8] Within the rights perspective, physical difference is acknowledged and even celebrated as an ethnicity might be by some, but the focus is away from the disabled individual as the problem and on society's structures instead.

For the analysis of news framing[9] of assisted suicide, this chapter primarily looked at stories in *The New York Times* during 1996-1998. These were the last three years Jack Kevorkian was part of the narrative of assisted suicide. He was convicted and imprisoned for committing assisted suicide in 1999.[10] Following media researchers Clifford Christians' and James Carey's notion[11] that the qualitative researcher should assess all aspects of the media texts, this qualitative analysis looked at story sources, direct and indirect quotes, language/terminology used, pro or con narratives about assisted suicide, and missing perspectives about the issue. From this analysis, several major news narrative frames were found in the assisted suicide stories, some of which tied to historic meta-narratives about eugenics/euthanasia and disabled people.

News frames and assisted suicide

With an issue such as assisted suicide, news frames enable us to understand a larger symbolic system of cultural representations of disabled people. Media scholars S. Elizabeth Bird and Robert Dardenne assert that news frames provide understanding of the values and symbols in a culture.[12] For disabled people, cultural definitions within mass media have become the naturalized beliefs about disability that inform ableist ideology today. (Disability studies scholar Joy Weeber calls ableism "a belief in the superiority of being nondisabled that assumes everyone who is disabled wishes they could be nondisabled – at any cost.")[13] This ideology that disabled people are "less than" can become a dominant cultural belief that imbeds news narratives in assisted suicide coverage.

We can see evidence of this narrative frame in historical coverage of the forerunners of assisted suicide: eugenics and euthanasia. The topics entered modern news discourse in the U.S. in the early 1900s, when some physicians actively allowed babies with disabilities to die by denying treatment. In 1915 Dr. Harry J. Haiselden persuaded the parents of a boy born with multiple disabilities not to allow him to have life-saving surgery but to let him die. Haiselden gained media attention in Hearst's *Chicago American* for his efforts to eliminate "defective" babies, whom he said "would be better off dead," according to Martin Pernick's book on the subject.[14]

Disability activists argue that this type of long-held cultural belief that disabled people are "better off dead" has become a naturalized understanding for much of modern society. Consequently, the disability rights activists have had to resist this message very strongly with an alternative that states the obvious: They are "not dead yet." Activists groups such as Not Dead Yet are concerned that both disabled people and terminally ill people may not be receiving supports, treatment for clinical depression, or proper pain management that would allow them to make a rational decision about voluntarily ending their lives if they choose to do so, according to Diane Coleman, the leader of Not Dead Yet.[15] "As a policy, it [assisted suicide] singles out ill and disabled people as fitting subjects for dying. Meanwhile, neither the public nor health professionals endorse this so-called 'autonomous' decision for young, healthy Americans. If there is a Constitutional right to control one's death through assistance, it should apply to all citizens, not just those judged (or misjudged) to have a deficient life," Coleman says.[16]

This cultural narrative that people with disabilities are "incurable" and "better off dead" becomes clear when it is contrasted with the treatment of non-disabled people who are suicidal. When a person without an apparent disability asks to die, he or she is quickly referred to a psychiatrist or psychologist or treated for clinical depression. However, if a person with a disability asks to die, society usually says "of course." Legal scholar Paul Miller explains that "the different attitudes society has about the death of a disabled person, as opposed to that of an able-bodied person, are rooted in the stigma associated with being disabled. Many able-bodied persons are tremendously fearful about becoming disabled. This fear is based upon the notion that a disabled person's life is inferior to, and less precious than, an able-bodied person's life."[17]

Miller adds that these cultural biases against disabled people reinforce self-hatred, which makes even disabled people consider suicide "a rational choice." "The irony about assisted suicide is that concepts of personal autonomy, freedom and dignity are used to empower people with disabilities to kill themselves, rather than enabling them to live independent lives with dignity," Miller says.[18] Because people with disabilities are actively stigmatized and seen as "invalid" in society, many receive no support for independent living, employment, and proper health care and equipment. In addition, the author of *Forced Exit*, Wesley Smith, fears disabled people will become the most prominent victims of assisted suicide because, in an economics-driven medical climate, the message may be that they are too "costly" to keep alive.[19]

News framing of assisted suicide in *The New York Times*

It is these cultural beliefs about disabled people that this chapter explores in the news coverage of assisted suicide in *The New York Times* during 1996-1998. This newspaper was selected because it is the pre-eminent agenda-setting newspaper in the U.S..

Because past media and disability research illustrates that news media sometimes represent disability issues within a medical framework,[20] this analysis discovers whether there is a "medicalization" of the assisted suicide issue in the news coverage. This medical frame is in direct conflict with the disability activists' frame, in which assisted suicide is seen as human rights issue. Disability activists argue that when news media use "medical reasoning" to frame the debate on assisted suicide, they are creating a major falsity that ties into cultural beliefs that misunderstand disabled people's lives. Disabled people and terminally ill people are not usually living similar experiences, although media images typically merge them.

This analysis also looks at the implications of a major U.S. newspaper such as *The New York Times* covering an important societal issue such as assisted suicide, and not using disability rights organizations as sources. The analysis focused primarily on news and feature stories in the newspaper; however, editorials, opinion columns, and letters to the editors were also analyzed because they represented some of the only editorial sites articulating disabled people's perspectives.

A Lexis-Nexis search found all the news/feature stories, opinion columns, and letters to the editor during the period from 1996 to 1998 in *The New York Times* that used the terms "disabled," "disability," "disabilities," or "handicapped" with the term "assisted suicide." There were 39 stories with these combined terms. (A search of the term "assisted suicide" without any disability terms resulted in 476 articles from 1996 to 1998.) These materials were analyzed to reveal the narrative themes or news frames they contained about assisted suicide.

One finding that was clearly apparent was the journalistic exclusion of the U.S.'s most active and well-known anti-assisted suicide organization, Not Dead Yet (NDY). (*The New York Times* only had two references to the organization in 1996-1998.) Based in Chicago, NDY has arranged actions at Kevorkian trials and Supreme Court rulings since its creation in April 27, 1996, but only rarely gets to comment in the mainstream media.

Another obvious finding in any analysis of assisted suicide in the 1990s is that American news media have tended to focus most of the discussion about the issue on one person, Dr. Jack Kevorkian. In *The New York Times*, for example, he was mentioned 160 times with the term "assisted suicide" from 1996 to 1998. Robert Kalwinsky's cultural analysis of the *New York Times* coverage of assisted suicide also confirmed that the newspaper tended to associate coverage of the issue primarily with Kevorkian's activities.[21]

Because Kevorkian's place in the story has been amply studied, this analysis focuses on additional non-Kevorkian news frames as well. The following news frames were found in *New York Times* content about assisted suicide:

1. The issue is about being for or against Dr. Jack Kevorkian.

2. Kevorkian associates are prominent news sources and crucial to defining the assisted suicide issue.

3. Assisted suicide is presented as an ambiguous religious and legal issue, rather than a human rights issue.

4. Disability issues are medicalized in the assisted suicide debate.

5. Better dead than disabled.

News Frame 1: The issue is about being for or against Dr. Jack Kevorkian

By November 1998, Kevorkian admitted to assisting in upwards of 130 deaths and had become the focus of the assisted suicide debate by becoming a kind of "anti-celebrity." Kevorkian's anti-hero status grew through several trials from 1996 through 1998, reaching full-blown media circus status in late 1998 when his video of killing Thomas York appeared on the long-running CBS news program, "60 Minutes." With this action, the New York *Daily News* wrote, Kevorkian moved past the notion of "doctor-assisted suicide to outright euthanasia."[22] The framing imbedded within this phrase seems to be that Kevorkian has moved from a more socially acceptable place on the continuum, "doctor assisted suicide," to a less acceptable one, "outright euthanasia." This illustrates that his grab for the ultimate celebrity attention – having one of his assisted deaths on TV – turned some of the media narratives against him.

But *The New York Times* showed over and over its fascination with Kevorkian (456 stories about him and assisted suicide from 1990 to 2009) and the ease with which he could garner media attention. For example, in 1997, the paper gave him coverage when he held an art show in a suburb of Detroit, where he displayed "a collection of 13 oil paintings depicting severed heads, moldering skulls and rotting corpses." It comes off as a publicity stunt by Kevorkian, but *The New York Times* is there to cover it. However, the newspaper does report that the stunt may have backfired because many visitors to the show found the artwork disturbing – "visitors to the exhibit here today said the paintings presented a disturbing side of a man sometimes portrayed as a humanitarian trying to relieve the suffering of the terminally ill. 'I used to respect what he did,' said Frida Macki, a 30-year-old Detroit accountant. 'These paintings changed my view,' she said. 'He's a sick person – how do I know he doesn't do what he does because he enjoys killing people?'"[23]

The media circus aspect of the Kevorkian-related stories illustrates that many times the news media moved away from covering the issue of assisted suicide and were instead mired in covering the trials and tribulations of Jack Kevorkian, who was sentenced to prison for murder in 1999.

News Frame 2: Kevorkian associates are prominent news sources and crucial to defining the assisted suicide issue

During the news coverage, Kevorkian's lawyers and other advisers garnered much media attention and dominated as sources, thereby creating a pro-assisted suicide frame within a significant segment of the coverage. Kevorkian's lawyer, Geoffrey Fieger, was specifically mentioned or cited as a source in 74 articles in *The New York Times* from 1996 through 1998.

In a case in 1996 in which Kevorkian assisted in the death of a woman with multiple sclerosis, the only spokesperson for "her side" of the story is Fieger. *The New York Times* uses a quote from Fieger as an authoritative source on her condition before death: "She had pain all over and huge open ulcers. Dr. Kevorkian had tried to encourage her to continue, to go on for a while longer, but she was unwilling," Fieger is quoted as saying in the *Times*.[24]

A few months later, Fieger again speaks for a woman with degenerative spinal disease who was not terminally ill, whom Kevorkian helped to kill herself in June 1996. He says she was "in horrible, horrible pain."[25] In general, through his quoted comments, Fieger creates a frame in the news stories that rationalizes physician assisted suicide for its victims. He says: "I am not aware that he (Kevorkian) has ever been present at any suicide. He has sometimes been present when people have ended their horrific suffering."[26] This type of sourcing in a news story by Kevorkian's handlers allows them to speak in favor of the "service" of assisted suicide. Few alternative options to assisted suicide appear in the stories to counter the pro-assisted suicide narrative.

News Frame 3: Assisted suicide is an ambiguous religious and legal issue, rather than a human rights issue

In many news stories, assisted suicide is presented as an ambiguous issue, covering physical, religious, moral, and legal uncertainties. In the U.S. specifically, the anti-assisted suicide movement is linked to the anti-abortion, "right-to-life" movement. For example, the Archbishop of Chicago explained personally why he didn't choose assisted suicide. He sent his message against assisted suicide to the U.S. Supreme Court very powerfully: "'I am at the end of my life,' wrote the Cardinal, who had terminal pancreatic cancer. 'There is much that I have contemplated these last few months of my illness, but as one who is dying, I have especially come to appreciate the gift of life.'"[27] The Vatican also voiced its opposition to assisted suicide when Australia used its voluntary euthanasia law in the Northern Territory to give a lethal injection to an elderly man with cancer.[28] Although the framing from individual Catholics and the Church is powerful and very much against assisted suicide, these sources tend to shift the framing away from the human rights of disabled people and onto specific conflicts based on religious beliefs.

News framing through legal narratives resulted partly from the numerous legal cases involving Kevorkian and also from the U.S. Supreme Court, which ruled in 1997 that the U.S. Constitution does not allow assisted suicide, although states can possibly legalize the practice themselves.[29] The implication from these stories of legal wrangling is that the assisted suicide story is about a legal fight between physicians and attorneys, rather than about deaths of disabled people at the hands of someone like Kevorkian.

The legal twists and turns also were represented in news stories in the 1990s about assisted suicide laws in Oregon and New York. For example, when *The New York Times* wrote a long feature analyzing the ethical conundrums of assisted suicide, it quotes a law professor who agrees that the legal argument alone is a problematic way to discuss assisted suicide. "We're talking public policy here, not individual cases that are moving," he complained.[30] However, his concerns about human rights focused specifically on the impact of assisted suicide on poor people and ethnic minorities, and he did not mention disabled people. The entire article, which tries to analyze the opinions of ethics experts, covers a good range of perspectives on both sides but still does not bring disabled people into the discussion except to explain that "[o]pponents (of assisted suicide) say that society's attitudes toward the poor, the old, the infirm, and the demented would inevitably harden."[31] In contrast, legal scholars who study disability discrimination understand how susceptible disabled people are when a society turns to assisted suicide to eliminate its more vulnerable members of society, disability studies scholar Jerome Bickenbach explains.[32]

News Frame 4: Disability issues are medicalized in the assisted suicide debate

The involvement of the medical profession in the assisted suicide debate in the U.S. continually frames the debate in medical terms. Obviously, there is a medical component related to people who have terminal illnesses and request death, but the media, not understanding the disability rights perspective, continually use the ableist frame, which merges disabled people into a "sickness" category. *The New York Times* characterizes the list of people assisted in suicide by Kevorkian as "seriously ill people," even though many were actually disabled people and not people with terminal illnesses.[33]

One of the more controversial assisted suicides that Kevorkian performed was on Marjorie Wantz, who said she had chronic vaginal pain after several unsuccessful operations. Even Kevorkian's lawyer agreed she had no fatal disease, and the prosecutors said that her pain was psychosomatic. But once again *The New York Times* allowed Kevorkian and his lawyer to speak for the victim and frame her as "terminally ill." Fieger said: "We can show she was in horrific shape."[34] What's missing from the story is a frame that might have come from disabled activists about the support services and counseling that were probably missing in Marjorie Wantz' life. The only sources in the story are Fieger, Kevorkian, prosecutors, and court records.

News Frame 5: Better dead than disabled

This repeated framing in the press that disability and terminal illness are equal derives from ableist ideology, citing disabling conditions as a reason to die. "Ableism causes pain because it convinces us that there is something fundamentally wrong with us, that we are not acceptable just as we are," Joy Weeber explains.[35] This "better off dead" frame can be seen as a meta-narrative that is imbedded in much of the assisted suicide coverage. And to provide the rationale of being disabled as reason to die, it enlists the voices of disabled people who have chosen assisted suicide.

As mentioned, the mainstream press rarely goes to disability rights groups for comments, either in individual stories or on the assisted suicide/euthanasia debate as a whole. Instead, in framing the stories, news media rely on doctors, lawyers, and the last words of a few people who have made the decision to die. For example, *The New York Times* uses Sherry Miller and Austin Bastable, both of whom had MS, to put the voices of disabled people who supported assisted into the story. In this way, *The New York Times* puts forth a personal narrative of the "horror" of disability to provide reasoning for assisted suicide. Bastable is quoted as saying his MS is "like being imprisoned in your own body – kind of like being sentenced to life imprisonment with no chance of parole – for a crime you didn't commit."[36] And *The New York Times* presents Sherry Miller's quote as a "common sense" approach to assisted suicide: "I want to die. I waited too long, and I can't do anything for myself."[37]

According to the disability rights perspective, this is internalized prejudice, and a repudiation of the independent living movement, which allows people who are severely disabled to be in charge of their own lives, according to *Ragged Edge* editor Mary Johnson.[38] Disability rights advocates argue that many who do choose assisted suicide do so for reasons that are caused by external factors, not their actual disability: They may be clinically depressed and not receiving treatment; they may not have adequate pain management or health care; they may not have proper attendant services; they may not have access to assistive technology; or they may incorrectly feel they are a burden to their loved ones.

However, the news media do not acknowledge these reasons for assisted suicide but instead use disabled sources in the stories to "naturalize" the reason of "better dead than disabled." As media scholar Stuart Hall has explained: "The ideological concepts embodied in photos and texts in a newspaper, then, do not produce new knowledge about the world. They produce recognitions of the world as we have already learned to appropriate it."[39] The framing of assisted suicide fits with pre-existing meta-narratives of disability – inferior in ability, less human, a damaged/defective persona, and lives not worth living – long identified by disability studies scholars.[40] Media studies scholar Todd Gitlin argues that the ways in which media frame an issue reveal the unconscious dominant beliefs of a society.[41] News coverage of assisted suicide reveals how the dominant ableist perspective of "better dead than disabled" flows through media in an uncontested "common-sense" way.

Oppositional news frames from disability groups

Many of these examples of major news frames within the news coverage of assisted suicide in *The New York Times* embody long-held cultural beliefs about disability. The general public through this coverage many times receives the message that when people are disabled, their quality of life is so poor and undignified that they are "better off dead."

Some oppositional perspectives do exist to undermine these news frames of the mainstream media. To find those perspectives, however, one must turn to the disability press and disability rights organizations. There, the frame is one of finding value, quality, and dignity in the experiences of disabled people. Disability magazine editor William Stothers explains that what he calls "Kevorkian's relentless evangelism" about assisted suicide feeds society's already negative impression of the quality of disabled people's lives. Instead, he says, society should understand that "many people with disabilities offer shining examples of the possibilities of life – rich, full, expressive, vital life."[42]

Not Dead Yet, the anti-assisted suicide group, has made one of its goals confronting ableism. It insists that the cultural beliefs that feed ableism cause public acceptance of assisted suicide. The organization says legalized assisted suicide represents bigotry against disabled people made life-threatening:

> Like racism, bigotry against people with disabilities can be deadly. Kevorkian's ableism is as extreme as the racism of the Ku Klux Klan. . . . Why is society creating a double standard based on a person's health? Why don't disabled people receive the same suicide prevention that others can take for granted? If Kevorkian's assisted suicide is really "voluntary," then why isn't it available to anyone? . . . While ableist bigots like Kevorkian are showered with public attention, the real experts are never asked: How does someone with significant health impairments achieve a good quality of life?[43]

As Not Dead Yet co-founder Diane Coleman explains, "Each of [Kevorkian's] victims [was] denied a chance to get the support to live to the point of natural death."[44] Disability studies scholars who oppose assisted suicide use a similar frame of the "double standard" when referring to a society quickly helping disabled people to die, when non-disabled people would be given every chance to live.[45]

The message of Not Dead Yet and others against assisted suicide may rarely make it into the mainstream press; however, it fills the alternative and disability press as a way to embolden the disability community to fight what it sees as a new form of eugenics. Writing in the alternative press publication *Utne Reader*, Kathi Wolfe, a visually impaired writer who covers disability issues, easily saw the link between assisted suicide and eugenics. She said the fear of Not Dead Yet is that "the 'right to die' could all too easily become an obligation – not only for those disabled, but for anyone whose life the society feels isn't worth saving."[46] As Not Dead Yet's Coleman pointed out in the *Utne Reader* article, "[Our culture] transmits the message that disability is a fate worse than death. Many people believe that people with disabilities have a 'low quality of life.' In this era of managed care, society thinks, 'Why help these people? Their life has no value. It would be more compassionate to give them the right to die.'"[47]

77

The most important frame from disability activists is that banning assisted suicide is a human rights issue. As mentioned, this news frame rarely makes it into news coverage. Activists argue that because people with disabilities receive little support for independent living, employment, and proper health care and equipment, they have little chance to experience value and quality in their lives. Society provides the option of death through assisted suicide to disabled people, but not the option of living in a supportive culture that values them as human beings. Patti Mullins, a lawyer with a disability and leader of Access International, explains that "we shouldn't allow euthanasia in a society that doesn't provide adequate health care to its entire citizenship," as in America.[48] With increasing health care costs, the disability community fears assisted suicide could easily become an inexpensive alternative to providing disabled people with the resources they need to lead independent lives.

The analysis of *The New York Times* from 1996 to 1998 reveals that the news about assisted suicide gave little voice to the disability perspective. If journalists had understood the political and social issues that inform the disability experience in the U.S., they might have focused some of their stories on why most disabled people do not choose assisted suicide. This type of frame would have illuminated the disability rights perspective. Although the issue of assisted suicide is not a simple one, it is clear from the news frames found in *The New York Times* that many significant aspects of the debate as it relates to disabled people are ignored or misrepresented. By merging together categories of terminal illness and disability, making an anti-hero of Jack Kevorkian, and looking to legal, medical, and religious sources, rather than disability activists, the news stories validate the ableist message of disability as "a fate worse than death."

News about assisted suicide in the current era

From a disability rights perspective, it would be wonderful to report that Western society had come to reject assisted suicide since *The New York Times* content was studied in the late 1990s. However, assisted suicide appears to be gathering more, not less, support and that is reflected in the continued media coverage of the Terri Schiavo case, new state laws permitting assisted suicide, and Jack Kevorkian's release from prison. For example, when Washington State passed its assisted suicide law in 2008, its citizens supported it by a margin of 59 percent to 41 percent.[49]

The case of Terri Schiavo in 2005 added a whole new layer to advocacy against assisted suicide, and had a long-lasting effect on subsequent media coverage. The Florida woman who had been in a persistent vegetative state since 1990 was at the center of a family conflict that at first pitted her parents (who wanted her to remain alive) against her husband (who wanted to remove her feeding tube). This family drama escalated to a national debate in March 2005 when a Florida judge granted husband Michael Schiavo's request to remove Mrs. Schiavo's feeding tube. Protests against this action brought together an unlikely cohort – disability rights activists, right-to-life religious groups, and conservative Republican lawmakers.

Several days after Mrs. Schiavo's feeding tube was removed, Congressional leaders, primarily Republicans, worked to move the Schiavo case into federal court in an effort to restore her feeding tube. President George W. Bush returned to Washington from his Texas ranch in anticipation of signing special legislation. *The New York Times* reported that these extraordinary measures polarized the country, with many Americans upset by Congressional intervention in what average citizens saw as a private family matter.[50]

Social conservatives commenting on the Schiavo case echoed the rhetoric of disability rights activists who had long protested against assisted suicide, which left many liberal Americans now connecting disability activism with socially conservative Republican beliefs. Said Tony Perkins, president of the Family Research Council, one of many groups pushing Congress to act, in *The New York Times*: "'Today it's Terri, tomorrow it's another disabled person. We've tolerated abortion in this country for the last 30 years, and now we're talking about eliminating those who cannot speak for themselves.'"[51] The Congressional efforts failed to restore Mrs. Schiavo's feeding tube and Terri Schiavo died March 31, 2005.

Even though the Terri Schiavo case wasn't always called an "assisted suicide" case, it had a far-reaching effect on that issue – by marrying the right-to-life rhetoric of social conservatives to the human rights language of disability rights activists. And the more liberal journalists were never to forget this connection in their subsequent reporting on the topic of assisted suicide. This case was a kind of "tipping point," in which many journalists saw even less to question about assisted suicide and its impact on the lives of disabled people.

As mentioned in the 1990s study, some of the *New York Times* stories did report on Jack Kevorkian in less than heroic terms. Not Dead Yet's efforts, coupled with Kevorkian's own outrageous antics, did have some success in getting the news media to recognize that Kevorkian crossed a line in his killing of people with disabilities. But the Terri Schiavo case tipped some of the attitudes about assisted suicide back in Kevorkian's favor. A *New York Times* article about assisted suicide during the Schiavo case reported on the growing discussion about right-to-die issues:

> 'People are definitely more open about it than in the past,' said Rabbi Leonard A. Sharzer, a doctor and bioethicist at the Jewish Theological Seminary in New York who opposes suicide on religious grounds. News coverage of assisted suicide and controversial end-of-life issues, from Dr. Jack Kevorkian and Ms. Schiavo to the fight over Oregon's law, has made patients more comfortable talking about death, he said.[52]

In the *New York Times* reporting about Kevorkian's release from prison in 2007, a story tried to provide "balance" by quoting both those for and against him. But some pro-assisted suicide advocates tried to distance themselves somewhat from Kevorkian because they had begun to push for legislation in several states that would sanction assisted suicide: "'He did a lot for the national dialogue way back when, but he also got carried away,' said Lloyd E. Levine, a Democratic assemblyman in California who is sponsoring a bill – due for a vote next week – that would allow some terminally ill patients there to legally seek lethal drugs under a set of guidelines."[53] *The New York Times* went on to report that "Mr. Kevorkian's friends welcomed his return, calling him a caring leader who had aided the wishes of the terminally ill and who, in return, had been grossly abused by the legal system. They had little patience with national advocates now distancing themselves from Mr. Kevorkian."[54] As usual, the newspaper talked about assisted suicide without including the voices of people with disabilities. The anti-assisted suicide source in this story was from Right to Life of Michigan; Not Dead Yet was not mentioned.

Controversy over Kevorkian continues – An HBO film about him was released in spring 2010. The movie, "You Don't Know Jack," directed by Barry Levinson ("Rain Man") stars acclaimed actor Al Pacino as Kevorkian, and even before its appearance it raised the ire of those both for and against assisted suicide, according to ABC News.

"'I am worried that they are going to do the Hollywood take on Kevorkian and turn him into a heroic martyr,'" Arthur Caplan, director of the Center for Bioethics at the University of Pennsylvania, told ABC News.

Caplan and others who support assisted dying with strict guidelines have said Kevorkian was 'cavalier and insensitive' to the dying who turned to him. They also have said Kevorkian preyed on the mentally ill, who, with further evaluation, could have been helped. Caplan said he once asked Kevorkian if he had been aware that one of his victims had a long history of depression. The doctor reputedly responded, 'How am I supposed to know the details of her life?'[55]

It's become clear from the ongoing debate about assisted suicide since 1998 that passions about the topic have not lessened; but because of Kevorkian and the Terri Schiavo case, discussions about the issue have become much more nuanced. Discussions about living wills and palliative care are much more frequent, and the assisted suicide laws passed in places like Washington State and being considered by the Montana Supreme Court have very specific guidelines that will hopefully make the issue clearer so disabled people won't fall victim to the laws. Under the Washington State law, "state residents requesting this assistance must be mentally competent, have six months or less to live according to two physicians, wait 15 days after their request and then repeat that request orally and in writing. They must be capable of administering medication themselves and agree to counseling if their physicians request it. The patients also must be told of alternatives."[56]

The more nuanced discussion of assisted suicide is finally allowing more input from Not Dead Yet into media coverage. In 2009, *New York Times* coverage of the Montana Supreme Court's consideration of legalizing assisted suicide included a spokesperson from Not Dead Yet. Bob Liston, a wheelchair user, "contends that aid in dying could backfire on people with debilitating conditions, leading not to more autonomy, but less. Mr. Liston, an organizer for a national disability-rights group called Not Dead Yet, said he envisioned people like himself being nudged toward life-ending choices by their doctors or families, out of compassion or perhaps convenience. 'People with disabilities don't get to live with dignity, let alone die with dignity,' he said."[57] *The New York Times* seems to finally understand that the disability rights perspective exists in the assisted suicide debate.

But that doesn't mean this major newspaper understands this perspective. The most prestigious paper in the U.S. still seems to be mired in ableism and what its reporters and editors see as the "tragedy" of disability. The paper's cluelessness about disability rights and assisted suicide became apparent when its editors selected someone who has written in favor of selective euthanasia for disabled babies – Princeton professor Peter Singer – to write the essay in *The New York Times Magazine's* annual memorial issue to memorialize the outspoken disability rights activist, lawyer, and writer Harriet McBryde Johnson, who died in 2008.[58] Even though Johnson had debated Singer on the topic of assisted suicide/euthanasia, most in the disability community felt that someone who shared Johnson's disability rights beliefs should have written the essay about her. In 2009, *The New York Times* turned to Singer once again to discuss the concept of health care rationing. He wrote:

> Health care does more than save lives: it also reduces pain and suffering. How can we compare saving a person's life with, say, making it possible for someone who was confined to bed to return to an active life? We can elicit people's values on that too. One common method is to describe medical conditions to people – let's say being a quadriplegic – and tell them that they can choose between 10 years in that condition or some smaller number of years without it. If most would prefer, say, 10 years as a quadriplegic to 4 years of nondisabled life, but would choose 6 years of nondisabled life over 10 with quadriplegia, but have difficulty deciding between 5 years of nondisabled life or 10 years with quadriplegia, then they are, in effect, assessing life with quadriplegia as half as good as nondisabled life.[59]

Singer's formulaic approach to health care cannot work in a culture awash in ableism because it doesn't take into account that most non-disabled people see little quality in a life with a disability. In a letter to the editor *The New York Times* did not publish, the Disability Rights Education and Defense Fund (DREDF) tried to protest Singer's perspective. In the letter, DREDF's executive director Susan Henderson wrote that Singer's essay

> reproduces tired prejudices about people with disabilities. As a graphic for the piece illustrates, Singer also ignores what his arguments fuel. He discusses the comparative value of people with and without quadriplegia. On Singer's cue, the graphic's designer blithely summarized that discussion: '___ YEARS OF A NONDISABLED LIFE IS WORTH ___

YEARS OF A DISABLED LIFE.' This is one consequence of Singer's price on life. In the lens of prejudice, life breaks down into 'nondisabled' or 'disabled,' worth it or not.[60]

Whether it is reporting on Jack Kevorkian in 1996, or an essay in 2008 about an important disability rights activist who campaigned against assisted suicide, or the volatile health care reform debate in 2009, *The New York Times* appears to be stuck in its ongoing framework of ableism.

Notes

Parts of this chapter appeared in Beth Haller and Sue Ralph, "Not Worth Keeping Alive? News Framing of Physician-assisted suicide in the United States and Great Britain," *Journalism Studies,* 2001, 2:3.

1. Lennard Davis, "J'accuse!: Cultural imperialism – Ableist style," *Social Alternatives,* 1999, 18, pp. 36-41; Simi Linton, *Claiming Disability: Knowledge and Identity.* N.Y.: NYU Press, 1998.

2. Joy Weeber, "What could I know of racism?" *Journal of Counseling & Development,* 1999, 77, pp. 20-24.

3. Marilyn J. Phillips, "Damaged goods: The oral narratives of the experience of disability in American culture", *Social Science & Medicine,* 1990, 30, pp. 849-857.

4. Hugh Gregory Gallagher, *By Trust Betrayed.* New York: Holt, 1990; Robert N. Proctor, *Racial Hygiene: Medicine Under the Nazis.* Cambridge Mass.: Harvard University Press, 1988.

5. William G. Stothers, "Death and Life – it's time to choose up sides," *Mainstream,* Feb. 1996, p. 42.

6. Kimberly A. Lauffer, and Sarah Bembry, "Investigating media influence on attitudes toward people with disabilities and euthanasia." Paper presented at the Association for Education in Journalism and Mass Communication annual meeting, New Orleans, Aug. 1999.

7. Richard K. Scotch, "Disability as the basis for a social movement: Advocacy and politics of definition," *Journal of Social Issues,* 1988, 44, pp. 159-172.

8. Frank Bowe, *Handicapping America.* N.Y.: Harper & Row, 1978.

9. Robert M. Entman, "Framing: Toward clarification of a fractured paradigm," *Journal of Communication.* 1993, 43, 51-58; Robert M. Entman, "Framing U.S. coverage of international news: Contrasts in narratives of KAL and Iran Air incidents," *Journal of Communication,* 1991, 41, pp. 6-27.

10. MSNBC, "Kevorkian released from prison after 8 years," June 1, 2007, msnbc.msn.com/id/ 18974940/.

11. Clifford Christians and James Carey, "The logic and aims of qualitative research," in G.H. Stempel and B.H. Westley, eds., *Research Methods in Mass Communication.* Englewood Cliffs, N.J., Prentice-Hall, 1981, pp. 342-362.

12. S. Elizabeth Bird and Robert W. Dardenne, "Myth, chronicle, and story," in James W. Carey, ed., *Media, Myths, and Narratives.* Newbury Park, Calif.: Sage, 1988, pp. 67-86.

13. Weeber, op. cit., p. 20.

14. Martin Pernick, *The Black Stork: Eugenics and the Death of "Defective" Babies in American Medicine and Motion Pictures Since 1915.* New York: Oxford University Press, 1996, p. 15.

15. Diane Coleman, Testimony before the Constitution Subcommittee of the Judiciary Committee of the U.S. House Of Representatives, Washington, D.C., Apr. 29, 1996.

16. Coleman, op. cit.

17. Paul S. Miller, "The impact of assisted suicide on persons with disabilities – Is it a right without freedom?" *Issues in Law and Medicine,* 1993, 9, pp. 47-62.

18. Miller, op. cit., p. 48.

19. Wesley J. Smith, *Forced Exit: The Slippery Slope from Assisted Suicide to Legalized Murder.* N.Y.: Times Books, 1997.

10. John S. Clogston, *Reporters' attitudes toward and newspaper coverage of persons with disabilities,* unpublished doctoral dissertation, Michigan State University, 1991; John S. Clogston, *Disability Coverage in 16 Newspapers.* Louisville: Advocado Press, 1990; John S. Clogston, "A theoretical framework for studying media portrayal of persons with disabilities." Paper presented at the Annual Meeting of the Association for the Education in Journalism and Mass Communication, Washington, D.C., August 1989; Douglas Biklen, "Framed: Print journalism's treatment of disability issues", in A. Gartner and T. Joe, eds., *Images of the Disabled, Disabling Images.* New York, Praeger, 1987; and Deni Elliott, "Disability and the media: The ethics of the matter," in *The Disabled, the Media, and the Information Age,* Jack Nelson, ed., New York, Greenwood Press, 1994, pp. 73-79.

21. Robert Kalwinsky, Analysis of physician-assisted suicide in *The New York Times."* Paper presented at the Association for Education in Journalism and Mass Communication annual meeting, Chicago, August 1997.

22. Helen Kennedy, "Dr. Death's reel," New York *Daily News,* Nov. 23, 1998, p. 5.

23. Keith Bradsher, "Kevorkian Is Also Painter. His Main Theme Is Death," *The New York Times,* Mar. 17, 1997, p. A10.

24. "Kevorkian attends another death; woman's body is left in vain," *The New York Times,* Jan. 30, 1996, p. A11.

25. "Ailing woman kills herself with help of Kevorkian," *The New York Times,* June 22, 1996, p. A20.

26. Jack Lessenberry, "Kevorkian is arrested and charged in a suicide," *The New York Times,* Nov. 7, 1996, p. A19.

27. Gustav Neibuhr, "Dying Cardinal asks court to rule against suicide aid," *The New York Times,* 1996, Nov. 13, 1996, p. A18.

28. "News in brief: Vatican 'horror' at euthanasia," *Guardian*, Sept. 27, 1996, 16.

29. Joan Biskupic, "High court allows ban on assisted suicide," *The Washington Post*, June 27, 1997, pp. A1, A5.

30. Gina Kolata, "Concerns grow that doctor assisted suicide would leave the powerless vulnerable," *The New York Times*, Oct. 20, 1996, p. 14.

31. Kolata, op. cit., p. 14.

32. Jerome Bickenbach, "Protecting the innocents from physician-assisted suicide: Disability discrimination and the duty to protect otherwise vulnerable groups," in M. P. Battin, R. Rhodes, and A. Silvers, eds., *Physician-assisted Suicide: Expanding the Debate*. N.Y., Routledge, 1998, pp. 13-132.

33. Tamar Lewin, "Ruling sharpens assisted-suicide debate," *The New York Times*, Mar. 8, 1996, p. 14.

34. Jack Lessenberry, "After victory, a new trial for weary Kevorkian," *The New York Times*, Mar. 11, 1996, p. A13.

35. Weeber, op. cit., p. 21.

36. Clyde H. Farnsworth, "Tape recalls a Canadian's gratitude to Kevorkian," *The New York Times*, May 9, 1996, p. A17.

37. "Trial turns to statements about death on videotape," *The New York Times*, Apr. 28, 1996, p. A21.

38. Mary Johnson, "Right to life; fight to die: the Elizabeth Bouvia saga," *Electric Edge*, 1997, ragged-edge-mag.com/archive/bouvia.htm.

39. Stuart Hall, "The Determinations of News Photographs," in Stanley Cohen and Jock Young, *The Manufacture of News. Social Problems, Deviance and the Mass Media*. London, Constable, 1981, pp. 226-243, P 239.

40. Weeber, op. cit.; Phillips, op. cit.

41. Todd Gitlin, *The Whole World is Watching*. Berkeley, Calif.: University of California Press, 1980.

42. Stothers, op. cit., p. 42.

43. Not Dead Yet, "Not Dead Yet! Disabled civil rights activists protest assisted suicide epidemic," May 12, 1997, notdeadyet.org/ablism.html.

44. Justin Hyde, "Kevorkian convicted, but suicide debate still on," *The Atlanta Journal-Constitution*, Mar. 28, 1999, p. 4A.

45. Anita Silvers, "Assisted suicide, terminal illness, severe disability, and the double standard," in M. P. Battin, R. Rhodes, and A. Silvers, eds., *Physician-assisted Suicide: Expanding the Debate*. N.Y.: Routledge, 1998, pp. 133-148.

46. Kathi Wolfe, "Suicidal tendencies," *Utne Reader*, 1997, pp. 22-24.

47. Wolfe, op. cit., p. 22.

48. Vicki Quade, "What is the value of human life?" *Human Rights: Journal of the Section of Individual Rights and Responsibilities*, 1992, 19, pp. 12-17.

49. Jane Gross, "Landscape evolves for assisted suicide," *The New York Times*, Nov. 11, 2008, p. D8.

50. Robin Toner and Carl Hulse, "Congress Ready To Approve Bill In Schiavo Case," *The New York Times*, Mar. 20, 2005, p. A1.

51. Toner and Hulse, op. cit.

52. John Schwartz, "New Openness in Deciding When and How to Die," *The New York Times*, Mar. 21, 2005, p. A1.

53. Monica Davey, "Kevorkian Freed After Years in Prison for Aiding Suicide," *The New York Times*, June 2, 2007, p. A8.

54. Davey, op. cit.

55. Susan Donaldson James, "HBO Film Inflames Dr. Death's Critics," ABC News, July 6, 2009, abcnews.go.com/Entertainment/MindMoodNews/story?id=7989806&page=1.

56. Gross, op. cit.

57. Kirk Johnson, "Montana Court to Rule on Assisted Suicide," *The New York Times*, Aug. 31, 2009, p. A1.

58. Peter Singer, "Happy Nevertheless," *The New York Times Magazine*, Dec. 28, 2008, p. 34.

59. Peter Singer, "Why we must ration health care," *The New York Times Magazine*, July 19, 2009. nytimes.com/2009/07/19/magazine/19healthcare-t.html?pagewanted=1&_r=1.

60. Susan Henderson, "___ YEARS OF A NONDISABLED LIFE IS WORTH ___ YEARS OF A DISABLED LIFE," Disability & Media Alliance Project blog, July 31, 2009, d-map.org/DISABLED-LIFE.

5.

Autism and inclusive education in the news media

Hartmann v. Loudoun County Board of Education: A case study

Inclusive education for disabled children has been a major focus for disability activists and parents of disabled children since the Individuals with Disabilities Education Act (IDEA) became law in 1975. Although a prominent topic in the minds of Americans with school-age children, the issue has only recently begun to attract media attention. News coverage of education issues in general has improved over the years,[1] and with that has come more attention to high-profile cases of inclusive education. In 1999, my research confirmed that in general coverage of disability issues, the news media most often focus on topics related to disabled children (23%) and inclusive education (17%). General education issues were also a popular topic in disability-related stories at 10 percent.[2]

One explanation for the news media's growing interest in inclusive education is that 20 years after it was first passed, IDEA was updated and re-authorized in 1997. IDEA has resulted in taking disabled children out of institutions and segregated special education settings and integrating them into regular classrooms and school activities. The U.S. Department of Education reports that before IDEA, 90 percent of children with developmental disabilities received an education in state institutions.[3] The Department of Education says that due to inclusive education programs today, three times the number of people with disabilities attend college, and double the number of 20-year-olds with disabilities are working, when compared to pre-IDEA figures.

However, inclusive education remains controversial in some school districts. When inclusive education programs were only directed at children with minor learning disabilities or slight physical disabilities, the issue was less controversial. But parents of nondisabled children have long been concerned that children with more severe disabilities, such as autism, can be disruptive to their children's education. Others worry about finite educational resources if large amounts may be needed for severely disabled children. Studies show that although approximately one third of children in the U.S. with special education needs receive an education in standard classrooms, few of these children have severe disabilities.[4] The controversy has grown as these more severely disabled children and their families fight for inclusive education.

This chapter concerns one high-profile case that rocketed the topic of inclusive education to national media attention in the mid-1990s. Beginning in 1995, *Hartmann v. Loudoun County Board of Education* tested whether or not schools must include severely disabled children in regular classrooms. At the time of their three-year legal battle in Northern Virginia, the Hartmanns and the inclusion movement became almost synonymous. The child at the center of the case, Mark Hartmann, who is autistic, became a symbol in a national debate over whether, and how often, disabled youngsters should be educated alongside their non-disabled peers.[5]

Using Walter R. Fisher's narrative paradigm (see page 92),[6] this chapter analyzes four years of the extensive media coverage of the Hartmann story to provide a synopsis of the narratives that address the central issues of inclusion. Through the press, competing interests told their stories to the public, hoping to win the moral high ground and persuade others of the "good reasons" that support their understanding of the costs or benefits of inclusion. Pedagogical issues concerning students with disabilities, who represent 11 percent of the school population in the U.S., raise complex questions of finance, ethics and academic standards. Varied state standards for the education of disabled children further complicate the discussion. Furthermore, as the inclusion debate continues, the diagnosis of disabled children steadily increases.[7]

Given the importance of the issue of inclusive education and the notoriety of this case, the narratives about *Hartmann v. Loudoun* warranted scholarly attention. Understanding these narratives also adds to the growing academic analysis of disability discourse,[8] which challenges preconceived "readings" of disability-related texts. Narratives told by the Hartmanns, and their allies, and the stories of those opposed to inclusion, constitute stories that present "good reasons" for adopting a point of view, according to Fisher's analytical structure.[9] The narratives are more or less persuasive, offering positive values that constitute "good reasons" to accept a claim. The narrative themes offered by the parties involved in the inclusive education controversy reveal that although the Hartmanns lost their court battle, their narratives and others on behalf of inclusion resonated more persuasively in the news media's court of public opinion, thus advancing the national inclusion movement.

Before discussing the narrative themes, it is important to note that this chapter is not an evaluation of inclusive education policy or any educational methods used for disabled children. This chapter focuses only on news media narratives about inclusive education as a policy and its implications for the U.S. education system.

The Hartmann case

This section outlines the facts of the Mark Hartmann story as reported by U.S. media, both local and national. After moving from a suburb of Chicago in 1994, Roxana and Joseph Hartmann enrolled their 9-year-old son in second grade at Ashburn Elementary School in Loudoun County, Va. Officials of the northern Virginia school district reported that Mark hit, pinched, screeched, and threw tantrums when placed in a standard classroom. Although the school reduced the class size and assigned an aide to work individually with Mark, his behavior made learning and classroom management problematic, according to school authorities. By the school year's end, officials concluded that the autistic youngster should be removed from a regular class and placed in a Leesburg school with four other autistic students in a "mainstream" program. In this type of "mainstream" program, the Leesburg school placed students with autism in regular classes only for music, art, and gym classes.

Mark's parents refused to accept this decision.[10] They agreed that their son's experience at Ashburn had been a disaster, "but they blamed the school system for not providing enough training to Mark's teacher and full-time instructional aide. They pointed to Mark's progress at an Illinois school, where he attended kindergarten and first grade, and they argued that it was crucial to Mark's social development that he go to school with his non-disabled friends," according to *The Washington Post*.[11] So began a lengthy battle "that stands as a troubling example of how bitter placement disputes can become," according to *The New York Times*.[12]

The Hartmanns believed the law supported their case. In line with historic American values of equal access to education by all, IDEA was created to guarantee disabled children the right to free and appropriate education in the least restrictive environment. Furthermore, an earlier 1988 update of IDEA prevents schools from sending disabled children to special education programs, such as the one at Ashburn, without their parents' permission. However, when Loudoun Country did not receive the Hartmann's approval to remove Mark from a regular classroom, the school district asked the State Supreme Court to appoint a hearing officer to decide Mark's academic future.[13] The officer ruled that the boy's educational needs were not served by inclusion and gave school officials permission to transfer him to Ashburn. A spokesperson with the American Federation of Teachers indicated this was the first time any school district had been allowed to remove a disabled child from classes since passage of IDEA.[14] The Hartmanns appealed.

Although the legal battle had just begun, within months Mark's story had appeared in *People* magazine, on network morning news programs, and in numerous newspapers as far away as Costa Rica, his mother's native country.[15] During the next three years the enmity between the Hartmanns and Loudoun County school district officials took on the character of a difficult divorce, according to NPR.[16] Meanwhile, the Hartmanns sought out another public school system that promotes inclusion. First, to enroll Mark in a Montgomery County school in Southwest Virginia, Roxana Hartmann established residence in Blacksburg, Va., and then had to stop a Montgomery County injunction to prevent Mark's enrollment.[17] Montgomery County, which has a national reputation for a progressive inclusion program, lost its argument that the mother and child did not have legal residence status. During the school year the mother and child traveled 250 miles (each way) to be with Mark's sister and father in their North Virginia home on weekends.[18]

The family's appeals and lawsuit against Loudoun County continued as Mark successfully settled into school in Blacksburg. Eventually the case moved to the federal court system,[19] where the Hartmanns won a battle. In December 1996 U.S. District Judge Leonie Brinkema ruled that Loudoun County inadequately trained staff to supervise Mark. Her decision was based on evidence that included videotape of Mark in a general education classroom at Kipps Elementary School in Blacksburg, Va., as well as testimony that he had advanced academically and socially at a school in Illinois before the family moved to Virginia.[20] However, the Hartmanns kept Mark at Kipps in Blacksburg; they chose to wait and see if the case would be appealed by Loudoun. It was, and the 4th U.S. Circuit Court of Appeals reversed the Brinkema decision, ordering the case to be dismissed. The three-judge panel wrote that Brinkema placed too much emphasis on the testimony of advocates for inclusion rather than school officials.

Finally, the Hartmanns' attorney filed a petition with the U.S. Supreme Court, arguing that Mark's case had significance for the nation, according to NPR.[21] Again the story made national news on NPR and in *The Washington Post*,[22] but the high court declined to act on the case.[23] The Hartmanns, who spent more than $200,000 in legal fees arguing for inclusion for Mark,[24] vowed to continue their struggle for the inclusive education movement.[25]

After the legal battled ended, three commentaries, numerous letters to the editor and a lengthy story on inclusion[26] appeared in the major daily newspaper that serves Southwest Virginia, *The Roanoke Times*. One opponent of inclusion added to the discussion by writing a commentary that said he was "distressed to read that the recent court decision not to allow autistic and other learning-challenged children into regular classrooms applied to a Northern Virginia school district but not to Montgomery County Schools. In this regard, I recently questioned my daughter about her experiences with such children. Her words were shocking."[27] The writer's commentary apparently shocked a number of readers. Over the next month Mark's mother responded to the attack with a long commentary for the paper,[28] followed by seven letters to the editor supporting her and berating the earlier writer's point of view. The Montgomery County Schools superintendent and school board chairman also contributed a lengthy piece on the issue.[29]

The *Hartmann v. Loudoun County Board of Education* case focused national attention on the inclusive education issue, placing the narratives of competing points of view before the general public. Therefore, the narratives of this case merited closer critical analysis.

Readers may notice one specific narrative is missing from the media coverage – that of Mark Hartmann's own stories told in his own voice. I can only speculate that some of the legal and ethical issues the media face may have caused them to avoid interviewing an autistic person who is not a legal adult. Media law specialists warn journalists that children cannot give legal consent to be interviewed; only their legal guardian can give the consent. Whatever the cause for the "exclusion" of Mark's voice in the coverage of the case, it suggests a significant issue in the discussion about inclusion and education in general: Most media stories about any education issue fail to include the "voices" of those most affected by the issue: children and teens.

Narrative analysis of themes in *Hartmann v. Loudoun*

Walter R. Fisher's narrative paradigm provides an appropriate methodology to analyze this case study about inclusive education and autism. Narrative inquiry emphasizes an interpretive thrust. Interpretive research seeks to expand understanding of how meaning emerges and is used by people in specific contexts. The approach discovers how people create meanings through stories by interpreting their texts – in this case, the texts are quotes and other comments in news stories and radio reports, as well as letters to the editor and op-ed commentaries. Narrative analysis seeks to discover how social actors perceive reality and it evaluates the respondents' stories about their reality.[30]

Fisher argues that human reality is composed of sets of stories from which we must choose.[31] Storytelling is seen as central to all human discourse and interaction. Narratives include all symbolic actions, all "words and/or deeds – that have sequence or meaning for those who live, create, or interpret them."[32] Reality, then, is composed of stories from which people must choose in a never-ending process. People make choices based on "good reasons," which vary in form and according to context. Fisher describes good reasons as those we perceive as: "(1) true to and consistent with what we think we know and what we value, (2) appropriate to whatever decision is pending, (3) promising in effects for ourselves and others, and, (4) consistent with what we believe is an ideal basis for conduct."[33]

Within this framework, narrative includes "traditional" forms such as novels or films, as well as nontraditional forms, such as the content of conversation, an interview, or editorials and quotes printed by the media. Media scholar Michael Schudson notes the shaping of news through use of traditions in narrative, storytelling, human interest, etc. This ties into the historical nature of culture. "All of this work recognizes that news is a form of literature and that one key resource journalists work with is the cultural tradition of storytelling and picture-making and sentence construction they inherit, with a number of vital assumptions about the world built in," Schudson says.[34] These news narratives contain key themes that display humans' experiences as well as their values. Through stories we explain our actions and beliefs, as well as lend meaning to our lives. The stories told in the *Hartmann v. Loudoun* tale illustrate the tellers' "good reasons" for supporting inclusion or opposing the practice.

Following are brief narratives and the "good reasons" embedded in themes drawn from press coverage of the case. The chapter examines eight themes that evolved from the inclusive education debate in the Hartmann case. These themes express "something that people believe, accept as true and valid; it is a common assumption about the nature of their experience."[35] The themes have a high degree of generality. Although they were not counted to determine frequency, the themes recurred in the media coverage of the case and in editorial comments. When participants expressed a single idea, at different times, in different settings, through similar stories, this suggested a possible cultural theme. People know and use cultural themes to organize their behavior and interpret experience, even if they cannot express them with ease.

The process of identifying narrative themes began after more than 90 news stories, editorials, commentaries, letters to the editor, and three radio transcripts about the case were gathered and analyzed. The media stories came from a variety of sources but most prominent were *The Roanoke Times, Richmond Times Dispatch, The New York Times, The Washington Post*, National Public Radio's (NPR) "Morning Edition" and "Talk of the Nation." The themes are divided into those that support the Hartmanns or inclusion, and those that support the Loudoun School District or are against inclusion (four narrative themes each). This division obviously oversimplifies the nature of the public discussion about inclusion; there are more than two sides to this complex issue. However, this division provides a more concrete, linear way to discuss the narratives and themes.

The themes found in narratives told by the Hartmanns' and inclusion supporters include:

1. Everyone wins with inclusive education

2. Inclusion is cheaper

3. Human rights should apply to everyone in a civilized society

4. Inclusive education has proven itself

5. Not in my kid's school

6. Protect the sensitive "normal" students

7. School is about academics

8. Attendance is not the same as integration

Narrative theme 1: Everyone wins with inclusive education

This narrative connects to an overarching theme imbedded within the IDEA legislation – that inclusive education benefits disabled children in the short run with better learning and in the long run with more employment and post-secondary educational opportunities. The benefit of inclusive education for non-disabled children is the ability to understand and cope with a more diverse society and people who are different from themselves.

For example, a *New York Times* analysis piece on inclusive education embraces the narrative of IDEA that it benefits all children, not just those with disabilities:

> Many educators and parents believe that segregating children with disabilities is bad, both educationally and morally. They say such a policy undermines the development of both disabled children, by failing to give them a chance to develop the skills and relationships that they will need as adults, and other children, by preventing beneficial contact with the full range of people in their communities.[36]

Mark Hartmann's mother, Roxana, most often provides this "everyone wins" narrative, in both her quotes to media and her *Roanoke Times* commentary on her son's case. In the following narrative from her commentary, she explains the benefits of inclusive education for all children.

> . . . [Mark] has demonstrated that there are no long-term harmful effects on the classmates of a disabled child. In fact, full inclusion gives them an opportunity to embrace diversity and grow in compassion and understanding – honorable goals that will serve our children well through their lifetime. In sum, through inclusion, we can make our communities a better place for people with disabilities one child and one family at a time, if we work together. It's the best thing to do for our future together.[37]

Roxana Hartmann's quotes for the newspaper also explain the difference inclusion made for Mark in terms of his less volatile behavior specifically:

'He understands language. I can talk to him like I can talk to you. I don't have to speak differently,' Hartmann explained.

'The other day it was raining and I didn't feel like taking him swimming, so I said to him that I didn't want to go. He just waved his hand a little, saying we didn't have to go. There was no screaming, no tantrums.'[38]

Joseph Hartmann, Mark's father, presented this same narrative nationally when he was part of a NPR "Morning Edition" story on inclusive education:

JOSEPH HARTMANN: He's becoming able to cope in society as society is, with his peers in the classroom. He knows when his teacher says: "OK, class, everybody be quiet" that it is his job to be quiet. He knows when the teacher says: "OK, class, it's time to go to lunch," – OK, I've got to get my lunch box and stand in line with everybody else and go on. . . .

If you have him in an autistic class, three or four other autistic kids, and they sit around and play with blocks all day, you don't take them out into the world except to visit.[39]

The news media also relied on prominent pro-inclusion sources, which made the narrative compelling. In articles about the broader inclusive education topic, such as the following *New York Times* article, Judith Heumann, an assistant secretary in the Office of Special Education and Rehabilitative Services at the U.S. Department of Education at the time, who is herself a wheelchair user, explains the "everyone wins" narrative in a national community context:

'Education is academic, but it's also social, learning how to live in a community, learning about differences,' she said. 'I tell parents who are afraid to send a child with disabilities into a regular setting that over-protection does no service when that disabled child becomes an adult. If your child was out of sight, out of mind, that doesn't change. People who might have become their friends in school won't know them.'

Academically, too, she said, all children can benefit from inclusion.

'The methods that teachers learn from working with the disabled and individualizing instruction, are useful with other students, as well,'

Ms. Heumann said. 'In a way, you can see every child as having special needs. So the ideal is a system in which every child gets an individualized education.'[40]

The narrative takes on even more strength when adults with disabilities who were the product of inclusive education enter the discourse. The following was a letter to the editor in *The Roanoke Times*, written after a commentary disparaged the benefits of inclusive education:

> I have cerebral palsy and a hearing impairment. I spent most of my school years in 'regular' schools in Connecticut in the 1960s and 1970s, so I am a product of inclusion. I shudder to think what I would have become had I not been given the challenges and intellectual and social stimulation I received. It motivated me to get a good education and to try to make a difference in the world.
>
> The parents of children with disabilities in Montgomery County only want what I was given. These children are more likely to learn appropriate behavior if they are 'included' in regular classes. Able-bodied children learn about acceptance, tolerance and compassion toward those who are 'different,' and perhaps something about 'the power of the human spirit.' Not all education is gained from books and facts. Holladay's misconceptions tell me we still have a long way to go toward understanding and accepting people with disabilities.[41]

These letters to the editor from disabled people fit with Swain and Cameron's notion of "coming out" for disabled people.[42] They say that when people embrace their social identity as disabled persons, they begin challenging oppression and "campaigning for equal opportunities to access education, employment, transport, housing, leisure facilities and control over personal lives."[43] The narratives from disabled people who are proud of their identity have even stronger resonance because they demonstrate the success of inclusion and the potential for Mark Hartmann to grow into an adult with a positive self concept.

Narrative theme 2: Inclusion is cheaper

This narrative appears in two ways. One implied theme is that society benefits in general from inclusive education because well-educated disabled children mean future contributing, tax-paying members of society rather than tax burdens. But typically the narrative was more overt: Inclusive education costs less than institutionalization of severely disabled children.

Roxana Hartmann makes the argument that institutionalization is expensive and has long-terms costs for society:

> But the commonwealth does support large institutions. A large chunk of your tax dollars are spent in institutions. It costs more than $80,000 per year to support a person in an institution, and it's getting more expensive all the time. By the year 2000, the national average will reach $113,000 per person in an institution. There are 189,000 Virginians with mental retardation alone – the greater majority housed in institutions. But why is this relevant to the education of a disabled child?
>
> We know from experiences of our sister states that it all begins with decisions focused on educating the disabled child. Early-intervention strategies and an inclusive education posture are proven as an effective approach to integrate our disabled citizens into the community with jobs that they can be trained for and normal home settings to live in. Community-based living and care works better than institutions, and costs far less.[44]

The message from the U.S. Department of Education about IDEA is similar. It estimates that educating students in neighborhoods, who would previously be institutionalized, saves $10,000 per child.[45] Consistent with notions of American pragmatism, this narrative ties to capitalistic notions of "the bottom line," in which citizens embrace policies that reduce taxes or give the most benefit for the least amount of tax dollars.

Narrative theme 3: Human rights should apply to everyone in a civilized society

Typically this narrative is tied to every American's right to a free public education. The right to an education is presented as a human right available to all equally. Roxana Hartmann puts it succinctly:

> After contemplating this response, I have decided to review some facts that may be overshadowed by accusations (real or imagined) and that may not be obvious to a casual observer.

First of all, public education is the right of all children. The Individuals with Disabilities Act guarantees access for disabled students into the 'least restrictive environment.' The only measure is that the school must demonstrate that the disabled child is able to learn in the LRE with appropriate support, services and accommodations.

... In all our debate, we should remember that each and every child in our community, including the disabled, is a valued human being who has a basic right to opportunity – whether we are talking work, education, housing or access to public buildings. To consider it otherwise will take us back to the 1860s.[46]

Several members of the local southwestern Virginia community continue the free and public education narrative in a number of letters to *The Roanoke Times*.

How does Holladay justify saying that his daughter has more of a right to an education than my brother? Holladay is concerned about students who "can learn algebra and Spanish, children for whom the schools are intended, and whose futures will depend on what they learn now." All children's futures are determined by what they learn. This is a public school system, and everyone has a right to an education.[47]

Our community has chosen (inclusion) for more than 10 years, with all its pitfalls, challenges and magic, because we care about children. All children have a future, and, in America, schools are intended for everyone.[48]

Public schools aren't for the learning elite. They are public schools, and by law must provide an appropriate education in the least restrictive environment for all children. There is no such thing as separate but equal.[49]

Although an explicit link is not made in the statements, the theme within these statements is reminiscent of the education reforms that African Americans fought for in the 1950s and 1960s to bring about integrated public education for black and white children. The inclusion movement puts forth the same notion, that separate but equal does not fit with American ideals.

Narrative theme 4: Inclusive education has proven itself

Specifically, this narrative tied into Mark Hartmann's success in an inclusive education environment before moving to Virginia, and broadly, the success of such programs nationally and in Blacksburg, Va., where Mark Hartmann was placed early in the case. Jamie Ruppman, an education consultant who works with disabled children, saw Mark's success back in Illinois destroying the case of Loudoun County. Educators from Illinois did testify that Mark was successful in their inclusion program before the family moved to Virginia.[50]

As Roxana Hartmann explained: "All you have to know about this case is that Mark was successfully included in Illinois and in Montgomery County. The only place he could not be successfully included was Loudoun County, and that's clearly because the school system did not have the commitment to do it."[51] Hartmann continued this argument by explaining why she chose to move to Montgomery County: "[That county] is one of the few school districts in Virginia to honor and abide by IDEA – the law. Among other states, Virginia is ranked 46th in its support of people with disabilities and their families."[52] Others made similar arguments:

> 'I have heard nothing negative about having this child stay,' the president of the Montgomery County Council of PTAs said. 'What I have heard is: Why did the school system take a negative stand against this child in the first place? From a parent standpoint, this woman did everything she could for her kid [in Loudoun County], then set out to find what she could for him somewhere else.'
>
> . . . We need to show that it works so other school systems can try to do the same thing.[53]

The successful inclusive education program narrative is also connected specifically to Mark's educational growth. Roxana Hartmann says: "He has blossomed in a very nurturing environment here with people who are dedicated and understand him and his disability. He'll stay here until he finishes school."[54] The Timmy Clemens case also bolsters the narrative of inclusive education "proving itself:"

> Four years ago, Timmy Clemens could not walk near a classroom without becoming so scared he couldn't enter the room. His autism required a full-time aide and much patient coaxing to get him through a day.

By his senior year last year, Timmy could walk to classes in Blacksburg High School on his own. With the help of his aide, Marc Eaton, and a special board that lists the alphabet and short words such as 'yes' and 'no,' he did homework and took tests in courses such as algebra and honors history. Today, as a postgraduate, he works with an aide in a job at Blacksburg's Municipal Building.

'Some truly believe in it; some think it's a waste,' said Judy Clemens, Timmy's mother. But other people's opinions don't matter, she said, because she can see the improvements in her son.

'I don't think inclusion is perfect. But I think it's going to get better and better, and I'm proud of Montgomery County.'[55]

Although these narrative themes in the Hartmann case advanced the cause of inclusive education, many who opposed the Hartmann arguments and/or inclusion were included in media coverage or wrote commentaries against the issue. Their oppositional narratives suggested the following themes:

Narrative theme 5: Not in my kid's school

This narrative presupposes that inclusive education will always have a disruptive effect on nondisabled children in the classroom and therefore should not be allowed. It is based on some anecdotal reports that a few severely disabled children, such as those with autism, have been disruptive. However, there is also much anecdotal evidence of disruptive nondisabled children, which is rarely mentioned in anti-inclusion narratives.

One parent, Steve Holladay, a Blacksburg, Va., parent, stated this narrative through his commentary piece in *The Roanoke Times*. The Virginia Tech professor claimed to quote his daughter, whose words were "shocking":

Many of these children (inclusion students) are uncontrollable. They enter your classroom in the middle of a class, and it may take 15 minutes for their aide to return them to the classroom they are assigned to. They break into loud crying fits or other noise making episodes regularly, at unpredictable times and without apparent cause, bringing a halt to teaching until control is re-established.

They wander around the class while the teacher is trying to teach, sometimes selecting a student to sit with and engage in an up-close, face-to-face staring contest. They may unexpectedly slap you in the fore-head when you walk by them in the hall. . . .

It cannot be denied that many of these children are extremely disrup-tive. And if they have been found to be too disruptive for normal class-rooms in other school districts, why do we place them in our classrooms where our children have their only opportunity to learn many founda-tional concepts? Do they magically behave better here? . . . Montgomery County has become an island that will accept highly disruptive children into our schools, children impaired to the point of being totally oblivious to the educational process going on around them, children incapable of learning in any way marginally related to the original intent of the school's programs, or to the expectations placed on other children in the class-rooms.[56]

Other parents present this narrative of the disruptive effect of inclusive edu-cation. Even the mother of an autistic child wrote:

I am the mother of an autistic child, and I agree with Steve Holladay. . . . I do believe in mainstreaming, where the child is placed in a regular classroom for short periods of time and gradually works up to a full class period. With mainstreaming, 'normal' children get the education they deserve and need without disruption by our 'learning-challenged' children.[57]

A teacher continued the narrative of disruptive inclusion kids:

'Our biggest problem is putting up with emotionally disturbed kids when they are disruptive and distracting to other children,' she said. 'That's a waste of time and that's where we're losing ground.'

Hall, [a] language arts teacher, also resents having to design different tests and notes and other material for some students and fears it inevi-tably watered down the lesson for all students.[58]

Narrative theme 6: Protect the sensitive "normal" students

Those who question inclusion also argued that it may be traumatic for non-disabled children to be in the presence of severely disabled children.

Beyond lost education, what effect might this have on the sensitive child who isn't yet ready to experience this type of behavior and instability?

I am sincerely sympathetic for Ms. Hartmann and her situation, and very thankful that my own children are healthy. I further admire her obvious determination to provide what she believes to be the best growing and learning environment possible for her son. However, she and others who move here to take advantage of our inclusion policy seem to have little concern about the effect their children may have on other children in the classrooms.

. . . Does Ms. Hartmann care about the boy or girl who sits in front of the inclusion child during the uncontrollable screaming fit? What about the child whose personal space is invaded by stares or inappropriate touching? Or my own daughter, who receives a stunning slap on the forehead out of the blue?

I asked other adults for their views about our inclusion policy. Not one spoke positively about it. One individual told of a girl whose earring was torn off by an inclusion child, and who subsequently was terrified of going to school. Another said her son quit Scouts because an inclusion child had selected him to shadow and touch.[59]

The mother of an autistic child adds to the narrative, believing her son's behavior might upset other children. "He couldn't tolerate all the activities and stimulus, nor would it be fair to the other children in the classroom."[60]

Narrative theme 7: School is about academics

In contrast with the inclusive education argument that it benefits children in many more ways that just academics, those opposed to the practice argue schools' primary goal should be to provide an education in reading, writing, arithmetic, etc. The attorney for Loudoun County illustrates this narrative in her comments to NPR's "Morning Edition":

KATHLEEN MAYFOUD, ATTORNEY FOR Loudoun COUNTY, VIRGINIA SCHOOLS: Socialization is part of that, but academic and educational instruction is obviously the primary responsibility. So, Loudoun would have had to totally overlook the educational requirements in favor of a minor goal.[61]

The anti-inclusion parent Holladay ties the idea of a proper learning environment with this narrative and argues that inclusive education is its antithesis.

> Doesn't it seem obvious that loss of teaching time to disruptive or ongoing distractive behavior isn't conducive to learning?
>
> Similar to Ms. Hartmann, we [the other parents] are also determined to provide our children the best possible learning environment. As an educator myself, I don't like our inclusion policy. I would never tolerate such disruption in my classrooms unless, as has become the case in Montgomery County, I was mandated to do so by law.
>
> I truly do care about Mark. However, I care more about his classmates who can learn algebra and Spanish, children for whom the schools were intended, and whose futures will ultimately depend on what they learn now.[62]

Narrative theme 8: Attendance is not the same as integration

This narrative questions definitions of inclusive education. It also re-interprets various aspects of inclusive education as having a negative effect. For example, Richard Schattman, a Vermont principal who believes in inclusion, explains how inclusion, when poorly implemented, gives those opposed to inclusive education fodder to urge its dismantling.

> 'A student can be more isolated and segregated in a normal classroom than in special education,' Mr. Schattman said. 'Inclusion isn't about placing the kid. It's about making the placement successful both for the kid and for the rest of the class. And it's not easy. You need small classes, lots of planning time, and staff that believes in it.'
>
> Some special education experts worry that the inclusion movement may lead to dumping children with special needs into classes where they will be ignored or taunted, and eliminating the special services and support that they receive in settings intended just for them.
>
> 'It has not been demonstrated that regular classrooms, even fortified regular classrooms using the best practices can accommodate all children all the time,' said Douglas Fuchs, a professor of special education at Vanderbilt University. 'The full inclusionists honestly believe that creating a situation in which teachers individualize instruction for each

student is a terrific goal we should all dedicate our lives to. So we should kick away the crutch of special education. But that's a high stakes game, and I'm not sure it's realistic.'

Nor are all parents and advocates for children with disabilities convinced that it is the correct goal.[63]

This narrative supports those opposed to inclusion by noting that it may not be the right accommodation for every disabled child. This type of theme turns inclusive education on itself, i.e., because it may not be appropriate for all disabled children, maybe be it should not be used at all. The *New York Times* story above continued this narrative by explaining that because of disruptive, abusive, and violent children, Vermont, a premier state for successful inclusive education, is placing such children in separate settings.[64]

Conclusions

As noted in this chapter, narrative themes were divided into those that support the Hartmanns/inclusive education and those that do not. This reflects a problem that is imbedded within the debate itself, by creating a division that oversimplifies the nature of inclusive education. The public discussion about this case reflects standard news coverage of a controversial issue – what language scholar Deborah Tannen calls the "either-or" dichotomy, i.e., debate rather than discussion.[65] When the news narratives follow lines of "yes" or "no" about inclusive education, they miss an opportunity to critically assess the issue for all children in U.S. public school systems. When the focus is on a two-sided debate, rather than a multi-faceted discussion, the news media are also more likely to drop coverage of the topic if one side of the debate tires of presenting their narratives.

The media stories and commentaries, and the themes they illustrate about inclusive education, lend insight into the participants' beliefs, actions, and world views, as well as their conflicts of opinion and perception relative to the setting.[66] Although this chapter touched on just a few of the prominent themes about inclusive education in the news in the Hartmann case, the themes offered in this analysis dominated the discussion. This analysis concludes that even though some parents of nondisabled children are vehemently opposed to inclusive education, it was the more numerous and more vocal parents of severely disabled children, educators, and proponents of IDEA who set the tone of the debate and framed inclusion as a workable approach to educating disabled children. In this case, the conclusion is that though the Hartmanns lost their case against Loudoun County, the narratives they inspired actually won in the court of public opinion.

It has taken almost 25 years for pro-inclusion narratives to take hold. As programs in Montgomery County, Va., Illinois, and Vermont show, school districts need not only well-trained faculty and well-financed programs to succeed, but public support as well. When parent Steve Holladay wrote to criticize inclusive education in Montgomery County, Va., his criticism was met with seven letters to the editor positively endorsing inclusive education. In the pro-inclusion environment of Montgomery County, Va., the local newspaper, *The Roanoke Times*, seemed to present the proponents' narratives wholeheartedly. Even when the Hartmanns lost their case, the newspaper published a family-provided color photo of Mark Hartmann on its front page. In the photo, Mark Hartmann, wearing T-shirt and shorts, grins broadly as a picture-perfect "average" kid. The image alone provides a "good reason" that Mark should be in a regular classroom, because he is presented visually as a "regular kid." Earlier, the newspaper published a large two-page spread on inclusive education in the county, providing a location for thoughtful discussion of the issue and primarily "good reasons" for inclusive education.

Some opponents of inclusive education fear the public and policymakers may be swayed by an underlying message of pity for the "poor, little disabled children." The conservative *National Journal* feared during the re-authorization of IDEA in 1997 that:

> Overhaul of the Individuals with Disabilities Education Act is tailor made for policy decision by anecdote. The facts and figures are sparse and conflicting; the horror stories are stark and vivid. And the interest groups are well organized, disciplined and loaded with heart-tuggers or spine-chillers, depending on their legislative goal.
>
> In the past, organizations representing the disabled could count on their substantial political clout in Congress. 'Politicians are terrified of them – that they'll trot out people in wheelchairs,' a lobbyist for an education organization said enviously. 'It's very easy for a Member to feel virtuous voting for their issues.'[67]

Yet the findings from this narrative analysis illustrate that proponents of inclusive education have no need to trot out hackneyed pity images of disabled children. They rely on much stronger and more salient narratives: Inclusion is a win-win situation for everyone; public education is every child's right; inclusion is cheaper than institutionalization; and inclusion has proven itself successful nationally. These "good reasons" hold the most persuasive power because they appeal to the audience's general understanding of equality and humanity, which most Americans embrace. As one woman with cerebral palsy and a hearing impairment explained the good reasons from her personal inclusion experience, disabled "children are more likely to learn appropriate behavior if they are 'included' in regular classes. Able-bodied children learn about acceptance, tolerance and compassion toward those who are different, and perhaps something about 'the power of the human spirit.' Not all education is gained from books and facts."[68]

These themes/stories in support of inclusion are consistent with American values of equality – the country has determined that schools cannot be separate and truly equal. Furthermore, the effects of inclusion, while perhaps detrimental to a few students, largely have promising effects for students both with and without disabilities. Inclusion represents Fisher's notion of a powerful narrative being representative of an ideal basis for conduct. While many of the stories against inclusion suggest pragmatic or traditional bases for educational policy, readers of the narratives are likely to find the rationality of the pro-inclusion arguments more consistent with U.S. history and culture. The 1960s civil rights movement, which successfully dismantled separate but unequal educational systems for blacks and whites, suggests the type of ideal conduct to which Fisher refers. The civil rights movement forced the U.S. to once again acknowledge the central narrative of its founding – that all citizens are created equal and deserve equal opportunities in all aspects of U.S. society, including education.

After the loss of her son's case, Roxana Hartmann said she would continue to lead national discourse about inclusive education: "'This is the end, but it's not going to stop me from talking about inclusion,' Roxana said. 'No, if anything, it's made me more of a believer than ever. . . .This is not about winners and losers; this is about schools doing the right thing for the children,' she explained."[69] Widespread media coverage of Hartmann's narrative and those of other supporters of inclusion should also prove to help make others believers in the movement's aims.

Current media coverage of inclusive education

After the U.S. Supreme Court refused to take the Hartmann case, it fell out of the news media. But coverage of autism continues in the news media, and, anecdotally, it appears to be *the* disability that the news media take notice of much of the time. In December 2009, *The Washington Post* wrote about an initiative in Maryland that teaches children with mild autism about social skills in a separate setting. Interestingly, the story quotes school officials who discuss the program in the context of inclusive education:

> Prince William and Prince George's counties have also designated schools with extra services for children with mild autism. But other districts, philosophically committed to mainstream inclusion as the best way to teach children how to cope with their challenges, have chosen not to. 'I know there's a certain pull to isolate, but I don't know that that is the answer,' said Flo Bosch, coordinator of adaptive curriculum for Fairfax County schools, where officials have emphasized inclusion for more than 10 years. 'I'm not so sure how that prepares them for being in the world."[70]

So the media still write about some of the nuances of autism and inclusive education, but given the ongoing collapse of traditional print journalism, I wonder if the news media will ever cover the complex issue of inclusive education with the multi-voice perspective they did in the Hartmann case.

One positive change began occurring in 2007, when autistic people[71] began speaking out in the news media for themselves. The autistic rights movement has gained momentum in U.S. society and given autistic people a platform to talk about the issues that affect them.

The autistic rights movement got the attention of the news media when it protested against the "ransom notes" ad campaign from the New York University Child Studies Center, which portrayed autism and other disabilities like ADHD as "kidnappers" that steal children from their parents and society. The autistic rights movement and other disability rights activists protested the campaign as stigmatizing and negatively stereotyping both children with disabilities and their parents. The activists felt the campaign would be detrimental to efforts toward inclusion and respect for individuals with these disabilities.[72] The most prominent rights group, the Autistic Self Advocacy Network (ASAN), led the fight against the ad campaign and got it taken down in two and a half weeks.

ASAN, unlike most autism groups that are run by parents and focused on cure, is run by and for people on the autism spectrum. It

> seeks to advance the principles of the disability rights movement in the world of autism. Drawing on the principles of the cross-disability community on issues such as inclusive education, community living supports and others, ASAN seeks to organize the community of Autistic adults and youth to have our voices heard in the national conversation about us. In addition, ASAN seeks to advance the idea of neurological diversity, putting forward the concept that the goal of autism advocacy should not be a world without Autistic people. Instead, it should be a world in which Autistic people enjoy the same access, rights and opportunities as all other citizens.[73]

ASAN's response to the NYU ad campaign was featured in articles in *The New York Times, The Washington Post,* and New York *Daily News.* The recognition ASAN received led to a in-depth story in *New York* magazine about the autistic rights movement.

ASAN's founder and president Ari Ne'eman says the NYU ads followed a "tragedy-centric paradigm" that sees people with autism as less than human. And he says many other autism groups, usually led by parents, reinforce this same notion with their emphasis on cures, the vaccine controversy and the medical model. He calls the narrative the "stolen child phenomenon," which "tells parents their (autistic) children are not there."[74]

ASAN is part of the neurodiversity movement, which insists that many people have neurological differences and don't need to be "cured" of them. Ne'eman says the focus should be on supporting people with autism and helping to integrate them into society. The *New York* magazine article explaining the term "neurodiversity" in the popular press, reported that the term comes from Judy Singer, an Australian who is on the autism spectrum and has several family members on the spectrum. "I was interested in the liberatory, activist aspects of it – to do for neurologically different people what feminism and gay rights had done for their constituencies," Singer said.[75]

Ne'eman explains that some characteristics of autism are not negative. (Many in the autism community cite people like Charles Darwin and Albert Einstein, both of whom were believed to be on the autism spectrum.) He also likens the autistic rights movement to the early gay rights movement, which rejected the medical model whereby homosexuality was diagnosed as a psychiatric disorder, in favor of civil rights for gays and lesbians.

The autistic rights movement and the idea of neurodiversity are culture-changing concepts that can potentially advance society's acceptance of all people with disabilities. With the advent of online media, autistic people are now able to easily tell the world about themselves and bypass the gatekeepers in traditional news media. Amanda Baggs, an autistic woman who uses a speech synthesizer, has been blogging and creating videos about her life experiences since 2005. Her YouTube video called "In My Language" captures how she interacts with the world. She says she creates her videos because "[i]t's one thing to describe the way I interact with my surroundings, it's another to actually show people, as in 'In My Language,' the ways that have always (whether I've had words or not at the time) come more naturally to me than standard language has. Also, a lot of people online tend to think that I and other autistic bloggers all somehow magically 'look normal'. Videos counteract that impression quite well, I've found."[76] Her "In My Language" video had almost 900,000 views on YouTube as January 2010.[77]

Notes

Much of the content of this chapter comes from the article: Beth Haller and Bruce Dorries, "The News of Inclusive Education: A Narrative Analysis," *Disability & Society*, 2001, 16:6.

1. Ernest C. Hynds, "Survey finds large daily newspapers have improved coverage of education," *Journalism Quarterly*, 1989, pp. 692-696, 780.

2. Beth Haller, *News Coverage of Disability Issues: A Final Report for the Center for an Accessible Society.* San Diego: Center for an Accessible Society, 1999.

3. U.S. Department of Education. "Overview of IDEA," (2000), ed.gov/offices/OSERS/IDEA/.

4. Peter Pae, "Loudoun can take autistic boy out of regular class," *The Washington Post*, Dec. 16, 1994, C1.

5. Debbi Wilgoren, & Peter Pae, "As Loudoun goes, so may other schools," *The Washington Post*, Aug. 28, 1994, p. B1.

6. Walter R. Fisher, "Narration as a human communication paradigm: The case of public moral argument," *Communication Monographs*, 1984, 51, pp. 1-22.

7. Tamar Lewin, "Where all doors are open for disabled students," *The New York Times*, Dec. 28, 1997, p. A1.

8. Marian Corker and Sally French, eds., *Disability Discourse*. Buckingham, U.K.: Open University Press, 1999.

9. Fisher, 1984, op. cit.

10. *The Washington Post* extensively covered the case in the following stories: Debbi Wilgoren, "Loudoun wants autistic boy out of class," *The Washington Post*, Aug. 16, 1994, p. B1; Debbi Wilgoren, "Mother says regular school is crucial for autistic boy," *The Washington Post*, Oct. 28, 1994, p. B3; Debbi Wilgoren, "Ruling due on boy's schooling," *The Washington Post*, Dec. 8, 1994, VI, Virginia Weekly section; *The Washington Post*, "Educating Mark," Dec. 17, 1994, p. A26.

11. Pae, 1994, p. C1.

12. Lewin, 1997, p. A1.

13. M. Rosen. and R. Jones, "Odd child out," *People*, Oct. 17, 1994, p. 113.

14. Rosen and Jones, op. cit.

15. Debbi Wilgoren, "In autism case, hearing is over, but battle isn't," *The Washington Post*, Dec. 27, 1994, p. D1.

16. Larry Abramson and Alex Chadwick, "Disabilities," NPR Morning Edition, Nov. 6, 1997, (transcript # 97110611-210).

17. This event was covered extensively in the Roanoke, Va., newspaper and mentioned in *The Washington Post*: Melissa Devaughn, "Autistic pupil not welcome," *The Roanoke Times & World News*, Feb. 10, 1995, p. A1; Melissa DeVaughn, "Judge hears from autistic boy's mom, school board," *The Roanoke Times & World News*, Feb. 17, 1995, p. B1; Melissa DeVaughn, "Judge lets autistic boy attend Montgomery school," *The Roanoke Times & World News*, Mar. 4, 1995, p. A1; *The Washington Post*, "Loudoun parents seek new school for autistic son," Feb. 17, 1995, p. D3; T. Campbell, "Suit on mainstream dismissed," *Richmond Times Dispatch*, July 9, 1997, p. B1.

18. Debbi Wilgoren, "Autistic Loudoun boy enters school in SW Va.," *The Washington Post*, Mar. 11, 1995, p. B2.

19. "Finding on autistic boy upheld," *The Washington Post*, May 6, 1995, p. B2; Victoria Benning, "Autistic boy doing well," *The Washington Post*, May 20, 1996, p. B3; Louie Estrada, "Parents' suit seeks to return autistic son to Loudoun School," *The Washington Post*, Sept. 10, 1996, p. B5.

20. Lisa Applegate, "Autistic child can go back to Loudoun school, judge says," *The Roanoke Times*, Dec. 6, 1996, p. B1; Lisa Applegate, "For autistic boy, school's open," *The Roanoke Times*, Dec. 7, 1996, p. B1; Louie Estrada, "Loudoun must mainstream autistic boy," *The Washington Post*, Dec. 6, 1996, p. A1.

21. Abramson & Chadwick, 1997, op. cit.

22. Ray Suarez, "Inclusion," NPR's Talk of the Nation, Nov. 17, 1997, (transcript # 97111701-211); Abramson & Chadwick, 1997, op. cit.; Larry Abramson and Alex Chadwick, "Mark Hartmann: Part II," NPR Morning Edition, Nov. 7, 1997, (transcript # 971101709-210).

23. "Loudoun disability case won't be heard," *The Washington Post*, Jan. 14, 1998, p. B3.

24. Lewin, 1997, op. cit.

25. Kathy Lu, "Autistic pupil loses fight to be 'included'", *The Roanoke Times*, Jan. 14, 1998, p. 1A.

26. Lisa Applegate & Kathy Lu, "Seeking best place to learn," *The Roanoke Times*, Feb. 1, 1998, p. A1.

27. Steve Holladay, "Learning-challenged kids shouldn't be in regular classrooms," *The Roanoke Times*, Feb. 7, 1998, p. A7.

28. Roxana Hartmann, "My son's right to an education doesn't hurt others," *The Roanoke Times*, Feb. 16, 1998, p. A7.

29. James Klagg & Fred Morton, "Balancing the needs of special and regular students," *The Roanoke Times*, Mar. 13, 1998, p. A9.

30. Catherine Kohler Riessman. *Narrative Analysis*, Newbury Park, Calif.: Sage Publications, 1993.

31. Walter R. Fisher. *Human Communication as Narration: Toward a Philosophy of Reason, Value, and Action*, Columbia, S.C.: University of South Carolina Press, 1989.

32. Fisher, 1984, p. 2.

33. Fisher, 1989, p. 194.

34. Michael Schudson, "The sociology of news production revisited," in: J. Curran and M. Gurevitch, eds., *Mass Media and Society*, London: Edwin Arnold, 1991, p. 155.

35. James Spradley. *The Ethnographic Interview*, N.Y.: Holt, Rinehart & Winston, 1979, p.186.

36. Lewin, 1997, p. 20.

37. Hartmann, 1998, p. A7.

38. Lu, 1998, p. A1.

39. Abramson and Chadwick, "Mark Hartmann, Part II," 1997.

40. Lewin, 1997, p. 20.

41. Susie Vass-Gal, "Parent's worries reflect misconceptions," (letter to the editor), *The Roanoke Times*, Feb. 23, 1998, p. A7.

42. John Swain and Colin Cameron, "Unless otherwise stated: discourses of labelling and identity in coming out," in: M. Corker and S. French, eds., *Disability Discourse*. Buckingham, U.K.: Open University Press, 1999.

43. Swain and Cameron, 1999, p. 76.

44. Hartmann, 1998, p. A7.

45. Department of Education, 2000, op. cit.

46. Hartmann, 1998, p. A7.

47. Lori Greenberg, "Everyone has a right to go to public schools," *The Roanoke Times*, (letter to the editor), Feb. 23, 1998, p. A7.

48. Steve Bickley and Patty Bickley, "Community supports inclusion policy," (letter to the editor), *The Roanoke Times*, Feb. 23, 1998, p. A7.

49. Marc Eaton, "Inclusion can help all students," *The Roanoke Times*, (letter to the editor), Feb. 23, 1998, p. A7.

50. DeVaughn, Feb. 17, 1995, p. B1.

51. Victoria Benning, "Court backs decision to remove autistic boy from regular class," *The Washington Post*, July 10, 1997, p. D1.

52. Hartmann, 1998, p. A7.

53. DeVaughn, Mar. 4, 1995, p. A1.

54. Lu, 1998, p. A1.

55. Applegate and Lu, 1998, p. A1.

56. Holladay, 1998, p. A7.

57. Debbie Kingery, "Mainstreaming can be done gradually," (letter to the editor), *The Roanoke Times*, Feb. 23, 1998, p. A7.

58. Applegate and Lu, 1998, p. A1.

59. Holladay, 1998, p. p. A7.

60. Kingery, 1998, p. 7A.

61. Abramson and Chadwick, 1998.

62. Holladay, 1998, p. A7.

63. Lewin, 1997, p. 20.

64. Lewin, 1997, p. 20.

65. Deborah Tannen. *The Argument Culture*, N.Y.: Random House, 1998.

66. Thomas A. Hollihan and Patricia Riley, "The rhetorical power of a compelling story: A critique of a 'Toughlove' parental support group," *Communication Quarterly*, 1987, 35, pp. 13-25.

67. R. L. Stanfield, "Tales out of school," *National Journal*, 1995, 27, pp. 33-34.

68. Vass-Gal, 1998, p. A7.

69. Lu, 1998, p. 1A.

70. Emma Brown, "Teaching the ABC's of crucial social skills; As number of autistic kids rises, schools and programs are being created to aid those with mild form," *The Washington Post*, Dec. 3, 2009, p. B1.

71. The autistic rights movement prefers the term "autistic" rather than "person with autism."

72. The Autistic Self Advocacy Network, "An open letter on the NYU Ransom Notes Campaign," Dec. 2007, petitiononline.com/ransom/petition.html.

73. The Autistic Self Advocacy Network, "About The Autistic Self Advocacy Network," 2009, autisticadvocacy.org

74. Ari Ne'eman, Presentation to "Disability and Mass Media" class, City University of New York Disability Studies Master's program, Graduate Center, New York, NY, Feb. 28, 2009.

75. Andrew Solomon, "The Autism Rights Movement," *New York* magazine, May 25, 2008, nymag.com/news/features/47225/. (Accessed 28th May, 2008).

76. Amanda Baggs, "How I Make My Videos," Amanda Baggs blog, Ballastexistenz.Austistics.org. 2007, Accessed on Feb. 20, 2009 at: ballastexistenz.autistics.org/?page_id=405.

77. Amanda Baggs, "In my voice," Jan. 17, 2010, [YouTube video], youtube.com/watch?v= JnylM1hI2jc.

6.

Disability media tell their own stories

D
isability media, like other types of alternative or dissident media in U.S. society, advocate on behalf of a distinctive U.S. group that has come together to form a political and social community. Over the years, these publications have vigorously covered the issues that affect the disability community. They're considered "alternative" or "dissident" media also because of the historic discrimination and exclusion people with disabilities have faced in society, as well as the negative stereotyping they have received from the mainstream news media.

Many people with disabilities have been isolated throughout U.S. history because of the architectural, occupational, communication, and educational barriers in society, but they have still played an integral part in the social and political development of the U.S. Their publications illustrate this. However, the publications of this community have never received much attention in mass media studies, even though many disability publications have a long history in the U.S.; some have been ongoing since 1907. Few scholars have analyzed disability media in any systematic way or at all.

This chapter fills that void by illustrating the vibrant diversity of disability media. It is based on a content analysis of a sample of the disability magazines, newspapers, and newsletters being produced in the 1990s (N-134),[1] evaluating demographic characteristics of the publications, as well as looking as content issues. This chapter discusses the ways in which many disability publications fall into media historian Lauren Kessler's alternative press model of dissident media.[2]

The alternative press model

Kessler theorizes that minority groups or alternative groups in society have historically had three typical forms of presentation by the mainstream press, all negative: 1) they are excluded completely from coverage by the mainstream press; 2) only their events/demonstrations are covered by the press, not their ideas or issues; 3) they are covered within the context of negative stereotypes and are held up to ridicule and insult.[3] This kind of coverage caused them to develop their own media.

In ethnic press history, the first African-American newspaper, *Freedom's Journal*, developed in the mid-1800s because the black community was not allowed to respond to anti-black editorials that were being run in the mainstream newspaper. The *Ram's Horn*, an early African-American newspaper, developed because Willis Hodges, a black man, tried to get his letter to the editor published in the *New York Sun;* he was made to pay $15 and the letter ran as an advertisement. He was told, "The *Sun* shines for all white men, not for colored men." Hodges was thus inspired to begin his own newspaper, *Ram's Horn.*[4]

A comparable modern example from the disability community occurred in 1998 when nationally syndicated *Washington Post* columnist William Raspberry complained that a blind man asking for the Bay Area transit system's Web site for bus and train schedules to be accessible under the Americans with Disabilities Act (ADA) was "a clear violation of common sense." Raspberry, who is African American and considers himself a "civil rights liberal," says he is angry with people with disabilities who insist "their disability be accommodated to and that we take no notice of it."[5]

As elite mainstream press, *The Washington Post* column reached hundreds of thousands of readers; however, Randy Tamez, the blind man who sued the transit authority, was never allowed to respond in a letter to the editor in *The Post.* The disability rights publication *Ragged Edge* (in three issues) had the only ongoing coverage of the Raspberry column. Tamez' full response to the column could only be found on the Internet as a reprinted email message.[6] There, Tamez confronts Raspberry's anti-disability and segregationist rhetoric with a civil rights narrative and reminds everyone that "it is obvious that the biggest obstacle to access is the attitudinal barrier."[7]

In line with Kessler's alternative press model, the modern disability media was reacting to the same kind of exclusion, stigmatization, and misunderstood consumer standing that other "outsider" groups have experienced. The development of the disability press also fits with Erving Goffman's theory of stigma. These publications allow people to pull themselves together as a community with similar goals and aspirations. Goffman says people with a stigmatized status in society develop their own publications because these media allow them to debate the societal issues related to them that rarely make the mainstream press. These publications allow them to define the friends and enemies of their community's goals, both inside and outside the community. They allow them to set expectations of behavior for the members of their community.[8] In the 1990s media scholar Jeffrey Alan John confirmed the place of disability magazines in bolstering disability community unity and culture.[9]

These factors have caused disability groups, just like other community, activist, or disenfranchised groups in society, to form their own publications.[10] Charlie Winston, who kept track of the disability press annually with his *America's Telability Media Guide*, estimated that in 1998-99 there were at least 1,200 mass media resources for the disability community in the form of magazines, newspapers, newsletters, radio/TV programs, and recurring newspaper columns.[11]

Winston says the disability media range from an individual creating a 2-4 page newsletter at a very low cost to a glossy lifestyle magazine such as *WE*, which, although now defunct, was directed toward people with disabilities with mid-to-high incomes. However, page count and financing are not indicators of the quality of these publications' content, Winston says. Many small newsletters report excellent and much needed information, he says, giving the example of a tiny newsletter from a nursery school for deaf children, which has two pages of useful information for parents of deaf children.[12] (Some of this newsletter content has now migrated to the Internet, in the form of blogs and Web sites, which were covered in Chapter 1.)

Media scholar Lillie Ransom also found in her study of 56 disability publications and through interviews with disability publication editors that the disability press's development fits with Kessler's alternative press model of being oppressed, having a different self perception than mainstream presentations, and exclusion from mainstream media. Ransom, however, did not find that the disability press was as thematically unified as the feminist press and black press are.

She identified three patterns among the publications: Activist/Political, Main-streaming/Assimilationist, and Special Interest. According to Ransom, a publication such as *Ragged Edge* was imbedded within the disability rights social movement, making it an Activist/Political model publication; *The Arc and the Dove*, a publication for the Association of Retarded Citizens of Maryland, fits within the Mainstreaming/Assimilationist model because they want people with intellectual disabilities to be accepted in the mainstream community; and a publication such as *The National Amputee Golfer* is a Special Interest model.[13]

As diverse as these models of publications are, however, they all serve the disability community as the disability press and have one common over-arching theme that functions within the very diverse disability community – each publication has the commonality of serving people who are outsiders and who face societal barriers due to physical or mental difference. Regardless of the orientations of the disability publications, they all share this quality.

Disability publication writer Douglas Lathrop explains that the disability press reflects that people with disabilities think of themselves as a "community":

> In the last couple of decades – particularly since the passage of the Americans with Disabilities Act in 1990 – more and more people have begun to see themselves not just as isolated individuals, but as members of a larger 'disability community,' with a set of common experiences, a common culture, and a common struggle for civil rights facing them. Like other minority communities did in the past, it has begun to build upon this common ground through the written word – through publications such as *New Mobility, Mouth, Mainstream,* and *The Disability Rag,* as well as others at the national and local or regional levels – reporting news, providing role models, exploring important issues, and otherwise covering the concerns of the community.[14]

In addition to giving a voice to the entire community of Americans with disabilities, disability media also remind us that people with disabilities are a multi-community community. Because different disabilities make for different societal barriers, specific publications are based on specific disability-related issues. Jeffrey Alan John found evidence of broad-based disability culture in a variety of disability magazines because they contained "tools and technology useful for the person with a disability; a largely shared value system in support of the individual with a disability; and an emphasis on events and information that promote interaction within the disability community and a subsequent empowerment through collective action."[15] The first two criteria can be found in most forms of the disability press and the third fits primarily with Ransom's Activist/Political model.

Disability publications in the U.S. media environment

Media and disability scholar John Clogston found from a number of studies of mainstream news media presentations of disability that, historically, articles about people with disabilities rarely made it into the news, and, when the articles were written, that they were misrepresentative and stigmatizing. His study of the *New York Times* coverage of the disability community from the 1940s to the 1990s found that before 1956 disability was most often dealt with in a charity story.[16] In coverage in the 1990s, Clogston also found that disability has yet to be covered in the beat structure of news reporting, meaning that it may only get covered in an event-oriented or feature story.[17]

In early 20th century America, as industrialzation and growing media influence added to the stigma of having a disabling condition, people with disabilities became more excluded from many of the activities of U.S. society than they had been in a pre-industrial agrarian, family farm-based society, where some were accepted for what they could contribute. After industrialization, people with disabilities, who were perceived as unable to participate in an industrialized economy, were devalued and stigmatized. The mainstream media did not consider them a worthy group to discuss, so they were, in essence, silenced because of the stigma of disability. Media scholar Carmen Manning-Miller says this inability to speak for themselves on issues affecting them caused different disability groups to begin their own publications.[18] Clogston's and Manning-Miller's findings support Kessler's alternative press model as explaining the development of the disability press.

The Deaf community has a long history of publications in this country. The North Carolina School for the Deaf began the first publication for Deaf persons in 1848 with its school newspaper, *The Deaf Mute*.[19] The American Deaf community is unique in being tied together not only by deafness, but also by a linguistic tradition, American Sign Language.[20] Although the Deaf community only rarely identifies itself as part of the disability community, its publications fit within the commonality of disability media by serving people who are outsiders in U.S. society and who face societal barriers due to a physical difference.

Deafness-related publications started when states began building residential schools for deaf children in the mid-1800s. These schools used sign language to teach and employed many deaf teachers. Thus, these schools became a location for the transmission of deaf culture to deaf children, and they began their own newspapers at these schools to help cement their community. Soon after the North Carolina school published the first school newspaper, the other school followed suit. The newspapers were known as The Little Paper family. They exchanged items of interest and stories and generally transmitted the Deaf community back to itself.[21] Deaf historian Edward Fay reported in 1893 that there were 50 of these residential school newspapers and they generously exchanged each others' news.[22] I studied the Deaf community's "Little Papers" in 1993 and found that they provided a significant cultural forum for the Deaf community to discuss important political events affecting the community, as well as small news events such as a new stained-glass window at a school.[23]

The blind community also has a long and vibrant publication history, and in terms of physical accessibility to news, the blind community was at the forefront with its growing number of Braille publications in the early 20th century. *The Matilda Ziegler Magazine for the Blind* began its Braille publication in 1907 to allow blind persons to read information accessible to them and is still being published today. *The Matilda Ziegler Magazine for the Blind* is the pioneering publication for blind Americans because its first editor, the former business manager of the Memphis *Commercial Appeal*, figured out how to publish the enormous number of embossed pages needed, although no such printing plant existed in the U.S. at the time. By 1907, the editor, Walter G. Holmes, discovered feasible modifications that would allow a regular rotary printing press to be used to produce the embossed pages.[24] The *Braille Book Review* began in 1938 and described the newest books in Braille from the National Library Service for the Blind. Once sound technology was more prevalent, *Talking Book Topics* was founded in the 1930s to give the blind community information about the most recent recorded books at the National Library.[25]

Disability-related publications fostered solidarity within the different subcultures of the disability community. After World War II, soldiers who had been disabled in war came home, which led to the Paralyzed Veterans of America's development of the magazine *Paraplegia News* in 1946.[26] Many disability publications target similarly distinctive audiences, from people with a specific disability to parents to health care professionals. For example, *Future Reflections* is a quarterly National Federation of the Blind (NFB) publication directed toward parents of blind and visually impaired children. *Future Reflections* editor Barbara Cheadle explains that the "disability community" that informs the publication's philosophy is the blind movement of the 1960s and 1970s, not agencies or professionals.[27]

In terms of overt disability rights activism, disability publications such as *Ragged Edge, Mainstream,* and *Mouth* helped fuel the disability community's civil rights agenda. Although many oppressed groups such as women, African Americans, Native Americans, etc. fought for their civil rights in the late 1960s, the disability community did not begin to assemble a strong disability rights movement until the mid- to late 1970s. After the Rehabilitation Act was passed in the 1970s but not given regulations to enforce it, the disability community began to organize protests and activism. Publications grew from these activities: *Mainstream* magazine started in 1975 (it folded in 1999) and *The Disability Rag* began in 1980. (*The Disability Rag* became the onliine publication raggededgemagazine.com, now an online archive of the publication's articles.) *Mouth* began in 1990 after its founder Lucy Gwin "escaped from what amounted to a nursing home." *Mouth* originally started to serve the community of people with neurological impairments but evolved into a general all-disability rights advocacy publication.[28]

Douglas Lathrop writes that these rights-based publications sprang up because many in the disability community were tired of the persistent negative media stereotypes of people with disabilities as inspirational or courageous. "In light of this persistent reliance on oppressive stereotypes, the disability press fills the void," Lathrop wrote.[29] Gwin, the editor of *Mouth*, explained: "Nobody [in the nondisabled media] is going to cover the disability-rights movement, so we're just going to have to cover it our own damn selves."[30] The activist disability publications fit squarely with what Kessler has termed the dissident press, which has thrived on the fringes of society and has even helped redefine and expand the American marketplace of ideas.[31]

The advertising dilemma

Charlie Winston reported that modern disability publications developed for consumer-based reasons as well, because the disability community was rarely seen as a worthy demographic segment in the U.S. capitalistic structure.[32] The argument is: If people with disabilities are not seen as a strong consumer group, the mainstream press may be less likely to cover their issues.[33] Caryl Rivers explains that publishers of major U.S. newspapers look for a specific middle- or upper-middle class socio-economic demographic to consume their information because this is what their major advertisers, such as chain stores, want.[34] Until the 1960s and 1970s, advertisers viewed the African-American and Latino consumers as low income and thus saw little need to advertise in their publications or diversify their advertising images.[35] However, in the 1990s, mass media became much more targeted, resulting in advertisers diversifying their placements in ethnic specialty magazines, newspapers, and TV programming. They also recognized the spending power of the African American, Latino, and non-English speaking communities in the U.S.[36]

However, such recognition as a consumer group rarely came for the disability community. Winston says, "People with disabilities [as an] advertising base is not understood by corporate America. No one thinks of a disabled person as a consumer, so why would they advertise to him?" He adds that the societal perception of people with disabilities as "sick" or unemployed causes advertisers to ignore them. Although people with disabilities are portrayed as poor, he points out, many have adequate financial means, whether it comes from insurance settlements, inheritance, full-time work, or Social Security.[37] "The disabled consumer not only purchases health-care services or medical equipment but clothing, jewelry, furnishings, food, travel services, and every conceivable consumer good and service. By reaching this market, businesses create a lasting relationship and brand loyalty that extends beyond the disabled consumer to relatives, friends, and associates," according to Carmen Jones of EKA Marketing.[38]

This non-consumer status has caused problems for disability publications too, because disability media who use advertising as part of their revenue base have struggled to attract major advertisers. In fact, the disability press lost a major voice in 1999 when *Mainstream* magazine stopped publication due in part to lack of advertising revenue.[39]

This history of exclusion from the U.S. consumer-based society continues today, even though estimates are that more than 50 million disabled Americans have annual spending of $800 billion.[40] Winston, who is visually impaired, says that many advertisers think they have solved the problem by including a few people with disabilities in their ads. "Using a disabled person in an ad is a warm and fuzzy feeling. [But] we are not treated as consumers," he explains, adding that this threatens the continued existence of an advertising-based disability press.[41]

In the late 1990s, advertising-based disability media were actively trying to woo national advertisers to the "disabled consumer" that they represent. Joe Valenzano purchased the magazine *Exceptional Parent* in 1993 and increased ad pages from 26 to 40 monthly in his first four years of ownership. As a publication for parents of children with disabilities with a circulation of about 65,000, it was able to attract major advertisers such as American Airlines, IBM, Carnation, and GM. One key seems to be that the magazine reaches a portion of the estimated five million parents of children with disabilities in the U.S. In addition, Valenzano was able to make subscription connections with many major disability charitable organizations and to get the magazine into 33,000 doctor and hospital waiting rooms. Valenzano, who has a son with a disability, says, however, even with increased circulation and ad revenues, the motto for the magazine stays the same: "Put the child first and the disability second." This is what one advertiser said attracted his company to the magazine: "its content and commitment."[42]

Content and character of disability publications

Using the Telability guide and using content analysis to examine the disability publications, I found the following general characteristics about the 134-publication sample used: That disability publications in the 1990s had small circulations, rarely used color photos (22%) but did use much black and white photography (68%), typically came out quarterly or bi-monthly, were many times provided in alternative formats such as audiotape or Braille (42.5%), and were primarily founded in the 1980s and 1990s.

Many of the publications had low circulation figures, but that should not mislead one to think that only a few people see disability publications. In many cases, circulation is a function of the organizational constraints of the independent living centers or disability service centers that publish them. Many are not well-funded and can only publish the number within their means. In addition, some of these centers are in areas of low population, so a small circulation is all that is needed: *Focus*, a publication of the Montana Independent Living Project, has a quarterly circulation of 2,200, in a state with a low general population. It is suspected, however, that due to the high salience of disability information for people with disabilities, these publications are probably well-read and passed along to other people who may not be on the subscription list.

123

The year of origin of these publications is an important indicator of their character. The fact that 70 percent were begun since 1979 illustrates the influence of new legislation and changing social attitudes toward people with disabilities and confirms Lathrop's argument that many sprang up from a new sense of "disability community."[43] Legislation aimed at ending discrimination based on disabilities began with Section 504 of the Rehabilitation Act, which forbade discrimination based on disability any place where federal dollars were received. That legislation finally began to be enforced in 1980, which led to much hope among Americans with disabilities that their issues were finally being addressed. However, enforcement was lax and by the late 1980s a bi-partisan group of advisers to the President, the National Council on the Handicapped (later renamed the National Council on Disability), saw that things were not changing for people with disabilities in the U.S. The Council laid part of the foundation for the 1990 Americans with Disabilities Act (ADA) in a 1986 report entitled *Toward Independence*, which assessed the current federal laws and programs affecting people with disabilities and made recommendations for legislative change. These recommendations, coupled with lobbying from disability rights activists, became the impetus for the ADA.[44] In this changing climate for people with disabilities, many disability groups saw hope and that manifested itself in creation of publications that could give a voice on their issues. This finding is analogous to the development of feminist publications, some of which emerged from the voting rights movement.[45]

Another more technological reason plays into the surge of disability publications after 1979 – the ease of desktop publishing. Underfunded and smaller disability groups probably couldn't afford the luxury of publications when they had to pay designers and printing companies. Mass communication studies report that by 1984 three new developments merged to allow desktop publishing – affordable personal computers that could handle graphics applications, affordable laser printers, and easier software that could design entire pages.[46] This desktop publishing revolution allowed disability publications at even the smallest disability organizations to be created if all they owned was a PC and printer. (A similar phenomenon is now occurring on the Internet, with template-based Web design for blogging and Facebook page creation. All one needs is a computer with an Internet connection and a desire to write to begin a blog, for example.)

This desktop publishing revolution meant that publications of all sizes could be developed – the only expense being the cost of photocopying and mailing. Interestingly, many of the publications, especially the newsletters, are funded by organizations. Only 36 percent of the sample carried advertisements and 38 percent had paid subscriptions. This is probably a result of the high percentage of independent living newsletters in the sample analyzed. The full-color magazines in the sample featured numerous advertisements, many with disability-specific products. *A&U*, a magazine for people with HIV or AIDS, has numerous full-page ads for the varieties of new medications that are being used to treat the disease. In a like manner, *Inside MS*, a magazine for members of the National MS Society, features many ads with medications related to multiple sclerosis, as well as wheelchair accessibility-related products.

In this study, the content of the publications was determined through an analysis of the issues covered in the articles, columns, and blurbs in the publications. The issue list was developed through an understanding of the important concerns in the disability community in the 1990s. A similar list of issues was also used to assess disability-related stories in the mainstream press in the fall of 1998.[47]

The only topic featured prominently both in mainstream and disability publications was children with disabilities. Because inclusive education for children with disabilities has been a major focus for local disability activists and parents of children with disabilities since the Individuals with Disabilities Education Act (IDEA) became law, I suspect that this is the reason children with disabilities/education issues have become a prominent topics for both types of publications. Also, the disability publications report on activities related to children because they are part of the "community" they serve – primarily any person with a disability and the families of people with disabilities. Therefore, the stories in disability publications about kids cover a wide variety of topics, not just education. For instance, the California-based World Institute on Disability's newsletter, *impact!*, presented a front-page story on a youth advocacy network in Russia for disabled youth activists,[48] and *Horizons*, a newsletter of South Dakota's Prairie Freedom Center for Independent Living, presented a front-page story on older teens with disabilities and a transition program in which they participated to learn independent living skills such as cooking or accessing transportation.[49]

Although none of the disability publications in the sample is a daily, a number of publications did cover what might be deemed general news. The Brain Injury Association's *TBI Challenge!* reported in detail about a Centers for Disease

Control (CDC) report on the latest statistics on brain injury in the U.S.. (The new information revealed that an estimated 5.3 million Americans, about 2 percent of the U.S. population, has disabilities resulting from traumatic brain injury.)[50] Although the story did not appear in *TBI Challenge!* until about two months after its release, a Lexis/Nexis search revealed that only one major newspaper in the U.S. had written a story on the CDC report (the *Journal-Constitution* in Atlanta, which is home to the CDC).[51] That potentially means only people with traumatic brain injury in Georgia might have been informed about the new report if *TBI Challenge!* had not done a story. This is an example of the alternative press model at work – these publications highlight stories for the disability community that the mainstream press may not have the time or interest to cover.

In another example of news coverage, the Northern Utah Center for Independent Living's *Options* proudly carried a front-page story on Judith Heumann's visit to the center to hear about problems facing people with disabilities in rural Utah.[52] Heumann was Assistant Secretary of the U.S. Department of Education and oversaw special education and rehabilitative services at that time. She is also considered a pioneer in the disability rights movement in the U.S. However, a Lexis-Nexis search revealed that Judith Heumann was only mentioned once in major mainstream newspapers in 1998 – in a three-paragraph blurb in the *San Francisco Chronicle.*[53]

In terms of disability-related topics covered by the disability publications, this analysis illustrated that they were covering specific issues of interest to disability community: the Americans with Disabilities Act (45%), recreation and sports access (31%), independent living (30%), access to transportation (30%), and advocacy of disability rights (28%); whereas the mainstream print media covered more general issues that might have an impact on people without disabilities as well: educational mainstreaming (19%), health care access/costs (12%), and attitudinal barriers (11%). Obviously, mainstream and disability publications have very different missions. Mainstream media have never understood the large number of people with disabilities (54 million Americans), their families, and disability support-related professionals who comprise the general news audience. Therefore, proportionally, the mainstream news media are under-covering issues that affect at least 20 percent or more of the U.S. population.

The most striking contrast in coverage between disability and mainstream publications is found with the most important topic – the Americans with Disabilities Act. I have argued[54] that although the ADA is trying to shift the social paradigm of how the U.S. perceives people with disabilities and their issues, mainstream media have yet to see this as a "big story." While about 45 percent of the disability publications covered ADA information, only about 4 percent of the mainstream news media mentioned it. On this particular topic, it could be argued that the publications have similar informational missions because of the ADA's impact on many nondisabled people, too. This makes the disparity in coverage all the more shocking. Disability publications assess the impact of the 1990 Act constantly; whereas the mainstream news media have almost forgotten it.

For instance, the Information Center for People with Disabilities in Massachusetts published a front-page analysis of the ADA's impact on employment in its *Disability Issues* periodical. The article cogently assesses the problems of people with disabilities, who were not previously working. The writer explains how ADA accommodations are being used by employed people with disabilities, but the Act has done little to assist the unemployed to break through barriers to obtain work.[55] In a more celebratory story about the ADA, *Reach News Lowdown* (a publication of three independent living centers in Texas) commemorated the 8th anniversary of the Act's passage with a front-page story.[56] This is the major anniversary for the disability community; however, no mainstream magazine covered it in 1998 and only a few national newspapers covered local celebrations; one prestigious newspaper that did, *The Boston Globe,* incorrectly reported the anniversary year.[57] Other ADA-related information in disability publications focused on educating people, such as an article in *Setting Sails* about the legal meaning of the term "reasonable accommodation" in the Act and its applicable definitions.[58] As the alternative press model explains, this lack of mainstream coverage spurs disability publications on to write many specific and detailed articles for their community.[59]

Other issues crucial to people with disabilities are independent living, access to transportation, housing, jobs, and advocacy of civil rights. All were heavily covered in disability publications. The New Jersey Developmental Disabilities Council magazine, *People with Disabilities,* featured numerous powerful profiles of people living independently in the community after being in now-closed residential institutions. One story explained that when Bob Hartwigson left the institution, he said, "I had a smile on my face." He explained in the article his dislike of being institutionalized: "Terrible place. Staff would give you cold showers. Here you have it how you like it. Glad that place closed."[60] Hartwigson now lives in a group home in the Matawan, N.J., suburbs and happily describes how he can now go for walks and is learning to cook for himself. Other aspects of independent living merge with issues such as accessible transportation. *Inside MS* magazine reported on the successful push by the Chicago MS Society to get the city to pass an ordinance providing accessible taxicabs.[61] Assistive technology is also important to independent living. *The Braille Forum* presented an article about the SOS phone, which quickly connects someone to a pre-programmed number, paratransit, or 911.[62]

Both mainstream and disability publications feature a particular article type – the personality profile; however, their execution of these articles is very different. Many mainstream magazines write profiles on people with disabilities that fall into a category known as the "supercrip" profile. They drip with pathos, pity, or an inspirational tone, and most give no "news" about any substantive disability issue. They illustrate the negative stereotypes presented in the mainstream press that Kessler refers to in her alternative press model, which lead disability groups to create their own publications. A *Parade* magazine cover featured a supercrip profile in its story on blind mountain climber Erik Weihenmayer taking his father on a climb.[63] Weihenmayer fits exactly with media scholar John Clogston's definition of a supercrip: The disabled person is portrayed as deviant because of "superhuman" feats (such as a mountain-climbing blind man) or as "special" because they live regular lives "in spite of" disability (i.e., deaf high school student who plays softball). This role reinforces the idea that disabled people are deviant – that the person's accomplishments are "amazing" for someone who is less than complete.[64] Disability activist George Covington explains how the media's supercrip stories cause problems. "Too often, the news media treat a disabled individual who has attained success in his field or profession as though he were one of a kind. While this one-of-a-kind aspect might make for a better story angle, it perpetuates in the mind of the general public how rare it is for the disabled person to succeed."[65]

But these inspiration-focused stories are much-loved by readers, and consumer magazines know their audiences and what they like, so they give it to them by writing many profile stories about disability that fit the supercrip model. Even high school journalists realize this is what the general public wants, according to Laura Miller, whose survey of high school journalism students, found that the majority of the students said they "would treat a person's disability as a news oddity, worthy of top placement in a news story."[66]

In contrast, even when disability publications focus on inspiring members of their community, it is "in-group" communication that promotes pride among its members. Because people with disabilities understand the barriers and discrimination the profile subject faces, they can properly give context to whether the person's life actually deserves "supercrip" treatment. As a result, personality profiles in disability publications typically cover more than just the superficial; they have issues important to the community as a whole imbedded within them.

A profile in the National Down Syndrome Society's *Update* illustrates this. The article focuses on Nannie Sanchez, who was the first person with Down syndrome ever to pass a placement test for community college. She has become an education advocate after her positive experience being mainstreamed throughout school. She decided to run for the New Mexico State School Board in her home state and collected almost triple the number of names she needed on a petition to get onto the ballot. Although she lost, Sanchez received 35 percent of the vote and brought the attention she hoped for to the issues of students with disabilities. The article refers to Sanchez as a "trailblazer," and that description is completely accurate. Nannie Sanchez is an "inspirational" role model for the disability community, but this designation comes not from her status as a person with a disability, as it might in the mainstream media; it comes from her actions and advocacy on behalf of her community.[67] This type of profile fits with the type of disability images the editor of *New Mobility* said he wants to present: "disabled people leading independent and active lives, as an antidote to the prevailing stereotype of helpless, dependent victims whose lives revolve solely around their disabilities."[68]

A look at personality profiles in disability publications reveals a difference in writing style that is significant. Although the publications were analyzed as a whole, not as separate stories, it was apparent that in many disability publications the writing style is different from that of mainstream magazines. It is the norm for most consumer or trade magazines to write with a perspective in mind. For example, a 1999 article in *Ladies Home Journal* on high-profile supercrip Christopher Reeve, and his wife, Dana, promoted her book, which is a collection of all the letters written to Christopher Reeve after his accident from numerous famous people and ordinary people, who wrote about how courageous he was to go on living.[69] In the article on the Reeves, the "slant" is that Dana Reeve was inspirational and courageous to stay with a husband who had such a serious disability.[70]

129

Disability publications also have slants to their stories – such as that Nannie Sanchez is an excellent advocate for her community and is a trailblazer. However, something more exists in much of the disability publications' writing: an information-heavy approach. The underlying theme to this writing style is "information is power." Even though some of articles are poorly executed in their writing style, they are information-rich, delving past the surface and digging deep into all aspects of the topic. These articles truly try to answer all the questions a reader might have, because disability publications know these articles have the highest level of salience with their audience.

A&U is well written and brutally honest because its writers know they are writing for an AIDS-savvy audience. In an October 1998 article, the magazine confronted culture clashes between gay, white people with HIV and Latinos who are HIV positive. An article about an AIDS education center in the Latino community explains that one in five new cases of HIV/AIDS is Latino/a, and Latina women with HIV/AIDS are one of the largest groups of new infections. Without judgment, the article investigates the unique cultural aspects of HIV infection in that community, such as silence about sexuality and the Catholic Church's stance on condoms. The article asks difficult questions but does not shy away from answering them: "So how do they even begin to educate teens when the governing culture works against such instruction, and when the prevailing attitude is 'Condoms are only for homosexuals'?"[71] The article then discusses how the center creates internal "families" of people who share the same sexuality and culture and those "families" meet at gatherings that may be social functions, rather than discussion groups.

The writing style in these types of articles is many times proactive. Members of the specific disability sub-community receive information about programs in which they can get involved or mirror in their own geographic area. Even in the smallest newsletter, many articles offer this kind of usefulness for the lives of the reader. As Winston explained: "The individual person does not have much money to supply a good looking or professional looking newsletter, but many are meaty, to the point and what the person with a disability wants to read."[72]

Conclusions

This analysis of disability media confirms the link between disability publications and Kessler's alternative press model. Previous research has shown that the mainstream media coverage of disability issues has been spotty at best, and the publications examined in this study illustrate how the disability press has stepped in to fill that void. Disability publications in the late 1990s were highlighting issues of concern to the disability community that the mainstream press may not have been covering. Without malice toward specific communities, many mainstream general interest publications just don't have the time, space, staff, or interest to cover their issues. And mainstream specialty publications such as women's magazines, computer magazines, or sports magazines must focus on stories that keep their audiences subscribing.

Kessler theorized that alternative media developed because many groups are covered within the context of negative stereotypes and are held up to ridicule and insult.[73] In the case of people with disabilities, they may be presented as supercrips, as pitiful, or as burdens on society. The disability publications in this study present a strong counter image to those stereotypes.

In actuality, people with disabilities feel more empowered today than ever before due to federal legislation that has brought down some barriers and alleviated some discrimination against them. However, even with these positive changes, stigma about disability remains, especially in mainstream media representations. As the mainstream news media continue to present hackneyed, trite images of people with disabilities and their issues, modern disability media will continue to fight those images and to provide accurate and up-to-date information for their community.

A unique aspect of the disability press that this chapter highlights is that unlike some dissident media, it is not monolithic. From disability rights to disability sports to independent living information, publications fit all the segments of the disability community. And new publications continue to start, finding new slices of the disability community to write about.

Disability publications show that a modern-day technological revolution is giving alternative voices easier methods to enter the marketplace of ideas. The revolution in desktop publishing, online publishing software, and technological advancements for disabled people themselves allow disability publications to thrive. Many new technologies such as speech synthesis, robotics, voice input systems, Braille text displays, and telephone relay systems allow people with disabilities to access information more easily both online and in print. John Hood writes that "the Information Age promises to expand the boundaries of human potential even further, as the mind – not the body – becomes the most valuable asset a worker or entrepreneur can bring to the marketplace."[74] Disability media reap rewards from these technologically empowered disabled people because print publications can readily create an accessible format by posting their content online, where people with disabilities who use screen readers or other reading devices and have access to the Internet can more easily read the content. Even the smallest disability publications began to put up Web sites in the late 1990s, because they are cheaper than paper and give more accessibility options to their readers.

Disability publications in the 1990s fall squarely within the alternative press model of their predecessors in the black press, the feminist press, or the immigrant press. Like the publications of these communities, disability media seek to "educate the 'unconverted' public by presenting a forum for ideas generally ignored by the conventional press."[75] As Kessler has explained, the U.S. marketplace of ideas has not just applied to the mainstream press, but for the alternative press "has meant the freedom to expand the marketplace – and ultimately, the freedom to speak."[76] For the disability community, its publications have created places where issues traditionally ignored can be discussed, where negative stereotypes can be challenged, and where there is still hope that societal barriers will fall.

Notes

The content of this chapter comes primarily from the following article: Beth Haller, "Content and Character: Disability Publications in the 1990s" in *Journal of Magazine and New Media Research*, Spring 2000, 1:3. It is used with full permission from the journal.

1. To find the disability publications analyzed in this chapter, I used Winston's 4th edition of the *Telability* guide (1998-99), which listed all U.S. disability media. A mailing was sent to approximately 260 disability publication editors in July 1999. The mailing list was selected from three sections of the *Telability* guide: the magazine listings, the newspaper listings, and the independent living listings. These were chosen because most cut across specific disability type and were focused on the general disability community and its issues. The only exclusions from the sample were academic journals, most of which were directed at health care service providers rather than people with disabilities. The mailing requested two copies of the publication, preferably from the fall of 1998. The resulting sample reflected the population centers of the U.S. New York was represented with the most disability publications (12 percent), California with 11.2 percent, and Texas with 7.5 percent. The only anomaly in terms of a larger number of publications in a lower population state was Maryland, but this can be explained by the large number of disability organizations surround-

ing the D.C. area. About 119 publications were received from the mailing; an additional 15 publications were added through library and Web versions, creating a total sample of 134 publications. Using the *Telability* guide, which lists circulation figures and origin years for the publications, and the first publications that arrived, a code sheet was devised that would assess a variety of demographic information such as circulation size, year of origin, type of publication, use of photographs or color, number of pages, and a variety of content information about the types of disabilities covered and the types of issues pertaining to the disability community covered. The disability issue list was developed in a previous content analysis in fall 1998 of mainstream media coverage of disability issues. The detailed code sheet assessed these 90 different disability issues in the disability publications, which were then compared to mainstream media coverage.

2. Lauren Kessler. *The Dissident Press*, Beverly Hills, Calif.: Sage, 1984.

3. Kessler, p. 14.

4. William D. Sloan, W.D., J.G Stovall, and James D. Startt, J.D., eds. *The Media in America*, Worthington, Ohio: Publishing Horizons, Inc., 1989.

5. William Raspberry, "Sometimes, accommodations for disabled defy common sense," *The Washington Post*, Nov. 17, 1998, p. A9.

6. Randy Tamez, Response to editorial, lists.w3.org/Archives/Public/w3c-wai-ig/1998OctDec/0318. html, November 1998.

7. "Raspberry's target denied response in print," *Ragged Edge*, Mar./Apr. 1999, p. 21.

8. Erving Goffman. *Stigma*, Englewood Cliffs, N.J.: Prentice-Hall, 1963, p. 23.

9. Jeffrey Alan John, "Indications of disability culture in magazines marketed to the disability community" *Disability Studies Quarterly*, Winter 1998, 18, p. 25.

10. Kessler, pp. 12-17, 154-159.

11. "Winston publishes media directory," *Telability Media*, 7, Oct. 1998, 1.

12. Charlie Winston, telephone interview by author, Mar. 26, 1999.

13. Lillie Ransom, *Disability Magazine and Newsletter Editors: Perceptions of the Disability Press, Community, Advocacy, Mainstreaming and Diversity*, Ph.D. dissertation, University of Maryland, College Park, Md., 1996, pp. 136-38.

14. Douglas Lathrop, "Challenging perceptions, " *Quill*, July/Aug. 1995, p. 37.

15. John, 1998, p. 25.

16. John S. Clogston. Fifty years of disability coverage in *The New York Times*, 1941-1991. Paper presented at the Association for Education in Journalism and Mass Communication annual meeting: Montreal, Quebec, 1992, p. 10.

17. John S. Clogston, *Disability Coverage in 16 Newspapers*. Louisville, Ky.: Advocado Press, 1990, p. 12.

18. Carmen Manning-Miller, "The disability press: A descriptive study." Paper presented at the Association for Education in Journalism and Mass Communication annual meeting, Kansas City, Mo., 1993, pp. 14-15.

19. John Van Cleve and Barry Crouch, *A Place of Their Own*. Washington, D.C.: Gallaudet University Press, 1989, p. 60.

20. Van Cleve and Crouch, p. 60.

21. Van Cleve and Crouch, pp. 102-103.

22. Edward A. Fay, ed., *Histories of American Schools for the Deaf, 1817-1893*. Washington, D.C.: Volta Bureau, 1893.

23. Beth Haller, "The Little Papers Newspapers at 19th Century Schools for Deaf Persons," *Journalism History*, Summer 1993, 19, pp. 46-47.

24. Michael Mellor, "A most notable benefaction: *The Matilda Ziegler Magazine for the Blind*," www.zieglermag.org/history.html.

25. Charlie Winston, *America's Telability Media*. Columbia, Mo.: National Telability Media Center 1995, pp. 38, 18.

26. Winston, 1995, p. 14.

27. Ransom, pp. 12-13.

28. MadNation, madnation.org/mouth.htm.

29. Lathrop, 1995, p. 37.

30. Lathrop, 1995, p. 37.

31. Kessler, p. 20.

32. Winston, 1999.

33. Estimates are that mainstream newspapers derive about 90 percent of their revenue from advertising, and magazines derive about 50 percent of revenue from advertising.

34. Caryl Rivers, "Covering the disenfranchised: A working reporter's notes," in *Small Voices and Great Trumpets: Minorities in the Media*, Bernard Rubin, ed., N.Y.: Praeger, 1980, p. 57.

35. Roland E. Wolseley, *The Black Press, U.S.A.*, 2nd ed. Ames: Iowa State Press, 1990, p. 307.

36. Clint Wilson and Felix Gutierrez, *Race, Multiculturalism and the Media*. Thousand Oaks, Calif.: Sage, 1995, pp.125-132.

37. Winston, 1999.

38. Carmen D. Jones, "Disabled consumers," *American Demographics*, Nov. 1997, letter to the editor, p. 4.

39. "*Mainstream* ceases publication," *Telability Media*, 8, Mar. 1999, p. 7.

40. Jeff Gremillion, "The disabled's strength in spending," *Mediaweek*, 17, November 1997, p. 30.

41. Winston, 1999.

42. Steve Wilson, "Accessible innovations," *FOLIO*, July 1, 1997, pp. 41-42.

43. Lathrop, 1995.

44. Sara D. Watson, "A study in legislative strategy. The passage of the ADA," *Implementing the Americans with Disabilities Act.* Baltimore: Paul H. Brookes Publishing, 1993.

45. Kessler, pp. 74-87.

46. Warren Agee, Phillip Ault, and Edwin Emery, *Introduction to Mass Communications.* N.Y.: Longman, 1997.

47. Beth Haller, *News media coverage of disability issues,* Fall 1998: A final report for the Center for an Accessible Society, San Diego: Center for an Accessible Society, July 1999.

48. "Youth advocacy network grows in Russia," *impact!,* Summer 1999, pp. 1, 6.

49. "Summer transition program a success," *Horizons,* Summer 1999, p. 1.

50. Monique J. Marino, "CDC report shows prevalence of brain injury," *TBI Challenge,* June/July 1999, pp. 1, 13.

51. Lillian Lee Kim, "Brain-injury study seeks to highlight 'silent epidemic,'" *The Atlanta Journal-Constitution,* Apr. 15, 1999, p. 3F.

52. "Assistant Secretary of Education visits Options," *Options,* Sept./Oct. 1998, p. 1.

53. "Honors for those who help disabled find jobs," *San Francisco Chronicle,* June 5, 1998, p. D7.

54. Beth A. Haller, *Disability rights on the public agenda: Elite news coverage of the Americans with Disabilities Act,* Ph.D. dissertation, Temple University, 1995.

55. Ray Glazier, "Jobs and the ADA: An update," *Disability Issues,* Autumn 1998, pp. 1, 6.

56. "ADA anniversary celebrated," *Reach News Lowdown,* Sept./Oct./Nov. 1998, p. 1.

57. Kathy McCabe, "Salem to observe disabilities day," *The Boston Globe,* July 19. 1998, p. 9.

58. "What is a reasonable accommodation and what does it mean to you?" *Setting Sails,* Aug./Sept./Oct. 1998, p. 4.

59. Kessler, p. 14.

60. Simon Fulford, "Bob Hartwigson," *People with Disabilities,* Nov. 1998, pp. 46-47.

61. Fred Reuland, "Hail accessible taxis," *Inside MS,* Fall 1998, pp. 42-43.

62. Nolan Crabb, "This simple cell phone could save your life," *The Braille Forum,* Dec. 1998, pp. 17-23.

63. Lou Ann Walker, "The day I took my Dad up the Mountain," *Parade,* October 31, 1999, pp. 4-5.

64. John S. Clogston, "Media models" (personal communication, March 8, 1993).

65. George Covington, "The Stereotypes, the Myths and the Media," Washington, D.C., *The News Media and Disability Issues.* Washington, D.C.: National Institute on Disability and Rehabilitation Research, 1988, pp. 1-2.

66. Laura Miller, The Supercrip Syndrome: A look at attitudes behind disability newsworthiness, (unpublished manuscript, March 21, 1995), p. 3.

67. "Nannie Sanchez wants to change her corner of the world," *Update,* Summer 1998, pp. 1-2.

68. Lathrop, 1995.

69. Melina Gerosa, "In sickness & in health," *Ladies Home Journal*, Nov. 1999, 182, pp. 238-239.

70. Gerosa, 1999.

71. Dale Reynolds, "We are family," *A&U*, Oct. 1998, p. 45.

72. Winston, 1999.

73. Kessler, p. 14.

74. John Hood, "Taking a byte out of disability," *Policy Review*, Mar./Apr. 1996, pp. 6-7.

75. Kessler, p. 158.

76. Kessler, p. 20.

7.

Pity as oppression in the Jerry Lewis Telethon

Happily, the subject of this chapter is becoming less and less relevant to the disability rights community. The rampant "pity party" that is the Jerry Lewis Muscular Dystrophy Association Telethon each Labor Day weekend has been gradually losing steam since 2000. Fewer local TV stations carry the telethon, and in 2009 even the newspaper supplement, *Parade* magazine, which had always featured the comedian and one of his "kids" on the cover to promote the MDA telethon, dropped it from the cover. *Parade* instead ran a cover story on medical research titled "Discoveries That Can Save Your Life " and, inside, the magazine only had a brief mention of MDA.

But the telethon is still a significant flashpoint in the representation of people with disabilities in American media. This chapter focuses on the results of a deep textual analysis of the rhetoric used by Jerry Lewis as he hosted the telethon in 1992.[1] Lewis rarely changes his telethon rhetoric each year, and its very outrageousness gives us crucial insight into this specific media narrative about people with disabilities.

The rhetoric of Jerry Lewis in the telethon broadcast

Since 1966 Jerry Lewis and his Muscular Dystrophy Association Telethon have been raising money for research and treatment of the 40 forms of neuro-muscular disease. Every moment of the annual Labor Day telethon is devoted to fundraising, and Lewis employs a variety of persuasive techniques toward that goal. But the discourse of the telethon also makes certain claims about the people with disabilities who are the focus of the fundraising.

As this chapter will show, the discourse of the telethon focuses on three areas: people with disabilities, the audience, and Jerry Lewis. For a number of years, disability activists have been focusing protest actions on the telethon and Jerry Lewis because of his rhetoric about people with disabilities. They say the telethon audience is made to believe certain things about disability in the effort to get donations. And finally Jerry Lewis himself makes an intertextual statement about disability through his comedic role as a "moronic" oddball and misfit.

Culturally, the narrative of the telethon has real ramifications for the ideology surrounding disability in U.S. society. Disability researcher Marilynn Phillips calls a telethon an "occasion of ideology," rather than an "occasion of social reality" in U.S. culture. Occasions of ideology invoke pity and charity in service of a belief of a cure, whereas occasions of social reality summon feelings of resentment and confusion over the "abnormality" of people with disabilities. During occasions of ideology, discourse focuses on the "defect" of the person, and disabled persons are homogenized as one. Phillips says, "primarily, these are events which define culturally appropriate handicapped behavior (being a good cripple), and which serve to demonstrate predictable interactions between nondisabled and disabled persons."[2]

Unfortunately, the rhetoric and behavior of Jerry Lewis on his telethon feel comfortable within an ableist U.S. culture. The nondisabled audience has a history of feeling pity and sympathy for people with disabilities. Culturally, as well, they embrace the optimism of the charity toward miracles and cures. They may reject the disability rights perspective because it causes discomfort and because it is rarely portrayed in U.S. media images. As Phillips questions: "Might installing a wheelchair ramp disaffirm the ideology of cure?"[3] These are some of the possible cultural paradigms with which the disability rights movement and its social constructionist model must contend. The oppressive message of the biological or medical model has been repeated throughout much of U.S. culture and its mass media images. However, the many years of loud opposition to the Jerry Lewis telethon may represent a gradual shifting of these cultural images.

This chapter theorizes that Lewis's telethon rhetoric makes claims about the bodies of people with disabilities – that disability is intrinsic to the body itself, a physical attribute that turns into a social category. The discourse surrounding

the audience constructs it as a threatened family who must put its fear of affliction to work to help others. And finally, Jerry Lewis – virtually equated with the
telethon – is constituted as an oddball parent-child through intertextual relations to his career as a film star/comedian.

The disabled body in society

One must consider the status of the disabled body in U.S. culture, because
the overriding theme of the MDA telethon is that the bodies of people with muscular dystrophy are "sick," and the telethon must raise money to heal them. This
claim rests on the fact that the people in need represented in the telethon have
one of the neuromuscular diseases called muscular dystrophy. They are thus
constituted as different from people who do not have a neuromuscular disease.
They must use wheelchairs and other equipment to assist them. They may lack
some muscle functions or may not have full motor control over all the muscles
in their bodies.

Their bodies do not fit with how the dominant U.S. culture defines what a
body should be able to do. Their bodies are seen as inferior in their physical
functioning when compared with people who do not have muscular dystrophy.
When the body becomes the focus of humanness, this inferiority of body means
the people become inferior as social beings as well, according to Claire Liachowitz in *Disability as Social Construct*.[4] Photographer and media critic David Hevey
explains how charities use bodies for the visual associations needed for awareness among the public:

> The task for the [charity] agency is to find an image which gives the im-
> pairment and its effects a symbolic but social identity. Since the impair-
> ment has to be the site of disablement, it follows that the body of the
> person with an impairment will be constructed as both the essence and
> symbol of disablement. Their body becomes fragmented and refocuses
> on the major fragment – the impairment. The object of this first stage,
> then, is to place the symbol of the impairment into social orbit but la-
> beled as the property or concern of the affiliated charity.[5]

With this in mind, we see that people with muscular dystrophy are constituted as inferior or subordinate to people without muscular dystrophy.

Most disabled people have been relegated to this inferior role because of their bodies, according to political scientist Harlan Hahn. They deviate from what he calls the "moral order of the body":

> The human body is a powerful symbol conveying messages that have massive social, economic, and political implications. In order to perpetuate their hegemony, ruling elites have attempted to impose what might be termed a moral order of the body, providing images that subjects are encouraged to emulate.[6]

Hahn argues that Western society promotes a certain moral order of the body that can be tied in modern times to mass media. In selling products, for example, mass media as an adjunct to capitalism has been most successful at selling an image of what the perfect body is. This, in turn, has strengthened the social and economic undesirability of people with disabilities and others who are physically different.[7]

At the sociocultural and aesthetic level, the disabled person's body may not conform to standards of beauty and wholeness emphasized in a culture.[8] Hahn argues that the value placed by 20th-century Western society on personal appearance affects the treatment of disabled people in society. He relies on a theoretical perspective that grows from Hanoch Linveh,[9] which he terms "aesthetic anxiety." These are the fears caused by someone who diverges from the typical human form and who may have physical characteristics considered unappealing. The culture reflects this anxiety through its rejection of people with physical differences and through its pursuit of superhuman bodily perfection. Hahn explains this aesthetic anxiety may send people who are seen as physically different into an inferior role in society.[10] After studying the influence of attractiveness in all types of relationships, Leonard Saxe deduced that unattractive people can be victims of injustice, whereas attractive people may be expected to perform at a superior level.[11]

In contrast, disability rights discourse relies on the notion that the body is a socially constructed concept. Therefore, disability actually comes from societal labeling, not from a specific physical attribute. Ability may be different, but humanness is the same. Within this claim, "handicaps" derive from society's architectural, occupational, and attitudinal barriers, not from the physical or mental differences of people. Currently, this perspective is a minority one in societal discourse but one which disability activists are fighting to promote.

Disability activists fight against images such as the telethon that still rely on the biological or medical model to portray them. The activists instead rely on a social constructionist model when creating images of themselves as people with disabilities. William Stothers, the former managing editor of disability activist publication *Mainstream*, explains that the disability rights perspective, unlike what telethons promote, attributes handicaps to environmental causes. "Modifying the environment – architectural barriers, discrimination and attitudes – is the order of the day," Stothers writes.[12] Outsiders to the disability perspective, like Jerry Lewis, associate disability with tragedy and inability. "Disability is attributed to the individual. The objective is to change the person, to offer help to reduce handicap," Stothers says.[13] Thus, the image promoted by Jerry Lewis and the one that many people with disabilities have of themselves collide at the site of the Muscular Dystrophy Association Telethon.

In his telethon rhetoric, Jerry Lewis presents a message of oppression within a biological or medical model rather than the social constructionist model used by disability activists. He presents muscular dystrophy as intrinsic to the body. His message is: People with muscular dystrophy are only half people, but with a cure, they can become whole people. This idea fits with a societal code that if someone is sick, he or she must be made well.

At one point during the 1992 telethon, he tells the audience: "We're going to give them a feeling of nobility, and we're going to help them be better people."[14] Thus, Lewis says, people with muscular dystrophy are not noble now, but they can be. If people will give enough money, afflicted persons can be transformed through a cure into full humans or "better people."

Disability/disease equates to a problem, as Lewis says, "because someone is disabled or somebody has a problem." Again, finding a cure will alleviate this "problem." In the past, Lewis has referred to this problem as almost divine providence. Mike Angeli of *Esquire* quotes Lewis from the 1973 telethon as saying, "God goofed, and it's up to use to correct His mistakes."[15] This comment touched off a barrage of criticism against him for his insensitivity to this "problem." So Lewis sets up himself and his telethon to correct these mistakes God has wrought – people with muscular dystrophy. And Jerry Lewis sets up his own version of religious thinking to find a cure – positive thinking:

> I just happen to think that the world is in such a state today that we
> get so pessimistic and so uncertain and so unsure anymore that I think

that maybe the answer to a better humanity is: We think positive and positive will come back to us. I think if you think positive it's going to work. I think if you think negative some ratfink hears that and makes it negative. But there's something wonderful about positive thinking. It's uplifting. It's spiritual. It's almost religious.

According to this, Lewis says humanity has problems because people with muscular dystrophy exist, but positive thinking can assist with the cure of these people. Finding a cure or donating toward a cure is set up as a spiritual act. And this positive thinking allows for the "uplifting" of people with muscular dystrophy from their inferior place in life. They can be "saved" from their disability.

The inferiority of the disabled person is played out even in the spatial relations between Jerry Lewis and the people who use wheelchairs on the telethon. In an interview sequence during the 1992 telethon between Lewis and Matt Schuman, a former poster child who works as a sports reporter for the Greeley (Colo.) *Tribune*, Lewis always stands. In the first shot of Lewis and Schuman together, Schuman's face is covered by the two lines of call-in numbers at the bottom of the television screen. The spatial difference exists because Schuman is seated in a wheelchair and Lewis, who is tall, is standing. This causes Schuman's presence in the shot to be negated because the call-in numbers cover his face part of the time and because only his head and shoulders are visible in the bottom left corner of the TV screen at other times. All attention is directed toward Lewis because he is standing. These spatial relations exist not just with Schuman but are repeated throughout the telethon whenever Jerry Lewis interacts with someone who uses a wheelchair. One way to diminish this superior-inferior spacial structure would have been to have an interview corner in which Lewis sits to talk to people who use wheelchairs. But instead Lewis stands throughout the days of the telethon.

Lewis's height and stature also play him as "parent" to the person with disability as "child." Throughout the telethon, he hugs and caresses the children and adults with muscular dystrophy, all of whom he calls his "kids." When Schuman completes his short speech, Lewis rubs and pats the back of Schuman's head. It is not a "good job" touch from one adult to another, as a pat on the back or a shake of the hand might be. It is a parent patting the head of a child to indicate the child has pleased him. In reality, Schuman is a working adult who happens to have a physical disability.

Another superior-inferior positioning comes from Lewis's use of the microphone with Schuman. The camera angle moves to a full-face, eye-level, direct address when Schuman speaks alone, but he is not given his own microphone. This allows Lewis to retain control over the message because he holds the mike, creating the question in viewers' minds as to whether Schuman is capable of holding the microphone himself.

Because Schuman speaks about Lewis and the MDA only in glowing terms, there is little need for Lewis to control the message. But by not letting Schuman hold his own microphone, Lewis denies Schuman the opportunity to show that Schuman can hold a mike. An earlier video clip showed Schuman typing at a computer terminal and taking notes as a journalist, indicating he has enough motor control in his hands to hold his own microphone. It becomes clear that the telethon coordinators made a decision not to provide clip-on lapel microphones for Schuman and many other people who use wheelchairs.

Because Lewis holds the microphone, Schuman must shift his eyes from direct address of the camera to look up at Lewis, who stands over him. Schuman shifts his eyes upward toward Lewis 10 times during his speech of less than one minute. The eye shifts give the impression of worship and raising eyes to a heavenly savior. Lewis has characterized the positive attitude needed for a cure as "spiritual, almost religious."

This relation to the religious gives people with muscular dystrophy a supernatural attachment. Although they are seen as lesser humans at the physical and mental level, people with disabilities are ennobled by their "suffering." Throughout the telethon, Lewis asks people to give to "these children and these adults and those who suffer from neuromuscular diseases." Beatrice Wright's research on attitudes toward disabled people explains that the stereotype assigned to people who have a disability is one of suffering misfortune and being enmeshed in tragedy.[16] Erving Goffman's work on stigma illustrates that this can translate into a stigmatized person being given desirable, yet incorrect, attributes such as superior understanding or ability to cope. He says this imputation of positive, yet undesired, characteristics can sometimes take on a supernatural hue.[17]

After the numbers representing millions of dollars in donations roll across the board during the telethon, Lewis tells a young man with muscular dystrophy: "You brought me luck." To a woman with muscular dystrophy, he says, "I never go on the air without my little note from Shelly wishing me well . . . gives me things to cling to." Lewis characterizes people with muscular dystrophy as amulets of good luck.

These "superpowers" given to people with disabilities add to the oppressive pity narrative needed to draw in the audience. They may be physically inferior, but they are good, virtuous people "suffering" without complaint, or, as Phillips says, performing the role of "good cripple."[18] They therefore deserve a hand-out. These superpowers also make them desirable as the objects of cure, so Jerry Lewis can better "sell" them to the audience as worthy of betterment.

The audience as a threatened family

The telethon rhetoric of Jerry Lewis uses specific techniques to "sell" the cure of people with muscular dystrophy to the moneyed audience. The primary discourse revolves around constructing the audience as part of the societal family that is also at risk from muscular dystrophy. This makes the pathos personal and helps people loosen their wallets to give to the cause.

Lewis is making his appeal within the framework of what Hahn identifies as the existential anxiety of nondisabled people. The bodies of disabled people threaten the body image of nondisabled people who fear that they, too, might become disabled some day. This anxiety is typically promoted in charity appeals to cause donors to count their blessings and give money out of fear for their own functioning and health.[19]

As Hevey explains, "Charity advertising sells fear, while commercial advertising sells desire. Charities promote a brand not to buy, but to buy your distance from."[20] Jerry Lewis tries to make his appeal based on the threat to one's own family:

> Any one of your healthy children could be one of my kids tomorrow. You must understand that what you are doing is preventative medicine and hopefully the medicine and research that will help Matt to continue to live a fulfilling life. We are begging you to have you help your own. While you're helping your own, the feeling of satisfaction is so wonderful that you're going to want to help Matt. And think about that.

First, the plea is literally personalized to the audience member's specific family. Their "healthy children" could turn into one of his inferior "kids" tomorrow. But if they cannot visualize their own family being affected, they are asked to bring Matt Schuman into their fold. Then they have a stake in Schuman's future. They must give, so he can "live a fulfilling life." The desperation of this need is emphasized because Lewis is not just asking, he's "begging" for help, he says. And if giving Schuman a better life is not enough, the plea becomes personal once again. The audience members can gain their own "feeling of satisfaction," thus bettering themselves.

Lewis also uses his own family as part of the discourse. Several times during the telethon, the camera is directed towards his wife, Sam, and daughter, Danielle. Danielle often serves as an example of what the cure can provide. Danielle appears to have no physical disability. In 1992 she was about one year old, with baby fuzz instead of hair and a bow tied around her bald head. She has a round angelic face with rosy cheeks. She looks like the picture-perfect, all-American baby. As one woman with muscular dystrophy says to Lewis, "I want a world of beautiful Danielle Sarahs." In essence, the telethon discourse says, this is what your money for a cure can buy.

Again, Jerry Lewis himself plays one role as parent within this constructed family involving his "kids." "Here's my girl," he says as he introduces a woman with muscular dystrophy. It signifies a father-daughter relationship. His message is that his "kids" are damaged, and therefore, the audience should give so the same thing will not happen to their families.

But Jerry Lewis also functions in a polysemic way in the telethon text. Therefore, who Jerry Lewis is constitutes part of the discourse.

The Jerry Lewis persona

Although Jerry Lewis said "God goofed" when creating his "kids," writer Mike Angeli has called Lewis "God's biggest goof."[21] This illustrates the connection between Jerry Lewis and people with muscular dystrophy. They both play the role of misfits or "goofs" in society.

The way Jerry Lewis is perceived by audiences in multiple personas (known as horizontal intertexuality) results from his long career as a film star/comedian. His intertextual meaning combines his stand-up comedy, his film characterizations, his off-screen personality, and his telethon appearances. Jerry Lewis is a "sign" formed by the intersection of these meanings. His horizontal intertexuality is linked by his predominate characterization as a "moronic misfit."

Lewis has maximized his deviance of appearance and voice for the sake of a laugh. When he was doing stand-up comedy in the late 1940s, he was funny

145

looking, had a screeching voice and emaciated body.[22] As his film career took off in the 1950s, he built his comic persona around creating grotesque and imbecilic yet lovable characters. His characters were many times almost hideous in appearance and moronic in intelligence, yet without malice. When the characters destroy through their bumbling and stumbling, they are trying to help, not hurt others. He combines lovability with repulsion, according to comedy film scholar Raymond Durgnat.[23] The characters Lewis creates parallel how society views people with disabilities. They somehow need more love and comfort because of their deviant appearance and behavior. Jerry Lewis exhibits an unpleasant voice, bizarre behavior, and disgusting jokes. The Jerry Lewis persona and people with muscular dystrophy are both what Raymond Durgnat calls the anti-hero. Seen as monstrous, they both attract and repulse.

When accepting a $600,000 check from Harley Davidson during the 1992 telethon, Lewis feigns annoyance at the size of the check. "That's awful," he says turning from the representative from Harley Davidson. "The guy took up my time. We have enough problems here, and the man takes up my time for $600,000. For crying out loud." He then squeals a high-pitched laugh, sticks out his front teeth mimicking the buck-toothed "Nutty Professor," and puts the head of the microphone into his mouth.

This behavior is acceptable as the Jerry Lewis "text." He gets his laugh and he casually introduces Leeza Gibbons for the next segment of the telethon. His telethon persona deviates little from his film star/comedian persona, which critics have characterized as in bad taste, physically disgusting, and insulting to people with mental disabilities. Durgnat argues that the Lewis characters are following a long history of tragi-absurd character in theatrical performances.

Another theme of the Jerry Lewis persona and people with muscular dystrophy on the telethon is a shared need for societal acceptance. Durgnat explains that a theme that pervades Lewis's films and filmmaking is one of searching for acceptance in a charitable world.[24] Unlike people with disabilities who often remain unempowered to change their level of societal acceptance, however, Lewis uses his power as a movie star, filmmaker, and MDA spokesperson to maneuver for more acceptance.

Born Joey Levitch, Lewis came from a poor Jewish entertainment family. He talks often about the odds he had to overcome to become successful. At the closing of the 1992 MDA Telethon, Lewis spoke with teary pride of his ability to make it in show business, although he never graduated from high school.

PITY AS OPPRESSION IN THE JERRY LEWIS TELETHON

He told the audience that education is not really necessary to have a full and prosperous life. "I'm not a dummy, but I didn't finish high school. Big deal. I don't recommend it. I don't recommend it to the young people. Finish it. It's good to have it in your pocket. But it ain't so terrible. You wind up a famous Jewish movie star like me. It couldn't be so terrible," Lewis says, punctuating this thought with exuberant laughter.

In this segment, Lewis realizes his signification as "a dummy" and tries to distance himself from it. It's like the famous TV commercial for aspirin: "I'm not a doctor, but I play one on TV." Lewis says he's not "a dummy," although he plays one on TV. And he acknowledges that he has inferior social status by not graduating from high school, but again tries to distance himself from that status by arguing that education was not necessary in his case. He overcame his "educational disability" to become "a famous Jewish movie star."

In his psychoanalytic analysis of Lewis as a filmmaker, Scott Bukatman theorizes that comedy provided a way to deflect the inadequacies Lewis felt at being different.[25] Comedy allowed a defense against pain for Lewis himself, according to Bukatman, who adds that Lewis's annual work with MDA illustrates his need to confront the pain of human suffering.

The telethon provides a vehicle whereby Lewis can gain acceptance, as well as help people with muscular dystrophy gain acceptance. His method of obtaining their acceptance is to raise money to "cure" them, thus alleviating what he sees as their physical and mental deviations and making them "better people." And in the process of transforming them, Lewis himself is seen as more lovable and acceptable. Lewis responds to a young man during the 1992 telethon saying, "There's nothing I can say or anything I can possibly provide that is more meaningful than when a young man says to me that what I've done is worth something. What he says to me is that I have value." Lewis says the telethon gives his own life meaning and gives him value as a person.

These acts of "helping," however, assign a certain status to people with muscular dystrophy. Beatrice Wright explains that helping leads to status judgments. The one who is always being helped ends up being categorized as inferior.[26] Therefore, the telethon's push to "help" people with muscular dystrophy to "become better people" through a cure actually stigmatizes and oppresses them further.

Sentimentality is another theme within the rhetoric of Jerry Lewis. When Jerry Lewis began directing his own movies, the characters he played were placed in story lines that dripped with sentimentality and contained moral lessons to be learned. Durgnat argues that in films such as "Cinderfella," "The Patsy," and "The Disorderly Orderly," Lewis is trying to mimic Charlie Chaplin and make a less bleak and sad "Limelight." He wants a sentimental result and even includes moralizing sermons, but he lacks the creativity and sincerity to make the films work at that level.[27] Gerald Mast in *The Comic Mind* says Lewis's devotion to sincerity is contradicted in his movies because his moralizing comes off as insincere and calculating.[28]

His desire to combine sincerity and sentimentality imbeds itself in the MDA Telethon text. His eyes well with tears as he introduces his newest poster child and the affliction he or she must endure as a "victim" of muscular dystrophy. A woman with muscular dystrophy tells of her sentimental attachment to Jerry Lewis:

> Dignity and pride are the epitome of what I feel when I'm next to you. And strong and determined are the epitome of who I am when I'm beside you, and when I'm not with you, I carry you in my heart because you're my miracle . . . Jerry, something that I want desperately to do one day is to put my arms around you and hug you. For now what I want you to do is to look deeply in my eyes because in my eyes is the biggest hug you've ever felt. I love you.

As Lewis caresses her face and lightly hugs her head, his face shifts from grimace to teary-eyed emotion, so he quickly cuts to the next segment on the show.

Jerry Lewis is constituted as not just a savior to people with muscular dystrophy but a "miracle." The woman's sentiment flows through her desire to "hug" Lewis and her "love" of Lewis. Yet his sincerity as a "miracle" slips because of his grimace and his light touch when hugging her. He had indicated that they have been friends for 10 years, but his show of affection is forced, rather than loving.

Disability activism and the Jerry Lewis Telethon text

The most important narrative about Jerry Lewis and his telethon comes from outside – the criticism he receives from disability rights groups. TV scholar John Fiske explains that when dealing with a television text, these secondary critical texts can activate the primary text in a distinct way.[29] Disability rights activists undertake an oppositional reading of the Jerry Lewis Telethon. But still Jerry Lewis and his rhetoric and behavior, more than the telethon itself, are constituted as the text for criticism.

The Jerry Lewis Telethon, even more than the Muscular Dystrophy Association, is the target of the activists' ire. The anti-telethon activist group Jerry's Orphans instituted a divestment plan, asking corporate sponsors to continue their donations to MDA but not to give their money on the telethon. Their goal was to neutralize the telethon, while allowing MDA fundraising to continue for research and equipment, according to a 1992 article in *The Disability Rag*.[30]

Jerry's Orphans consists of some former MDA poster children who are now disability rights activists. If Jerry Lewis is characterized as parent to his "kids," these activists chose to be orphans, or figuratively have Jerry Lewis dead and therefore not involved in the telethon. They reject the paternalism of Jerry Lewis's parent role in relation to people with muscular dystrophy. One former poster child, Laura Hershey, launched an anti-telethon campaign that also signified Jerry Lewis as locus of her anger. She advocated that people "Tune Jerry Out." People should literally turn off their television instead of watching the telethon, and not listen to the rhetoric of Jerry Lewis.

The Jerry Lewis telethon represents a modern day "collision of images," according to the disability activist group ADAPT. Throughout much of history, people with disabilities have been characterized as childlike, dependent, and helpless.[31] Since the 1970s, however, people with disabilities have been gaining more independence and civil rights through federal legislation and technological advancements. "These newer, adult roles challenge the older roles of childlike dependency," writer Douglas Lathrop said in the disability magazine *Mainstream*. Therefore, many people with disabilities no longer want to be Jerry's "kids."[32]

Outsiders to the disability perspective have difficulty understanding that many people with disabilities want the emphasis to be on independence for today rather than a cure for the future. "We are not all into being cured," said Ed Roberts, a disabled man who founded the independent living movement in the U.S.. "We are people who need to go on with our lives."[33]

The lingering death of the Jerry Lewis telethon?

Disability activists have long been advocating for a new meaning to the telethon text, one that does not involve Jerry Lewis. As people with disabilities, they see the power he has as a text – moronic misfit in society, lovable/repulsive, and dripping sentimentality – and the power of his rhetoric and behavior on the telethon. Many people with disabilities do not want to be associated with him. The activists see the rhetoric of Jerry Lewis and his telethon as a roadblock to the attitude changes toward people with disabilities that they want to see take place in U.S. society.

Many disability activists annually hosted protests against the telethon. Harriet McBryde Johnson, an activist and lawyer in South Carolina, led protests beginning in 1990 and kept them going for 17 years. When Johnson unexpectedly died in 2008, her fellow activists held the 18th protest in her honor. Here's how Johnson explained the oppression she saw in the narrative of the telethon:

> Our message is that people with disabilities want rights and respect, not pity. Over the years, Jerry Lewis has called us "half persons" and our beloved wheelchairs "steel imprisonments." He told a TV reporter (on camera): 'You're a cripple in a wheelchair and you don't want pity? STAY IN YOUR HOUSE!' It goes on and on . . . A real charity doesn't insult the people it is supposed to serve. A real charity wouldn't employ a notorious bigot as its spokesman. But disability prejudice is still considered OK. Need some proof? This year, Lewis is getting an Emmy (the "prestigious governor's award") for the Telethon. To add insult to insult, the TV Academy announced it on July 26 (1995), the 15th anniversary of the signing of the ADA. The ADA's philosophy couldn't be more opposite to what the Telethon represents.[34]

The protests galvanized nationwide in 1991 after Jerry Lewis in a 1990 *Parade* magazine article, called people with disabilities "half persons." Major protests sprang up in Las Vegas, Chicago, Colorado, and South Carolina. Lewis and the protestors began to clash and Lewis compared them to Nazi storm troopers. In 2001, Lewis famously said on "CBS Sunday Morning": "Pity? You don't want to be pitied for being a cripple in a wheelchair? Stay in your house."[35] His insulting attitude helped the disability activists' cause because in national media venues the general public could see his nastiness.

As the protests progressed over the years, some of the anti-telethon rhetoric did begin to take hold, as evidenced by Lewis being asked about it in the "CBS Sunday Morning" program. It appeared that fewer and fewer TV stations were showing the telethon (or if they did, the broadcast began late at night and showed overnight). MDA's 2009 data lists about 160 stations still running the telethon,[36] with many broadcasts beginning 9 or 10 p.m. Considering there are about 1,100 U.S. broadcast TV stations[37] affiliated with the major networks – ABC, NBC, CBS, FOX, and CW – this means only about 15 percent carried the telethon in 2009.

The more disability activists pushed against Jerry Lewis, the more he said outrageous things, which were covered by the news media. In 2000, Jerry's Orphans activists infiltrated a telethon broadcast and made a documentary about their anti-telethon protests called "The Kids are All Right."[38] The documentary is available online and is a powerful ongoing record of all the outrageous things Lewis has said over the years.

It should be noted that Lewis has gotten into trouble with other groups as well – in several instances, once on the telethon and once in Australia, he has made anti-gay slurs. In 2007 he used an anti-gay slur during the telecast of MDA Labor Day Telethon but finally apologized after pressure from the Gay & Lesbian Alliance Against Defamation (GLAAD),[39] and in 2008, he called cricket a "fag game" during a trip to Australia, but refused to comment about it.[40]

The protests seemed to be having an effect – more media coverage of the activists' actions and a few more nondisabled people understanding the harmfulness of pity each year. But then in 2009 the Academy Awards decided Jerry Lewis would receive the Humanitarian Award for his work with MDA. The Academy of the Motion Picture Arts and Sciences seemed to be oblivious to 20 years of telethon protests by people with disabilities.

The anti-telethon activists galvanized around the cause, creating a Web site, thetroublewithJerry.net, and planning protests at the Academy Awards headquarters. Even nondisabled writers questioned the award to Jerry Lewis; a *Los Angeles Times* columnist called the telethon "torture" to watch and reminded readers of the comedian's anti-gay and anti-women slurs over the years. "Lewis has been a self-aggrandizing embarrassment for years," he wrote.[41]

Another nondisabled writer at the *Chicago Tribune* said if Lewis deserved an Oscar, then it should been for his masterful comedy work in "The Nutty Professor" in 1963. Another argument can be made for an Oscar for Jerry Lewis for his technical developments as a director: "Lewis patented the video-assist playback system, which he first used on 'The Bellboy' in 1960."[42] He also wrote a highly regarded book on filmmaking in 1971 called *The Total Film-Maker,* which was used in many college film programs for years. Those were legitimate contributions to motion picture arts and sciences for which he could have been honored. He should not have been honored for years of heaping stigmatizing pity on people with disabilities via the MDA telethon.

But even with a Humanitarian Oscar for Jerry Lewis, the telethon appears to be on its last legs. With inclusive education and better accessibility in American society, many more nondisabled people can count people with disabilities among their friends. With those relationships comes understanding of the oppressive ramifications of pity. And parents of children with disabilities feel more empowered these days to fight for the rights of their kids and to complain about negative media images of disability, as evidenced by the anti-R-word campaign[43] (see Chapter 9).

Finally, the death of the telethon may result from changes in television itself. By 2009, millions of Americans watched shows online, rather than on a TV, through TV networks' Web sites, hulu.com, or with on-demand webcasting.[44] So it's likely a live broadcast like the telethon, which is also reviled by a growing segment of Americans, will not draw much of an audience anymore.

Notes

This chapter is based on Beth Haller, "The misfit and muscular dystrophy," *Journal of Popular Film and Television*, 1994, 21:4, pp. 142-149.

1. Tom Angleberger, "Vinton 'posts' are tubes to protect young trees," *The Roanoke Times*, Sept. 14, 2009, roanoke.com/columnists/angleberger/wb/218876.

2. Marilynn J. Phillips, "Damaged Goods: The Oral Narratives of the Experience of Disability in American Culture," *Social Science & Medicine*, 1990, 30:8, pp. 849-57.

3. Phillips, op. cit., 849.

4. Claire H. Liachowitz, *Disability as Social Construct*. Philadelphia: University of Pennsylvania Press, 1988.

5. David Hevey, *The Creatures Time Forgot: Photography and Disability Imagery*. London: Routledge, 1992, p. 34.

6. Harlan Hahn, "Can Disability Be Beautiful?" *Social Policy*, 1988, 18:3, p. 29.

7. Harlan Hahn. "Advertising the Acceptable Employable Image: Disability and Capitalism," *Policy Studies Journal*, March 1987, pp. 551-70.

8. See William Gellman, "Roots of Prejudice Against the Handicapped," *Journal of Rehabilitation, 1959*, 40:1, p. 4+, and Beatrice A. Wright, *Physical Disability – A Psychological Approach*. N.Y.: Harper and Brothers, 1960.

9. Hanoch Linveh, "On the Origins of Negative Attitudes Toward People With Disabilities," *Rehabilitation Literature*, 1982, 43.11-12, pp. 338-47.

10. Hahn, 1988, op. cit.

11. Leonard Saxe, "The Ubiquity of Physical Appearance as a Determinant of Social Relationships," in *Love and Attractiveness: An International Conference*, M. Cook and G. Wilson, eds, Oxford: Pergamon, 1979, pp. 33-36.

12. William G. Stothers, "Put Poster Children to Rest." *Mainstream*, Aug. 1992, p. 50.

13. Stothers, op. cit.,p. 50.

14. Unless otherwise indicated, direct quotes from Jerry Lewis on the telethon broadcast come from a transcript of Hour 18 of the 1992 MDA telethon.

15, Mike Angeli. "God's Biggest Goof," *Esquire*, Feb. 1991, pp. 99-107.

16. Wright, op. cit.

17. Erving Goffman, *Stigma*. N.Y.: Simon and Schuster, 1963.

18. Phillips, op. cit.

19. Harlan Hahn, "The Politics of Physical Differentness: Disability and Discrimination," *Journal of Social Issues, 1988*, 44:1, pp. 39-47.

20. Hevey, op. cit., p. 35.

21. Angeli, op. cit., p. 98.

22. Angeli, op. cit.

23. Raymond Durgnat, *The Crazy Mirror, Hollywood Comedy and the American Image*. N.Y.: Horizon Press, 1969.

24. Durgnat, op. cit.

25. Scott Bukatman, "Paralysis in Motion," in *Comedy/Cinema/Theory*, A. S. Horton, ed., Berkeley: University of California Press, 1991.

26. Wright, op. cit.

27. Durgnat, op. cit.

28. Gerald Mast, *The Comic Mind*. Chicago: University of Chicago Press, 1979.

29. John Fiske, *Television Culture*. London: Routledge, 1987.

30. "A Test of Wills. Jerry Lewis, Jerry's Orphans and the Telethon," *The Disability, Rag*, Sept./Oct. 1992, pp. 4-9.

31. Douglas Lathrop, "Telethons Caught in 'Collision of Images,'" *Mainstream*, Aug. 1992, pp. 17-21.

32. Lathrop, op. cit., p. 18.

33. Lathrop, op. cit., p. 18.

34. Harriet McBryde Johnson, "Harriet McBryde Johnson's 18th Annual Labor Day Telethon Protest," Media dis&dat blog, Aug. 26, 2008, media-dis-n-dat.blogspot.com/2008/08/harriet-mcbryde-johnsons-18th-annual.html.

35. Harriet McBryde Johnson, "Frequently Asked Questions about the Telethon Protest," Crip Commentary Web site, cripcommentary.com/faq.html.

36. MDA, "2009 Television Stations," mda.org/telethon/FindYourStation.pdf

37. Wikipedia, "List of United States over-the-air television networks," en.wikipedia.org/wiki/List_of_United_States_over-the-air_television_networks.

38. "The Kids are All Right," [Online video] thekidsareallright.org.

39. Beth A. Haller, "Jerry Lewis makes offensive comments again," Media dis&dat blog, Oct. 28, 2008, media-dis-n-dat.blogspot.com/2008/10/jerry-lewis-makes-offensive.html.

40. Alex Starritt, "Comedian Jerry Lewis says cricket is a fag game," *The Telegraph*, Oct. 27, 2008, telegraph.co.uk/sport/cricket/3267756/Comedian-Jerry-Lewis-says-cricket-is-a-fag-game.html.

41. Patrick Goldstein, "Jerry Lewis on live TV: Julius Kelp or Buddy Love?" *The Los Angeles Times*, Feb, 17, 2009, latimesblogs.latimes.com/the_big_picture/2009/02/oscars-scariest.html.

42. Michael Phillips, "Which Jerry Lewis will visit the Oscars?" *Chicago Tribune*, Feb. 15, 2009, archives.chicagotribune.com/2009/feb/15/entertainment/chi-0215-jerrylewis-phillipsfeb15.

43. Neda Ulaby, "Rethinking 'Retarded': Should It Leave The Lexicon?" NPR, Sept. 8, 2009, npr.org/templates/story/story.php?storyId=112479383.

44. Brian Stelter, "Web-TV divide is back in focus with NBC sale," *The New York Times*, Dec. 3, 2009 nytimes.com/2009/12/04/business/media/04hulu.html.

8.

The new phase of disability humor on TV

Disability and humor have an uneasy relationship. Cultural codes of conduct tell members of many societies not to laugh at people who are physically different. Also, many non-disabled people who fear disability perceive having a disability as tragic, pitiable, or just plain sad. A U.K. disability organization's publication explains, "There is little that is intrinsically humorous about having a disability. Concomitantly, there is little that is inherently morose, sorrowful or tragic about having a disability. Many people in the community at large perceive disability with sympathetic and lamentable attitudes. Because of that, they resist or oppose attempts to juxtapose humor and disability."[1]

This chapter looks at the transition of disability and humor from destructive humor – jokes that laugh at people with disabilities – to current disability humor on television in which disabled people are more in control of the humor – empowering humor.

Disability studies scholar Gary Albrecht says disability humor "raises a hidden paradox that makes people feel uncomfortable. What is so funny about having a disability when others think it is a tragedy?[2] Yet, historically, disabled people have been a source of amusement for non-disabled people. Individuals with disabilities were used as court jesters, exhibits of curiosity in "freak shows," or as cartoon characters with comical speech and sight problems. "Most of us have experienced negative forms of humor where we have been laughed at rather than laughed with," explains a writer for a U.K. disability organization. Con-

155

structive (positive) humor "creates positive environments where people support each other, promote self esteem and create mutually beneficial connections. Destructive humor does the opposite."[3] Destructive humor sets disabled people apart by poking fun at what are seen as their inadequacies.

There are genres of disability jokes and humor, just as there are ethnic jokes. One renowned disability humor genre is the Helen Keller joke. On the surface the jokes may seem mean-spirited by making fun of the famous deaf-blind woman (example: How did Helen Keller burn her face? Answering the iron). Joke scholar Mac E. Barrick argues that the jokes grew from media attention given to Keller's life through the movie, "The Miracle Worker," and its subsequent rebroadcast on television, as well as new federal legislation in the 1960s that began to mainstream disabled children in public education. Barrick reports that Helen Keller jokes grew from the "sick joke" genre, which often targets disabled people (example: What has 500 legs and can't walk? 250 polio victims).[4]

Humor scholar Alan Dundes argues that the growing visibility of disabled people in society spawned joke categories that focused upon them. He explains that sick jokes about quadriplegics "attempt to recognize and articulate the public's discomfiture in the presence of armless, legless, or otherwise disabled individuals."[5] Barrick agrees, saying Helen Keller jokes and those about disability in general assist society in dealing with more visibly disabled people mainstreamed into society and the accompanying civil rights that people with disabilities rightfully demand. He says ethnic jokes have cropped up in the same way; for example, a rash of Jewish jokes cropped up after the "Holocaust" was broadcast on TV in the late 1970s.[6] Other research has shown that the changing role of women in 19th-century U.S. society was reflected in magazine cartoons; Johnson suggests in that research that "the social humor represented in these cartoons helps society process the changes that are occurring within it. . . . The irony depicted in humor may reflect society's early awareness of the tension between the status quo and the new."[7] For instance, in a cartoon from 1887, a woman president is surrounded by female judges, politicians and generals. From below the podium observing the inaugural are female soldiers, sailors and businesswomen. A lone man in the corner cares for a child.[8] Such cartoons reflected male concern about the growing independence and power of American women.

Barrick believes the Helen Keller joke provides a similar purpose in society. "Like a classical drama, it has had the cathartic effect of erasing the pity normally felt toward the disabled, so that the joke teller and his listener now accept these people on equal terms. . . . How can you hate someone who makes you laugh?"[9] However, Barrick's thesis does not account for those missing in the construction of the jokes or humor: people with disabilities. Helen Keller jokes and sick jokes about quadriplegics were created by non-disabled people for other non-disabled people. Given that disabled people were not involved in the creation of humor, these jokes can be read as insulting and patronizing.

When people with disabilities create the humor it truly revolutionizes the disability humor genre. Quadriplegic cartoonist John Callahan's humor merges sick jokes and disability themes, coupling them with the powerful message of being drawn by an artist with a disability. "This exploration of bad taste in disability imagery could be seen as the antidote to tragic imagery, mocking and teasing, instead of displaying misery," according to disability language scholar Jenny Corbett.[10] Callahan "confronts disability with a raw humor in newspaper and magazine [cartoons] that have drawn praise and condemnation, with people who have disabilities taking both sides."[11] Other disabled humorists also have taken control of "sick humor." Sharon Wachsler, a cartoonist with chronic fatigue syndrome and multiple chemical sensitivity, on her Sick Humor Web site, wrote, "As I was confronted with the daily frustrations, indignities, and peculiarities of life with chronic illness, I started drawing cartoons that depicted my experiences – transforming my anger into comedy."[12] Most disabled humorists believe they get their messages across when their work is both hated and loved.

However, disabled humorists must contend with the legacy left by Helen Keller jokes and sick humor – that these jokes and humor are for children or insensitive adults. Most adults "know better" than to laugh at such things. Fred Burns, a disabled comic, noted, "The thing I found from the beginning is that when you're disabled, unlike other comics, audiences don't want to laugh at you. They're taught all their lives not to make fun of handicapped people. That was the challenge – to get them to laugh at their concepts of people who are disabled."[13] Rick Boggs, a blind actor and performer, says a focus on disabled people as inspirational, or only in the context of a serious subject, means society does not get to see the diverse qualities of people with disabilities – especially that they like to laugh and have fun just like anyone else. Boggs tried to counteract this in a series of cell phone commercials for AirTouch Cellular (now Verizon Wireless) in which he told the audience of the virtues of cell phone service from a chili dog stand, a museum, a Las Vegas wedding chapel, and behind the wheel of a convertible, which was hooked up to his friend's tow truck. Boggs says, "There are a lot of roles out there that portray how admirable people with disabilities are, but we need more like my character, someone who's not only capable, but fun. Someone you'd really want to know."[14]

An international disability organization, Rehabilitation International, reports that when done correctly humor can build bridges between disabled and non-disabled people. Barbara Kolucki in an article for Rehab International says humor is a good way to convey "messages concerning the assumptions that non-disabled people make about life with a disability or people with disabilities. Humor is a bridge over the awkwardness many people feel when approaching a new or unfamiliar situation."[15] She also suggests that messages received through humor are remembered longer than those presented without.

Humor has long been a way for many groups to confront oppression. A number of ethnic and social groups have used humor as a way to protest against those who would put them down. Simmons identifies seven forms of protest humor among oppressed groups:

> First and most basic is the belief that personal salvation is to be found strictly within the group and that acceptance of the customs of the majority group will lead to heavy personal loss. The second utilizes a favorite form of retaliation, the trickster motif, whereby a minority member scores by countering a specific insult delivered by a member of the majority. Third, a parody is devised against an alleged somatic or cultural image. The fourth logically follows the majority group's thinking but twists the conclusion to allow for the minority group to escape. The fifth derides the majority group by either depreciating its high status, demonstrating the inferiority of a majority group member, or disclosing how the majority member actually feels toward the minority. Sixth, the close relationship between the minority group and a prized majority personality is emulated but mimed. Last, the entire scene is reversed so that the images appear topsy turvy and the minority group emerges triumphant.[16]

Cartoons in disability publications attacking the helping and health professions by illustrating how little they understand about the disability experience fall into Simmins's fifth category. For example, the disability rights publication *Mouth* regularly runs cartoons by Scott Chambers, who often confronts the medical profession. One of his cartoons shows a doctor at a psychiatric hospital extracting a patient's brain, saying, "You won't need this any more!" Chambers mocks the views of mental health professionals who believe they always know best, even when it hurts the patient.[17]

Others have established the healthful benefits of humor. Many people with disabilities have incorporated humor into their worldview to cope with the barriers they encounter in society. Many newly disabled wheelchair users "incorporate humor to aid in the healing process and many are able to laugh at themselves and their situation," according to Chris Sheridan's analysis of disability in the media.[18] Humor among people facing problems indicates high self-esteem, according to a laughter expert.[19] "When the person with a sense of humor laughs in the face of his own failure, he is showing that his perspective transcends the particular situation he's in, and that he does not have an egocentric, overly precious view of his own endeavors. . . . It is because he feels good about himself at a fundamental level that this or that setback is not threatening to him."[20] Humor is a good method to cope with even horrific situations, from concentration camps to the September 11 attacks. "Humor was another of the soul's weapons in the fight for self-preservation," according to Auschwitz survivor and psychotherapist Viktor Frankl.[21] When confronting an event like Sept. 11, 2001, "humor is a release from the restraints of our personal powerlessness in confronting that evil."[22]

John Mythen, who created Claude, a cartoon character who is a wheelchair-using dog with multiple sclerosis, says, "Humor is good for the body and soul."[23] Sally Greenwood, director of the MS Society of Canada, says, "Through his book *MSing around*, John touches on many delicate issues surrounding MS and opens doors to further communication."[24] Carol Sowell says in a muscular dystrophy publication, "Laughter makes you stronger. No, it won't cure your neuromuscular disease, but it helps you master the things you can control – your own attitude and, sometimes, other people's reactions."[25] For John Callahan, too, cartooning became a way for him to vent his frustrations, as well as laugh at a world that does not easily accommodate a person with quadriplegia.

John Callahan as modern spokesman for disability humor

A car crash paralyzed John Callahan from the chest down at the age of 21. He retained limited use of his arms and learned to draw using his left hand to apply pressure and the right hand to guide the pen. For more than 20 years, Callahan has been known for his biting and controversial gag cartoons. He produced a number of cartoon books, numerous magazine cartoons, and a well-received autobiography, *Don't Worry, He Won't Get Far on Foot* (1990).[26] He has managed to anger many groups with his work, from feminists to disabled people. However, he remained steadfast in his cartoons' assault on political correctness. Callahan says, "America's got this horrible political correctness thing. I'm like a vulture feeding off political correctness."[27] Callahan says of his topics:

> I've never been the kind of cartoonist who is interested in cartoon themes like pets, dieting, the boss at work, etc. Life to me is major league, and I'm drawn to the aspects of it that typify the struggle: death, disease, insanity, feminism, tragedy, disability, etc. Though my work also includes themes of sweetness and frivolity, I'm afraid I've been cruelly and unjustly typecast as sick and twisted. Let it be known that I have never once answered any of the 'lively' letters aimed at me. Except once, when I could no longer abide the criticism that 'Mr. Callahan could not possibly understand the struggle of someone with a spinal injury.'[28]

His insightful work fits with a 1918 statement about the mission of someone who draws cartoons: "The cartoonist makes people see things."[29] Despite the controversial nature of his work, or perhaps because of it, Callahan's following grew. His cartoons and his notoriety as a quadriplegic cartoonist are now seen as moving disability humor forward.

The Miami Herald, which carried Callahan's work in its Sunday magazine in the 1990s, reported: "When we get complaints about his handling of the subject of disability, they are almost always from people without disabilities themselves. And whenever we hear from the physically disabled, individually and through organizations promoting their interests, what we hear is loud and enthusiastic applause."[30] Commenting on a cartoon showing a spinal cord injury center with a notice on the door saying "standing room only," the *Miami Herald* editor said, "The truth is you shouldn't have to know that Callahan himself is disabled to realize that his cartoons are not 'poking fun at the handicapped.' The reason why our disabled readers love Callahan is that they don't misread him." The cartoon doesn't make fun of wheelchair users. "Here's a clinic specifically designed for the disabled – presumably run by able-bodied doctors who don't understand the needs of the people they serve. Standing room only. The joke's on those of us who can stand."[31]

Callahan's work has helped change some of the disability stereotypes that the disability rights movement has long tried to challenge. Callahan's cartoons, while controversial, are evidence of the "slashingly dark humor"[32] used by disability activists attempting to challenge and transform "ablest" conceptions of disability. In his own unusual and bizarre way, Callahan is confronting attitudes about people with disabilities. "Whereas ableists have used quadriplegic jokes to exert social control over persons with disabilities, Callahan's gag humor serves as a cultural release of anxiety by engaging in a dialogue about disability and actively aggressing against an ableist perspective."[33] No subject is taboo in his cartoons for adults, including people with significant disabilities. Callahan successfully makes biting statements about ableism in society because he is quadriplegic. Kara Shultz and Darla Germeroth analyzed Callahan's gag cartoons and described how they "provide a force of resistance by taking the stereotypes against persons with disabilities to a ridiculous extreme and poking fun at the attitudes of those who cling to their status of able-bodiedness."[34]

Case study: Callahan creates a children's cartoon for TV

Having reached primarily adults with his humor, Callahan began to turn his attention to kids with the development of the "Pelswick" cartoon for the Nickelodeon TV network in 2000. "I've spent my whole career trying to do a style of cartooning that is really honest. And I think that is what kids are about," Callahan says.[35] He says Pelswick Eggert is different from all the other cartoon characters not only because he uses a wheelchair but "because of his spirit, his worldview. He sees things the way they are. He's fearless, extremely funny and doesn't define himself with this disability."[36] "Pelswick isn't anywhere near as rough as Callahan's print cartoons, but the show bears a healthy helping of its creator's irreverent edge," according to *USA Today*.[37] The series is "infused with the same wry sense of humor about living with paralysis as fills the artist's collection of cartoon and kids' books, including his autobiography," the *New York Daily News*[38] reported.

Pelswick Eggert, (voiced by Robert Tinkler) is a 13-year-old boy who is a power wheelchair user. Like his creator he is quadriplegic and paralyzed below the armpits due to a car injury. Both Pelswick and John Callahan have some limitations in the use of their hands. This leads to Callahan's unique drawing style of shaky lines and somewhat out-of-proportion character features. Pelswick always has one eye drawn about twice the size of the other. "'Pelswick' inhabitants have that mutant-bordering-on–grotesque look. In chinless Pelswick – who has golf ball eyes, a cucumber mouth halfway down his neck – Callahan is transferring to TV a kid who surfaced from time to time in his syndicated cartoons, but was not in a wheelchair."[39]

Callahan came up with the name Pelswick after seeing it in an old movie; Eggert comes from Callahan's love of Humpty Dumpty.[40] He says, "I've always had an obsession with Humpty Dumpty. I relate to his cockiness and of course his ignominious demise."[41] Pelswick likes music, enjoys his friends, gets into trouble, get bullied, likes adventure, plays jokes on his friends, has a healthy suspicion of authority, draws cartoons, has irreverence for school, is bright, and has a sharp tongue. In keeping with cartoon tradition that characters usually have only one outfit,[42] Pelswick wears red and white sneakers, a red baseball cap worn backwards, a purple/blue T-shirt with a red chest stripe worn over a long sleeved white shirt with baggy blue pants. He has red hair and freckles and a long nose.

Although named after Pelswick, the show features about 10 other characters prominently. Interestingly, another member of Pelswick's family also has a disability. His grandmother, Gram Gram, Priscilla Eggert (voiced by Ellen-Ray Hennessy) uses a walker. She has been described as "a tough-love Gram Gram – a crazy old lady who rides a skateboard with her walker in tow."[43] Because Pelswick has no mother, she functions as the mother figure in the Eggert household. Nickelodeon's "Pelswick" Web site says: "She can't hear or chew very well, but she'll introduce you to the pavement if you mess with Pelswick. This is a lady who played fullback for her high school football team. Who enjoyed a successful career as a professional wrestler. Who digs hang gliding, skateboarding and scuba diving in the lobster tank at the super market. And who has been known to fully immerse herself in mud, Green Beret-style, in order to spy on and ambush bullies who mess with Pelswick. Pelswick's grandmom is one tough old bird."

Pelswick's father Quentin Eggert (voiced by Tony Rosato) is an "oh-so sensitive"[44] politically-correct college professor, who allows Callahan to continue his humorous attacks on political correctness. Quentin always tries to see both sides of an argument, to never offend anyone, to respect everybody involved, and to never say anything mean or opinionated.[45] A typical comment from Quentin: "This is my chance to be creatively proactive, while respecting the unique personhood of my enemies and remembering that nobody's wrong, they're just differently right."

Pelswick has two siblings. Little sister Katie (voiced by Tracey Moore) is the typical pesky sister who always gets in his way. She is a pest who has a great sense of humor and likes to play practical jokes. Bobby Eggert is Pelswick's two-year-old brother. He doesn't talk much and speaks in one-word sentences. He spends most of his time in a baby carrier hanging from his dad's chest. He wants to be just like Pelswick.

Pelswick also has two best friends, Ace Nakamura and Goon Gunderson. These friends are both supportive of Pelswick and dependent upon him because he is the brightest one in the group. Ace Nakamura (voiced by Phil Guerrero) is intelligent and full of obscure facts and references. He likes to ride on the back of Pelswick's wheelchair as they speed down the hills in their San Francisco neighborhood. Ace appears to be Japanese American. Goon Gunderson (voiced by Peter Oldring) is not the brains of the group but despite his "hulking size and dim-bulb status, Goon is actually a sweet, gentle and sensitive giant."[46] Goon is a loyal friend to Pelswick but his first love is professional wrestling. In the episode "David and Goonliath," he achieves his life's dream and faces a real pro wrestler, despite Goon's noticeable lack of talent.

Other friends include Julie Smockford (the voice of Julie Lemieux), who is the object of Pelswick's affection. Although she remains just out of reach, Pelswick is always trying to get her attention. Julie's best friend is Sandra Scoddle (voiced by Kim Kuhteubl). Like Julie, she is bright, funny, strong willed, and independent. She is very similar to Julie, and they have many fights. They can be enemies one minute and great friends the next. Sandra differs from Julie only in that she's usually annoyed by Pelswick's antics. Sandra is African American.

Pelswick also has a type of guardian angel whom no one else can see. His name is Mr. Jimmy, described as a "white haired bearded magical mentor."[47] Mr. Jimmy is meant to remind one of ZZ Top guitarist Billy Gibbons and is voiced by actor David Arquette. Mr. Jimmy serves as a moral compass for Pelswick and through a series of bizarre stories helps Pelswick work out the answers to the many problems he faces.[48] Arquette says he likes the types of issues the show tackles. "Taking on the role of Mr. Jimmy allows me to have fun working with the creative wit of John Callahan, while raising kids' and parents' social consciousness of important issues," he said.[49]

One of Pelswick's biggest problems is the school bully who seeks him out for daily harassment. Boyd Scullarzo (voiced by Chuck Campbell) bullies Pelswick in a variety of ways, from competing in wheelchair races, even though he doesn't use a wheelchair, to teasing Pelswick when he listens to a "boy band" to get closer to Julie. However, even as school bully, Boyd won't hit Pelswick because "you can't punch a kid in a wheelchair," he says in one episode. So Boyd resorts to verbal abuse. Pelswick counters Boyd and his gang's abuse by "turning their mean spirited high jinx against them."[50] Pelswick and his friends attend Alcatraz Junior High in San Francisco. The school's Principal Zeigler (voiced by David Huband) also plays a role in the show. He is a kindly but nervous and absent-minded. Generally, he could be described as "clueless."

The "Pelswick" cartoon embodies some of Simmins's type-seven protest humor[51] because Pelswick usually triumphs over his nemesis Boyd, the bully. But Callahan's "Pelswick" also has moved past overt protest humor toward a humor of equality – the disabled character is equal in status and humor to all the other characters. "Pelswick" both normalizes and demystifies the disability experience for its youthful audience.

"Through Pelswick, Callahan can share with viewers his thoughts on kids and disabilities," according to *The Washington Post*. Callahan says, "I have a philosophy that all kids are created equal and they all have their challenges."[52] The focus of the show is on Pelswick's world as a kid in middle school, not his disability. Pelswick "is a typical 13-year-old navigating the treacherous teen years – only he does it from a wheelchair."[53] He refers to his wheelchair as an SUV, Spinal Utility Vehicle. The series focuses not on the fact that he is permanently seated (uses a wheelchair) but on the daily life and difficult issues of growing up, his very funny and fearless personality, his amusing friends and family. Issues tackled by the show include: censorship, the rights of disabled people, boy bands, the Pokemon trading card craze, pro wrestling, and reality TV. "These are probably the 'issues' that take up more cafeteria conversation than any others these days. And they all get skewered on 'Pelswick.'"[54]

As a character, Pelswick "refuses to let his disability cripple his life,"[55] and this is an innovative new direction in the presentation of a disabled kid on TV. Pelswick is the first physically disabled cartoon character with his own TV series.[56] Nicklodeon TV, which aired "Pelswick," reports that the network's goal was to show more diversity in children's programming. "'Pelswick' is part of Nickelodeon's goal of reaching out to all young people," according to a Nickelodeon vice president.[57] Those who report on the cable industry say Nickelodeon has led the way on inclusion, "producing scripted and non-fiction programs with diverse casts," and inclusion has quietly and successfully been embraced by a different group of networks: cable's family programmers."[58] Diversity matters to viewers, according to these cable networks. With "Pelswick's" premiere on October 24, 2000, cable gained the first disabled cartoon character written by a disabled cartoonist. The show also was carried on Canadian TV, UK's Channel 4, and in fall 2002, the show moved to American TV's CBS Saturday morning line-up.

While Callahan downplays the "gag" style humor in this Nickelodeon cartoon, he continues to focus on society's ableism, rather than making fun of people with disabilities. For example, when a bully calls Pelswick a "cripple," Pelswick retorts that he prefers the term "permanently seated." True to Callahan's controversial style, the show confronts patronizing attitudes and political correctness. Callahan says he wants the cartoon to be entertaining: "Kids need a certain amount of rudeness and grossness." But he also wants to "show kids that people in wheelchairs are just like everybody else and want to be treated like everyone else."[59] "Pelswick takes a no-nonsense, see-things-for-what-they-are attitude and he demands to be treated normally. He doesn't look for sympathy, and he doesn't get any."[60]

Most TV critics and children received the show well. "'I think (Callahan's experience) gives it authenticity and integrity that allows him to go boldly where he wants to go,' says Cyma Zarghami, Nickelodeon's executive vice president. She does say she would feel uncomfortable with 'Pelswick's' humor if the creator weren't in a wheelchair."[61] However, Callahan does not want special treatment from critics because he is quadriplegic, "although he says his experience gives him insight about disability." Arts critic and disabled actor Neil Marcus says Pelswick has "major disability cool. He's a regular kid, with what I thought were very well placed or balanced character traits. For example, disability seems to be the least of his problems or concerns. Should it be his main concern? No! After all, this is the new millennium and Pelswick is interested in . . . living."[62] As the disability rights publication *Ragged Edge* said, "Pelswick" "totally gets it right about cripdom. Who says you can't laugh at quads? Callahan shows how to do it the right way."[63] One media critic says, "Nickelodeon is changing the face of TV. And the skin color tones. And the physical capabilities. . . . Nick has made a commitment with its recent schedule by putting ethnic minorities and people with disabilities in leading roles."[64]

The show's humor represents a new phase of disability humor because it includes all the characters. Most of the characters have no disability and much of the laughter is directed at them. When Pelswick becomes the focus of the humor, it, therefore, is normalizing because he is represented like all the characters. When the humor focuses upon his disability, it is Pelswick poking fun at himself. For example, Pelswick quips in an early episode about the dangers of a school-sponsored camping trip: "I'm the only one in the class who can't get accidentally paralyzed."[65] *Business Week* disability issues writer John Williams says Pelswick, as "the likeable rascal who easily finds himself in trouble, is far more believable than most past TV portrayals of wheelchair-using youths – helpless, docile, angelic wallflowers."[66] As one media critic put it, Callahan "breathes bold honesty into Pelswick."[67]

Disability humor on TV in the current era

The Pelswick character illustrates how some TV images of people with disabilities are shifting to more equal and mainstream representations, as well as how disability humor is evolving. Callahan's more subtle approach to disability issues in the cartoon series has persuasive power with its young audience because Pelswick comes across as a smart, cool 8th-grader who gets into the usual scrapes with his friends. "Pelswick" both normalizes and demystifies the disability experience for its audience. The show focuses on Pelswick's interactions with others and the world around him, not his disability.

Other TV shows since "Pelswick" have added to these more empowering representations. The return of comic actor Daryl "Chill" Mitchell to the TV dramedy "Ed" was one such representation. Mitchell joined the quirky show about a lawyer who returns to his small hometown in Ohio and sets up practice in the local bowling alley he buys. Mitchell, who had been a regular cast member in "The John Larroquette Show" from 1993 to 1996, became a wheelchair user in 2001 after a motorcycle accident and returned to TV in "Ed's" third season.[68] Mitchell's character, Eli, came on board to manage the bowling alley. It was a wonderful portrayal in which a wheelchair-using actor led the show to include some subtle information about accessibility and the disability experience in America. In one particular scene in Season Three, an Eli-focused episode showed the character waking up in the morning and getting ready for the day. It was a powerful window into regular life of someone with paraplegia. Eli wooed women, worked his job, and pursued the comic antics of the supporting characters in the show. Chill Mitchell returned to TV in 2009 as the co-star of a short-lived sitcom called "Brothers," in which he played a sports bar owner in conflict with his NFL hero brother who returns home. Mitchell was a producer on the show and helped fashion its scripts and comic sensibility.[69]

A number of animated shows have regular disabled characters and, even though people with disabilities do not appear to be involved in the creation of the shows, the storylines illustrate that these shows "get" disability issues. "South Park" on Comedy Central, "Family Guy" on Fox, and "Rick and Steve Happiest Gay Couple" on Logo all have main or recurring characters with disabilities. In "Rick and Steve," Steve's best friend is Chuck, an HIV-positive wheelchair user, whose partner is Evan, a 19-year-old club kid. They pal around with Rick and Steve in the gay community. Although his connection to disability is unknown, the creator of the show Allan Brocka, when told that the Logo Web site referred to Chuck as being "confined to a wheelchair," quickly apologized and had the network fix the gaff.[70]

On "The Family Guy," the character of Joe Swanson, a macho and fit wheelchair user, contrasts to the doughy family guy, Peter Griffin. He arrived in Episode 5 of Season 1, when Peter asks him to play softball, not realizing he's paraplegic. Joe, of course, wins the game and becomes a hero, making Peter jealous. In another Joe-featured episode, "Ready, Willing and Disabled," Joe competes in a Paralympics-like sporting event. In another Joe-focused episode, "Believe It or Not, Joe's Walking on Air," he receives a leg transplant and becomes a jerk, so the gang decides to re-paralyze him. TV.com describes "Family Guy" this way:

> Sick, twisted, politically incorrect and freakin' sweet. The animated series features the adventures of the Griffin family. Peter and Lois have three kids – the youngest, Stewie, is a brilliant, sadistic baby bent on killing his mother and world domination. Chris, like his father, is obese, has a low IQ and no common sense. Meg desperately tries to be part of the popular crowd, and is coldly rebuffed. Their talking dog Brian keeps baby Stewie in check while sipping martinis and sorting out his own life issues.[71]

The empowering aspect of the Joe character is that he is just part of the comic landscape of the show.

"South Park" on Comedy Central is an irreverent satire featuring four foul-mouthed elementary school boys. The show occasionally spotlights their schoolmate Timmy, a wheelchair user with garbled speech, who was voted "The Greatest Disabled TV Character" in a poll by BBC's Ouch! website. Jimmy, who uses crutches, is also another disabled character, who sometimes teams with Timmy. *New*

Mobility reports on the popularity of Timmy among disabled voters at Ouch!:

> With his jagged teeth and can-do spirit, Timmy appears at first glance to uphold the condescending disability stereotypes that are gradually fading from mainstream entertainment. But like everything else in South Park, he's actually challenging preconceptions, toppling taboos, and weaving his uniqueness into the fabric of the show. He fits right in with the other South Park misfit kids (even the nefarious Cartman seems to enjoy his company), and he's never robbed of his disability pride. There will always be thick-headed morons who laugh at Timmy, but the character's popularity is largely determined by those who laugh with him.[72]

Ouch! said Timmy got the vote because of his badass activities on the show: "His capers have included becoming lead singer of Timmy and the Lords of the Underworld. They were hounded by a cartoon Phil Collins, who felt it wrong and shameful that a disabled person was fronting a rock band. Timmy also tried to join the notorious 'Krips' street mob, mistakenly thinking it was an empowering gang for cripples. And he was at the centre of a comical ethical debate over the question 'Do the handicapped go to heaven?'"[73] Although the creators of "South Park," Matt Stone and Trey Parker, aren't disabled, they seem to embrace the philosophy that the comedy landscape includes everyone, and even as important, that people with disabilities can be the focus of satire just like everyone else.

Parker and Stone took a second step to embrace disability humor beyond "South Park" when they became the executive producers of "How's Your News?" The concept for the show grew out a program at Camp Jabberwocky in Massachusetts, the nation's oldest sleepover camp for people with disabilities. The show began as a series of short films with campers working as reporters. Stone and Parker saw the films and backed a feature-length documentary that followed the camp reporters across America.[74] In 2009, "How's Your News?" became a six-part series on MTV, in which the reporters visited cities in America. The series, although not renewed, was embraced by the disability community and the mainstream media.

The show made *Entertainment Weekly's* "Must List" and received a good review from *The Washington Post*, as well as positive press in other U.S. news media. Tom Shales of *The Post* wrote: "The show isn't really 'about' mental disabilities;

it's just a chance to look through someone else's eyes and see the world in ways you've never seen it before. It could be part of a course in the humanities, or just a course in humanity. It's also a wickedly entertaining half-hour, one you'll never regret having surrendered to your television set."[75] The show truly is a refreshing take on life. Whether a reporter is asking a rock star about his favorite food or a reporter with a speech disability is asking Hilary Clinton a question she can't understand before a political convention, the show puts the audience into the reporters' shoes and their unique ways of viewing the world. From its beginning, the reporters and those who help create the films understood that some viewers may laugh *at* rather than *with* the show's stars. So they put a statement about their humor right out front – "Humor is an important part of life with a disability (and life in general!), so we'd like you to know that it's OK to laugh at some of this material. We're laughing right along with you . . ."[76] And even as important, the show allows people with intellectual disabilities to define their own humor and put it out there for the entire nation to see.

Disability humor on TV received its biggest boost in 2004 when Josh Blue, a comedian with cerebral palsy, won NBC's "Last Comic Standing." Blue jokes that "I realize that people are going to stare so I want to give them something to stare at." He says he uses his comedy to defy stereotypes and encourage others to overcome preconceived notions about people who are considered "disabled." And he says he gets great joy from "humbling condescending people."[77] His humor pokes fun at barriers in society and other's attitudes toward him, something he calls "reverse teasing." He has worked steadily as a stand-up comedian since winning "Last Comic Standing," and had a Comedy Central special in March 2009. With disabled comedians like Josh Blue on the national scene, disability humor is finally going mainstream.

Even Academy-Award-winning deaf actress Marlee Matlin will possibly be joining the TV comedy genre in 2010. Although known for her fire and intensity as a dramatic actress, Matlin has guest starred on several high profile comedies, most notably NBC's "Seinfeld" and "My Name is Earl." Matlin will star with "Sex and the City's" Mario Cantone in the Showtime comedy, tentatively titled "Mouthpiece," which will take place in a high-powered law firm. The creator of the comedy wrote the episode "Lip Reader," in which Matlin guest starred on Seinfeld in 1993.[78] Hopefully, finding the humor in fighting an ableist society will become a permanent TV comedy trend.

Conclusions

What do these TV comedies show us about disability humor? The most important thing they tell us is that even when a show has a main character with a disability, it need not focus solely on disability humor. "Pelswick" at its core is a show for pre-teens, and as such it combines a certain gross-out humor with important messages about the moral and ethical issues kids face. The humorous situations and in-depth messages are portrayed through all the characters equally – Pelswick, his friends, family, and the school personnel. Pelswick is just a regular member of this cast of characters, who just happens to use a wheelchair.

Disability humor has passed through three phases in the 20th century, and with the advent of shows like "Pelswick," "Brothers," and "How's Your News?" it has entered a fourth phase. Phase one was categorized by freak shows and using mentally disabled people as representative "fools." Phase two was represented by sick jokes, quadriplegic jokes, and Helen Keller jokes, which made fun of people with disabilities and emphasized their "limitations." In phase two, non-disabled people created the jokes and humor about disabled people.

The third phase of disability humor is characterized by people with disabilities taking control of the humor message. It represents the surge in number of disabled cartoonists such as John Mythen, Sharon Wachsler, Scott Chambers, and John Callahan, and the prominence of disabled comics such as deaf comedian Kathy Buckley, Fred Burns, a professional comic with spina bifida, and "Last Comic Standing's" Josh Blue. These disabled humorists poke fun at society's barriers and their own place in a world that has pitying or negative attitudes toward them. Callahan's humor is some of the most vehement in this vein because he takes on patronizing and pitying attitudes by protesting any form of political correctness in his gag cartoons for adults. This phase of disability humor doesn't just go for the laugh; it allows non-disabled people to see issues related to disability in a different light.

Shows like "Pelswick," "Brothers," and "How's Your News?" usher in a new phase of disability humor, one that illustrates an integrated approach rather than a disability-focused approach. In this phase of disability humor, the person with a disability is just another character in the humor landscape. The humor does not focus upon the person with a disability and much of the humor has no disability theme at all. This is the true innovation of these shows – disability is just part of the diverse humor panorama, not the reason for the comedy.

Within the third and fourth phases of disability humor, the power of the disabled cartoonists, comics, and actors is crucial. For non-disabled audiences to properly "read" the humor, they must understand that disabled people created it. If this is not understood, the humor is seen as cruel, rather than funny. Callahan explored this problem in the "Pelswick" episode "Draw." Pelswick's cartoon in the episode was considered to be offensive publicly until it became known that a disabled person drew it. With that information, the cartoon suddenly became acceptable. This mirrored Callahan's own experience as a cartoonist – many of his cartoons were read as funny only when it became widely recognized that he uses a wheelchair.

If phase two of disability humor represented a discomfort with people with disabilities gaining rights in U.S. society, such as in the Helen Keller joke cycle,[79] then phases three and four illustrate that the increasing visibility and integration of people with disabilities in society allow audiences to feel comfortable with humor that includes disability. Humor created by people with disabilities for all audiences challenges stereotypes and builds bridges to understanding. When comedies have disabled characters of equal status with all the other characters in the show, it sends a message to viewers that having a disability does not mean someone cannot have a full, interesting and exciting life. The disabled characters are fully participating member of their communities. Disabled people in TV comedies can illustrate disability humor at its best – everyone can laugh at our shared human experiences, and having a disability is depicted as just another unique feature about human beings.

Notes

Portions of this chapter were previously published in: Beth Haller and Sue Ralph, "John Callahan's Pelswick Cartoon and a New Phase of Disability Humor," *Disability Studies Quarterly*, 23:4, 2003.

1. R. Bruce Baum, "Humor and Disability," *The Bridge*, 1998, 8:4, pp. 3-5.

2. Gary L. Albrecht, "Disability humor: What's in a joke?" *Body & Society*, 1999, 5:4, p. 67.

3. Baum, op. cit., p. 4.

4. Mac E. Barrick, "The Helen Keller joke cycle," *Journal of American Folklore*, 1980, 93, pp. 441-9.

5. Alan Dundes, A. "The game of the name: A quadriplegic sick joke cycle," in *Cracking Jokes: Studies of Humor Cycles and Stereotypes*, Berkeley, Calif.: Ten Speed Press, 1987, p. 18.

6. Barrick, op. cit.

7. E. Johnson, "A case study of visual humor as prophecy: The portrayal of women in the cartoons of *Life* magazine (1884 to 1908)." Paper presented at the National Communication Association, Atlanta, 2001.

8. Johnson, 2001, pp. 172-3.

9. Barrick, op. cit., p. 449.

10. Jenny Corbett, *Bad-Mouthing: The Language of Special Needs.* London: Falmer Press, 1996, p. 53.

11. Bill Keveney, "Toon teaches teens from wheelchair," *USA Today,* Oct. 31, 2000, p. 5D.

12. Sharon Wachsler, Sick Humor postcards Web site, 2002, sickhumorpostcards.com/.

13. D. Coddon, "Disability is no handicap to laughter. He wields humor about, not despite, condition," *The San Diego Union-Tribune,* Feb. 22, 1996, p.8.

14. Kristin Tillotson, "Soothing society's woes: Generous portions of both humor and awareness can help produce the best response to disabilities," Minneapolis *Star Tribune,* March 9, 1997, p. 1F.

15. Barbara Kolucki and Barbara Duncan, *Working Together with the Media: A Practical Guide for People with Disabilities.* Geneva, Switzerland: International Labour Office, 1994, p. 9.

16. Donald C. Simmons, "Protest Humor! Folklorist reaction to prejudice," *American Journal of Psychiatry,* Dec. 1963, pp. 567-570.

17. Scott Chambers, "The joy of mental hygiene," [cartoon], *Mouth,* July/Aug. 2001, pp. 36-37.

18. Chris Sheridan, "A physical challenge for the media: The effects of portrayals on wheelchair users,"1996, youknow.com/disability/portrayals.html.

19. John Morreall, *Taking Laughter Seriously.* Albany, N.Y.: SUNY Press, 1983.

20. Morreall, 1983, p. 106.

21. Morreall, 1983, p. 104.

22. M. M. Melendez, "When faced with enemy, we spoof to conquer," *Contra Costa Times,* June 17, 2002, p. D1.

23. Claude's World Web site, 1998b, "My mission statement", claude-john.com/index.html.

24. Claude's World Web site, 1998a, "The Book Titled *Claude: MSing around,*" claude-john.com/book.html.

25. C. Sowell, "You've got to be kidding," *Quest,* Fall 1996, 3:4.

26. John Callahan, *Don't Worry, He won't Get Far on Foot.* N.Y.: Vintage Books, 1990.

27. S. Tilley, "Welcome to Maimed Manor. Nothing is sacred for partially paralysed cartoonist John Callahan," *Edmonton Sun,* Feb. 2, 2001.

28. John Callahan, *Will the Real John Callahan Please Stand Up?* N.Y.: William Morrow and Co., 1998, 65.

29. Stephen Hess and Sandy Northrop, *Drawn and Quartered: The history of American Political Cartoons.* Montgomery, Ala.: Elliott and Clark Publishing, 1996, p. 82.

30. Callahan, 1990, op. cit., p. 89.

31. Callahan, 1990, op. cit., p. 90.

32. Douglas Martin, "Disability Culture: Eager to bite the hand that would feed them," *The New York Times*, June 1, 1997, p. 1.

33. Kara Shultz and Darla Germeroth, "Should We Laugh or Should We Cry? John Callahan's Humor as a Tool to Change Societal Attitudes Toward Disability," *The Howard Journal Of Communication*, 1998, p. 9.

34. Shultz and Germeroth, op. cit., 233.

35. Keveney, op. cit., 5D.

36. Scott Moore, "Pulling No Punch Lines; Nickelodeon's Pelswick Features a Kid in a Wheelchair," *The Washington Post*, Oct. 23, 2000, p. C13.

37. Keveney, op. cit., p. 5D.

38. Donna Petrozzello, "Disabled? Not This Kid," *New York Daily News*, Oct. 23, 2000, 85.

39. Howard Rosenberg, "Searing spirit behind 'Pelswick', An animated quadriplegic," *The Los Angeles Times*, Oct. 20, 2000, p. F1.

40. Moore, 2000, op. cit.

41. Callahan, 1998, p. 71.

42. Christopher Wagner, "Boy's Costumes Depicted in Television Shows," Feb. 9, 2002, histclo.com/The/tv/itv/tvalb.html.

43. CNN Web site, Oct. 24, 2000, Entertainment- 'Pelswick' debuts on Nickelodeon. cnn.com/2000SHOWBIZ/TV/10/24/pelswick.ap/.

44. Keveney, op. cit.

45. Nickelodeon, Pelswick, Press Release, 2000.

46. Nickelodeon, Pelswick Web site, op. cit.

47. Moore, op. cit.

48. Pertozzello, op. cit.

49. Premier's Council on the Status of Persons with Disabilities. "CBC Brings Disability to Primetime," *The Quarterly Newsletter on Disability Issues in Alberta*. Feb. 2001. cd.gov.ab.ca/helping_albertans/premiers_council/Status_Report/February_2001_Status.asp.

50. Petrozzello, op. cit.

51. Simmons, op. cit.

52. Moore, op. cit., p. C13.

53. Keveney, op. cit., p. 5D.

54. Zillions.org, 2000, Your Reviews on Zillions Online: Pelswick zillions.org/rateit/Tvshow/pelswick.html.

55. M. Perigard, "Nick's Pelswick rolls away from stereotypes of disabled," *The Boston Herald*, Oct. 24, 2000, p. 55.

56. "Who's News," *Time for Kids,* Oct. 20, 2000, 6:6, p. 8.

57. S. Goode, "Cartoon Advocates for Disabled," *The Hartford Courant,* Nov. 18, 2000, p. B3.

58. S. Miller, "The Family Tree Branches Out; Cable's family programmers are industry leaders when it comes to showcasing diversity. But there's still plenty of work to be done," *Cablevision,* Jan. 29, 2001, p. 33.

59. Scott Moore, "Pulling No Punch Lines; Nickelodeon's Pelswick Features a Kid in a Wheelchair," *The Washington Post,* Oct. 23, 2000, p. C13.

60. Petrozzello, op. cit., p. 85.

61. Keveney, 2000, p. 5D.

62. Neil Marcus, "Who is Pelswick Eggert?" *Disability World,* 5, Oct./Dec. 2000.

63. "'Pelswick' is permanent chair in new Callahan cartoon," *Ragged Edge,* 2000, raggededgemagazine.com/extra/pelswick.htm.

64. Ricardo Baca, "Nickelodeon works to defy stereotypes," Corpus Christi *Caller-Times,* caller2.com/2000/today/ricardo/7199.html October 22, 2000.

65. "Pelswick: Meet the characters," Nickelodeon, 2000, nick.com.

66. John M. Williams, "Animated Hero for the Disabled," *Business Week* Online, Oct. 18, 2000, businessweek.com/bwdaily/dnflash/oct2000/.

67. Baca, op. cit.

68. Greg Braxton, "'Brothers' star Daryl Chill Mitchell beats the odds," *Los Angeles Times,* Dept. 25, 2009, latimes.com/entertainment/news/la-et-daryl25-2009sep25,0,269197.story.

69. Braxton, op. cit.

70. Allan Brocka, "Blog," [Email message], Mar. 19, 2008.

71. "Family Guy, Show Overview," TV.com. 2009, tv.com/family-guy/show/348/summary.html.

72. Jeff Shannon, "Krazy Kripples: South Park & Disability," *New Mobility,* Nov. 2005, newmobility.com/articleViewIE.cfm?id=1075#.

73. "The Greatest Disabled TV Character," BBC Ouch!, 2005, bbc.co.uk/ouch/.

74. "'How's Your News?' Main," MTV.com, 2009, mtv.com/shows/hows_your_news/series.jhtml.

75. Tom Shales, "Disabled get last laugh on MTV's 'News'" *The Washington Post,* Feb. 5, 2009, washingtonpost.com/wp-dyn/content/article/2009/02/04/AR2009020404010.html.

76. How's Your News? Web site, Home page, 2009, howsyournews.com/.

77. Josh Blue, "Bio," Josh Blue Web site, 2009, joshblue.com/

78. Nellie Andreeva, "Carol Liefer sets up at CBS, Showtime," The Hollywood Reporter, Oct. 1, 2009, hollywoodreporter.com/hr/content_display/news/e3i1c9f6a73741ca4f549fee3a186fe5745#.

79. Barrick, op. cit.

9.

Media advocacy and films
The 'Million Dollar Baby' effect

Films have long been a locus of disability representation, and disability studies scholars and writers for disability media have critiqued many of their clichéd or negative images of people with disabilities over the years.[1] One disability and film studies scholar said he began researching film depictions because he saw little resemblance between actual people with disabilities and disabled characters in the movies.[2] And some disability studies scholars argue the power of negative film images to add to the oppression of people with disabilities. Disability studies scholar Colin Barnes says that the social model of disability's notion that society's barriers cause "a disabling environment and culture" includes film images as one of those barriers. These images lead to "the devaluing of disabled people through negative images in the media – films, television and newspapers."[3]

But films have only rarely been a focus of disability activism. Film and disability scholar Martin Norden says there were some protests of film representations beginning in the 1990s. For example, the International Leadership Forum for Women with Disabilities in 1997 discussed the concern that so many media images of people with disabilities are negative: "The media have such stereotyped views of us that they only see us as either tragic but brave, overcoming the odds to become heroines or champions, or as pathetic and powerless objects of charity."[4] And deaf activists protested "Calendar Girl" in 1993 because a hearing actor played a deaf character; a man with kyphoscoliosis had a letter-writing campaign against "The Hunchback of Notre Dame" in 1996,[5] and the National Federation of the Blind asked Disney to abandon bringing "Mr. Magoo" to the screen in 1997.[6] (The movie was produced and released as scheduled.)

Although these protests garnered some media attention, this chapter argues that the 2004 premiere of the Clint Eastwood film "Million Dollar Baby" was a type of game-changer in ramping up disability rights media activism against film images, because that film was so odious to most in the disability rights community. And it pushed activism against films that misrepresent people with disabilities onto the permanent agenda of the disability rights movement, with the activists acknowledging that these film images feed the long-lasting oppression of people with disabilities. As Norden explains: "There is little question that Hollywood filmmakers have taken their cue from the dominant culture and frequently used fear and pity (and to a lesser extent, awe and humor) to separate people with disabilities from the rest of society. In so doing, they of course help perpetuate the culture."[7]

"Million Dollar Baby"

"Million Dollar Baby" represented a serious disconnect between dominant able-bodied culture and disability culture. This became readily apparent when film critics and Hollywood lauded the film, while the disability community was up in arms about its positive portrayal of the assisted suicide of a person with a disability. Disability studies scholar Lennard J. Davis put it succinctly: "You know there is something wrong when 100 of the major film critics in the U.S. say that Clint Eastwood's film 'Million Dollar Baby' is a great film and every disability scholar and activist rails against the movie."[8]

The disability rights movement has spent much protest time on issues such as assisted suicide, independent living, employment, transportation, and legal protections against discrimination, but has not directed much energy toward protesting a film. This all changed with "Million Dollar Baby." Anecdotally, some people with disabilities say they returned to disability rights activism because of the outrageous message of "Million Dollar Baby" – that seemingly the best option for someone with a spinal cord injury is death.

Hollywood typically has much success when it turns to disability themes. The accolades and awards tend to roll in. Films such as "Children of a Lesser God" (winner of best actress Academy Award for a deaf actress), "My Left Foot" (winner of two Academy Awards), "Rain Man" (four Academy Awards), and

"Born on the Fourth of July" (two Academy Awards) come to mind.[9] Even with their acknowledged flaws, these movies at least illustrated that disabled people have lives worth living and are filled with the full gamut of human experiences from joyful to tragic. These films also had some input from real people with disabilities. Marlee Matlin, a deaf actress, starred in and won the Academy Award for "Children of a Lesser God." Daniel Day Lewis for "My Left Foot" studied at a school for people with disabilities when developing his powerful characterization of Christy Brown, an Irish writer and artist with cerebral palsy.[10] "Rain Man" was based on an actual autistic savant, Kim Peek, whom Dustin Hoffman met with a number of times,[11] and Ron Kovic, the wheelchair-using Vietnam veteran whose life story was depicted in "Born on the Fourth of July," wrote the screenplay for the film with its director Oliver Stone.[12] However, the 2004 movie from Clint Eastwood, "Million Dollar Baby," which won four Oscars, follows another path: With no input from disabled people, it depicted a scenario of death as preferable to life as a disabled person.

Disability activists around the U.S. were vocal in their criticism of "Million Dollar Baby," but their counter-message to the movie was heard only sparsely against a roar of critical acclaim for the film. Some media coverage arose when the Chicago-based anti-assisted suicide organization Not Dead Yet protested the Chicago Film Critics Association in January 2005 because most critics in the association gave a rave review to "Million Dollar Baby," a film that Not Dead Yet said "promotes the killing of disabled people as the solution to the 'problem' of disability."[13]

Although primarily a movie about a female boxer (played by Hilary Swank) trying to achieve her dream of a boxing title, it features an important plot point in which the Clint Eastwood character assists the Hilary Swank character to die after she becomes quadriplegic due to a boxing accident. "It's a pro-euthanasia movie," according to Not Dead Yet. "But they don't want you to go in expecting that to be the main message. But it's the romanticized killing at the end that makes the movie 'great' for most of the critics."[14]

Ironically, the movie's characters are somewhat one-dimensional and devoid of emotional depth until the disability twist in the plot. Even the boxing sequences lack much detailed choreography because Hilary Swank's character knocks out her opponents so quickly. And even with minimal knowledge of boxing, it's obvious the film doesn't follow the actual rules of the sport. Hollywood's history with Oscar-winning disability themed films supports Not Dead

Yet's contention – the film critics give the movie credit for deeper performances and a stronger plot once a disability theme enters a fairly clichéd boxing film.

The National Spinal Cord Injury Association (NSCIA) in Bethesda, Md., also released a statement criticizing the movie for its portrayal of a person with a spinal cord injury. The Association wondered why, when the character in the movie becomes disabled, there is no long-term rehabilitation or mention of resources that could allow the person to return home and continue to live a productive life.

"Eastwood's message, that life with SCI, with a disability, is not worth living, is a prejudice shared by many," explains NSCIA in its release. "Eastwood fails to include mention that it is discrimination, poverty, and an inaccessible society that sometimes leads newly-injured people to abandon hope and choose death."[15]

Disability rights activists singled out Clint Eastwood's significant role in the problems of "Million Dollar Baby" because he drew much criticism from disability rights advocates in 2000 when he fought against Americans with Disabilities Act provisions that mandated he make his hotel in Carmel, Calif., accessible.[16]

Eastwood told *The New York Times* that he did not see the film's theme as being about the right to die. "The film is supposed to make you think about the precariousness of life and how we handle it," he said. "How the character handles it is certainly different than how I might handle it if I were in that position in real life. Every story is a 'what if.'"[17]

Eastwood added that the film is based on a story by F. X. Toole,[18] and as the director, he kept the movie close to the original's plot. The nuances of how Eastwood filmed the death scene were changed from the book, however. In the film Frankie, Maggie's trainer (Eastwood), looks Maggie in the face when assisting her to death, but in the Toole story "Frankie stands behind Maggie to avoid the full gravitas of his act."[19]

Disability rights activists say they protest so vehemently against assisted suicide because it is a human rights issue for disabled people. Activists argue that because many disabled people receive little support for independent living, employment, proper health care, or equipment, they have little chance to experience value and quality in their lives. Society condones the option of death through assisted suicide for people with disabilities, but not a culture that supports and values them as human beings, activists say.

"Million Dollar Baby" reinforces the narrative that devalues people once they become disabled. Many ableist narratives imbedded within Western culture tend to ignore or represent disabled people negatively. Disability studies scholar Joy Weeber says ableist narratives are akin to racism, calling them "belief in the superiority of being nondisabled that assumes everyone who is disabled wishes they could be nondisabled – at any cost."[20] When people are shown as "better off dead" than disabled, the underlying message is that they are inferior to non-disabled people, are "defective," or have a worthless status in society. In "Million Dollar Baby," the assisted suicide is actually compared to putting the family dog to sleep. Comparing a human life to that of a pet really illustrates the "worthless status" the person with a disability has in the movie.

Not Dead Yet has made one of its goals confronting society's "ableism." It says the cultural beliefs that feed ableism cause public acceptance of assisted suicide, and assisted suicide makes bigotry against disabled people life threatening. Disability studies scholars say society has a double standard – disabled people who ask to die are quickly helped toward death, whereas non-disabled people who want to commit suicide are given every intervention to prevent their deaths. The disability rights publication *Ragged Edge* explains:

> Life with a disability is so devalued, society is so bigoted against the idea that life with a severe disability can have quality, that in such a climate the 'right to die' becomes a 'duty to die.' Activists fear that people who become disabled will choose suicide over living with disability. They fear that people whose disabilities make them burdens on family members will be pressured – subtly or not so subtly – to end their lives. Disability studies scholar and historian Dr. Paul Longmore says that if it were legalized, 'assisted suicide would be practiced within a health care system rampant with disability prejudice and discrimination,' adding that people with serious disabilities report hospital staffers pressuring them to sign Do Not Resuscitate forms.[21]

This issue of someone's "state of mind" should be at the forefront of the discussion of assisted suicide and disabled people, but rarely is. In "Million Dollar Baby," a few suggestions were made about life after disability – getting a power wheelchair, going to college, etc. But the movie never dealt with the possible depression and sadness of someone who is newly disabled, so those life-affirming options were not seriously considered by Hilary Swank's Maggie character.

Any type of major change in someone's life needs emotional processing. Counseling to help the newly-disabled person cope with changes, or mentoring by other people with disabilities to help them understand the new direction of life is crucial. Hundreds of disability organizations exist world-wide to help people make the transition to a life with a disability. The late actor/director Christopher Reeve openly admitted in his autobiography *Still Me* that he considered suicide right after the riding accident that left him paralyzed. He ended up rejecting that idea due in part to the support of his family and friends who told him that, disabled or not, he was still the same person they had always wanted in their lives.[22]

Reeve counseled other newly disabled people against suicide, he said in an October 2004 interview in *Reader's Digest*. What kept him going, he said, was "the love and support of my family, and the fact that I am needed. I'm working. I focus on the opportunities that have come my way rather than on the things that haven't yet arrived."[23]

Reeve also spoke often about how being disabled changed his parenting style for the better. Because of his limited physicality, he had to actually listen to and communicate with his three children, he said.[24] In addition, by choosing life, he was able to give his youngest child, who was only two at the time of Reeve's accident, the precious gift of getting to know his father for nine more years.

Although he had one of the most serious spinal cord injuries a person can sustain, Reeve continued to pursue many aspects of his acting and directing career. He even directed a true story about a young woman with paralysis who completed her master's degree at Harvard University, "The Brooke Ellison Story," which aired on the A&E cable television channel in 2004.

Like the character in "Million Dollar Baby," both Reeve and Ellison have quadriplegia and use ventilators to assist with breathing. They illustrate what Marcie Roth, executive director of the National Spinal Cord Injury Association, asserts: "Many people with SCI and other disabilities survive, thrive, and contribute to our society."[25]

Disability rights advocate and journalist William G. Stothers of the California-based Center for an Accessible Society says that supportive messages about assisted suicide feed society's already negative impression of the quality of disabled people's lives. In contrast, he says, society should understand that "many people with disabilities offer shining examples of the possibilities of life – rich, full, expressive, vital life."[26] Unfortunately, most of American society never receives this message about the lives of people with disabilities, and there has been growing support of the "right to die" movement, with 84 percent of Americans supporting right-to-die laws in 2005 compared to 79 percent in 1990.[27]

Movies such as "Million Dollar Baby" reinforce the beliefs held by the American public. Disability rights activists tried to make it clear how the film does a disservice to attitudes towards disabled people by validating the negative, ableist message of disability as "a fate worse than death."

Continuing disability activism about films

For all its negative messages, "Million Dollar Baby" reinvigorated disability advocacy in the area of popular culture, specifically films. The next big movie protest came in 2008 over the film "Tropic Thunder." With a new, savvier way of dealing with Hollywood, protests spawned by this film remain in U.S. culture in the form of the R-word campaign.

In the summer of 2008, "Tropic Thunder" protests brought together hundreds (possibly thousands) of advocates, parents, and people with intellectual disabilities around the U.S. to voice their concerns about language use in the Ben Stiller film. The satirical comedy is about actors who go to Asia to make a movie and end up being in an actual war, but the concern from the disability community focused on a subplot poking fun at Hollywood actors who want to play a disabled character so they can win an Oscar.

In that subplot, the Ben Stiller character starred in a movie called "Simple Jack" in which he was advised to "never go full retard" in his attempt to win an Oscar by playing an intellectually disabled man. In the scenes about the film-within-a-film "Simple Jack," the term "retard" was used 17 times. This term, known as "the R-word" in disability rights circles, is a very derogatory slur but still is heard in many schoolyards taunts, in off-color comedy routines, and in everyday conversations.

Once the disability community was informed of the abundant use of the R-word in the film, local and national disability organizations from around the nation picketed outside the premiere of "Tropic Thunder" and subsequently at many openings of the movie at theatres across the country. Disability rights organizational leaders, parents, people with disabilities, and even legislators wrote opinion columns that appeared in national and local newspapers for weeks and weeks after the early August opening of "Tropic Thunder."[28]

Disability organizations began separate anti-R-word campaigns, held a Rally for Respect, made buttons and T-shirts, and created public service announcements to educate people about how hurtful they feel the word is.[29] The R-word campaign caught on and continued as a major effort of organizations like the Special Olympics.

The group's CEO Timothy Shriver explained the bigotry behind the R-word in *The Washington Post* in 2010:

> The point of the campaign by people who have intellectual disabilities, their friends, advocates and tens of thousands of individuals and dozens of organizations: We are fighting a word because it represents one of the most stubborn and persistent stigmas in history. Millions of people have a prejudice they often are not even aware of. It is much bigger than a word, but words matter. And the word 'retard,' whatever its history, reflects a massive problem. . . . Our coalition seeks no law to ban words and no official censorship against those who freely use 'retard.' But for our part, we are trying to awaken the world to the need for a new civil rights movement – of the heart. We seek to educate people that a crushing prejudice against people with intellectual disabilities is rampant – a prejudice that assumes that people with significant learning challenges are stupid or hapless or somehow just not worth much. They're, um, 'retarded.' And that attitude is not funny or nuanced or satirical. It's horrific.[30]

The "Tropic Thunder" protests and complaints about the R-word received much media coverage and many Americans received an important reminder about a hurtful disability slur. As most "nice people" already knew not to use the R-word, the protests did engender some backlash from those who felt some of the protests were calling for censorship or were a bid for political correctness.

But as one media-savvy disability rights advocate pointed out, the protests weren't about censorship or political correctness: they were about Hollywood's failure to talk to even one disabled person during production of "Tropic Thunder." Lawrence Carter-Long, executive director for the Disabilities Network of New York City and the founder/curator of the "disTHIS! Film Series: disability through a whole new lens," explained that Ben Stiller, the director, co-writer, and actor in "Tropic Thunder," made a conscious effort to get feedback from veterans about the film because of its war theme and, based on that, dropped a reference to "post-platoon syndrome" for fear of offending returning veterans with post-traumatic stress disorder. Stiller also screened the film before racially diverse audiences because the Robert Downey, Jr. character in "Tropic Thunder" is in blackface throughout the film.

Carter-Long calls the film "satirization without representation," meaning that Dreamworks Studios, producer of the film, and Stiller did many screenings of the film before its release and remembered to make sure they had veterans and people of color in the audiences but never thought to include disabled people. "Census figures put the disabled population of the U.S. at 1 in 5 – that's 54 million, arguably our largest minority – but culturally speaking disability is still considered a distant threat, something that happens to people segregated to telethons and fundraising campaigns," Carter-Long explains.

> Only when our brothers and sisters return from wars missing limbs or our parents are debilitated by hip or knee replacements do we take notice. Seldom do we consider people who 'join the club' like Christopher Reeve could one day be us. Seldom do we consider that the children hurt by schoolyard taunts could be our own. People with disabilities are simply not yet recognized as a constituency to be reckoned with and, as such, have not been afforded the same concern as other groups.[31]

The "Tropic Thunder" protests served as another flashpoint in continued media activism, and hopefully Hollywood may be beginning to take notice of disability concerns. More than 200 U.S. disability organizations signed a petition opposing the film and protests occurred in most American cities when the movie opened. "Media coverage has been unprecedented," Carter-Long says. "Hollywood can ill afford to dismiss the views of disabled advocates and their allies now. It didn't have to be this way, but by failing to consider the nation's 'largest minority,' Dreamworks created the controversy themselves."

Because the "Tropic Thunder" protests showed disability advocacy groups that they must continue fight against negative media messages about disability, the R-word campaign took hold throughout the nation. NPR's Neda Ulaby wrote about the changing attitudes toward the R-word in 2009:

> While the Tropic Thunder protests did little but provide publicity, there are signs that the word's status may be changing. Earlier this summer,

film critic Eric D. Snider was reviewing a DVD called 'Miss March.' It's a stinker of an insult comedy uniformly hated by critics when it came out in theaters last spring. Snider noticed that in the DVD version, actors' lips were clearly saying 'retard' repeatedly, but the word was dubbed out and replaced with 'stupid' or 'crackhead.' It's not just movies rethinking 'retard' as an easy laugh. The Black Eyed Peas recorded a 'clean' version of their song 'Let's Get Retarded' that changed that line to 'Let's Get It Started.' And a few months ago, popular sex advice columnist Dan Savage renounced his use of the word.[32]

The NPR story quotes *Atlantic* writer Ta-Nehisi Coates, who "says that in order for hateful language to become socially unacceptable, it needs to be linked with the kind of bigoted behavior no one wants to be associated with. And he suggests that there needs to be a fundamental cultural shift in empathy."[33] The years of activism surrounding the R-word since "Tropic Thunder" are arguing for exactly this shift in empathy.

The R-word debate entered the political arena in 2010 when President Barack Obama's Chief of Staff Rahm Emanuel, known for his penchant for cursing, called a plan to run ads attacking conservative Democrats "fucking retarded" in *The Wall Street Journal.*[34] Disability organizations used the gaffe as a "teaching moment" and met with Emanuel, who pledged not to use the word again.[35] Republicans, specifically 2008 Vice Presidential candidate Sarah Palin, who is the mother of a child with Down syndrome, used this incident to call for Emanuel's firing and to lash out at others who use the R-word.

The political dimensions of the R-word debate grew when conservative talk-show host Rush Limbaugh repeatedly used the R-word in talking about the Emanuel story. Palin chastised everyone but Limbaugh, instead calling his program "satire." When comedy shows like "Saturday Night Live," The Stephen Colbert Report," and "The Daily Show with Jon Stewart" satirized the R-word debate, the discussion of the R-word and comedy took the national stage once again and sensitized the American public – this time on both sides of the political fence – to the offensiveness of the word.

From high school students who embrace people with intellectual disabilities as their friends to self-advocates themselves, the R-word campaign seems to have staying power. The AP reported in April 2009 that the "Spread the Word to End the Word" campaign came from students who attended a Special Olympics youth summit in Idaho. Their efforts led to rallies around the country and events at high schools nationally that challenged young people to stop using the R-word.[36] In 2010, *The Washington Post* reported on the leadership role self-advocates have had in helping to eliminate the R-word:

As institutions close and the disabled are increasingly included in regular schools, people with intellectual disabilities are becoming increasingly articulate, self-confident and ambitious. Some are attending adapted college programs. Many self-advocates are being invited to sit on commissions or nonprofit boards or to intern in state legislatures. . . . Nationally, they have helped escalate protests against R-word references in popular culture and by public figures, joining the outcry over 'Tropic Thunder,' a 2008 movie laced with 'retard' punch lines, and over Emanuel's recently reported reference to liberals as retarded. During a People First meeting in Fairfax [Jan. 2010], members met with a facilitator from Toastmasters, a public speaking and leadership training program. They focused on making eye contact and keeping 'umms' and 'ahhs' in check during a series of impassioned speeches about the R-word. 'They need to completely erase it out of the ledger and the government books. If I find the R-word in a government document, I would just burn it until there was nothing left. That is how strongly I feel about it,' said Robbie Kelly, 35, of Dumfries. In many places, including Maryland, the change in terminology has been approved quickly. Nina Marcellino, an Anne Arundel County mother whose 7-year-old daughter, Rosa, has Down syndrome, was inspired by the campaign in Virginia and urged a Maryland legislator in 2008 to sponsor a bill. Less than a year later, it passed unanimously, and the term is being removed from education and health codes. Self-advocates were among the most vocal supporters, Marcellino said. Some wept when it passed. 'It was a change whose time had come,' she said.[37]

These sweeping language changes on the horizon for American society came primarily from disability rights activism about film images.

Bolstered by the success of the "Tropic Thunder" protests and the R-word campaign, disability activists no longer hesitate when a film that negatively stereotypes people with disabilities appears. The National Federation of the Blind publicly denounced the 2008 film, "Blindness," and hosted a number of protests at theaters showing the film. NFB's president Marc Maurer said:

> The National Federation of the Blind condemns and deplores this film, which will do substantial harm to the blind of America and the world. Blind people in this film are portrayed as incompetent, filthy, vicious, and depraved. They are unable to do even the simplest things like dressing, bathing, and finding the bathroom. The truth is that blind people regularly do all of the same things that sighted people do. Blind people are a cross-section of society, and as such we represent the broad range of human capacities and characteristics. We are not helpless children or immoral, degenerate monsters; we are teachers, lawyers, mechanics, plumbers, computer programmers, and social workers.[38]

However, as a mediocre and boring film,[39] "Blindness" quickly left theaters, having none of the staying power of an award-winning film.

In 2009, the long-awaited James Cameron film "Avatar" pushed the envelope of special effects, animation, and CGI. And its main character, Jake Sully, is a disabled wheelchair user. Although outright protests didn't occur, reviewers with a disability perspective and even the mainstream media questioned the seemingly random use of a character with a disability. All reviewers agreed that the animation and CGI in "Avatar" were amazing. (It was nominated for nine Oscars and won three, but more importantly it became the highest grossing film of all time in January 2010.)[40] But most said the plot was somewhat weak.

The disabled Jake Sully character enters a non-disabled avatar body and is able to go to the planet Pandora, home of the blue feline-appearing Na'vi people, whom his avatar resembles. In Disability Arts online, reviewer Alison Wilde questions why the film even made its main character disabled (played by non-disabled actor Sam Worthington):

> There is no apparent reason for this character to be disabled in the first place, other than to frame Jake's moral dilemma; whether to put the good of the Na'vi before the before evil of the invaders. Taking a decision to side with the native people means Jake will remain disabled, as a human being, spurning Colonel Quaritch's reward of 'new legs' for successful infiltration and relevant information. So although the film

is critical of Western military power, it simultaneously communicates a message of disabled warriors as heroes. And in the end, like many disabled male characters, Jake's heroism is rewarded by the full restoration of his masculinity; the girl, the legs, the cultural power and the biggest 'bird' on the planet.[41]

A science fiction Web site noticed a sci-fi trend that "Avatar" follows, in which mobility-impaired characters are many times able to walk again. Called "20 Science Fiction Characters Who Got Their Legs Back," the article points to the first captain in the "Star Trek" series, a time when Batman breaks his spine, and the character of John Locke on the TV series "Lost," all of whom were disabled but walk again their respective sci-fi worlds.[42]

Other disability reviewers rightfully questioned why a society set so far in the future would not have come up with new technology for people with disabilities. An article on gender and disability in "Avatar" wonders:

Though technology can fix many things in Pandora and in our world, it still apparently cannot or rather chooses not to fix human bodies. This is of great note in a film that both displays and is about the transcendent qualities of CGI and biotechnology. When Jack Sully transmits his consciousness into the hybrid Na'vi body that he eventually comes to occupy permanently, a world of limits is evoked. We can see that the bias against disabled people is exactly the same in the future as it is at present – one passing soldier refers to Sully as 'meals on wheels' and another replies 'that's just wrong,' apparently referring to Sully's very presence on Pandora. Sully's spinal injury is repairable, but he can't afford it. However, as we see during the avatar-training scenes, the disabled body is viewed as 'waste' that a thrifty military industrial complex can recoup. Disposable military bodies, often bodies of color in this film, are continually sacrificed: Sully is given the ability to acquire a prosthetic alien-soldier body not as compensation for his disability, but in spite of it – his genomic capital as the identical twin to his scientist-brother makes him the only possible match for the cloned Na'vi body, a technology far more expensive and precious than his own defective body.[43]

So the film has little consideration that things may change for the better for people with disabilities in the future. But some wheelchair users liked the film's use of a disabled person as the main character. ABC News interviewed people with spinal cord injuries about the film and they felt that it was wonderful to see a disabled main character: "The movie's greatest statement was to feature a paraplegic lead character in an action movie. 'I didn't feel like it was a pity story about someone in a wheelchair,' said [Santina] Muha, a communications associate at the National Spinal Cord Injury Association and the current Ms. Wheelchair New Jersey." Steve Coleman, of the Christopher and Dana Reeve Foundation, said he believed "Avatar" worked because it showed "the mental and emotional strength of disabled veterans. 'It showed you perspective that, although his legs weren't working, his heart and mind were working,' said Coleman."

The ABC News report allowed people with disabilities to once again explain why they had been upset about the disability myths perpetuated by "Million Dollar Baby." "'What I hated about "Million Dollar Baby," it showed all the worst things about having a disability,' said [Phil] Klebine, [a wheelchair user] who thought all the complications Maggie suffers after her accident could have easily been avoided with decent care." Because "Million Dollar Baby" was a flashpoint for media activism, other films featuring disabled characters are seemingly judged against it now. Disabled people in the ABC News report were happy the "Avatar" Jake character was not a "supercrip" and that his disability was not the focus of the film. "Muha and others were glad to see a disabled character in a movie about something other than disability. 'I do think that it's an advance in seeing people in wheelchairs in the entertainment industry,' said Klebine. 'I just wish people who have a disability get a chance to play those roles.'"[44]

Although little disability activism surrounded "Avatar," it appears even mainstream media outlets now remember the "Million Dollar Baby" controversy when other films appear that have disabled characters. So it can be argued that the activism surrounding that film had some long-lasting ramifications. That activism may not have been as explicit as the R-word campaign that grew from "Tropic Thunder," but clearly mainstream media have a growing awareness of negative or stereotypical images of people with disabilities in films thanks to the activism of disability advocates surrounding "Million Dollar Baby."

Notes

1. Some of the studies that have looked at disability and film: Paul K. Longmore, "Screening stereotypes: Images of disabled people in television and motion pictures," in A. Gartner and T. Joe, eds., *Images of the Disabled, Disabling Images*. N.Y.: Praeger, 1987, pp. 65-78; E. Keith Byrd, "A study of film depiction of specific characteristics of characters with disability in film," *Journal of Applied Rehabilitation Counseling*, 1989, 10:2, pp. 13-15; Otto F. Wahl, *Media Madness, Public Images of Mental Illness*. New Brunswick: Rutgers University Press, 1995; Martin F. Norden, "Resexualization of the disabled war hero in 'Thirty Seconds over Tokyo,'" *Journal of Popular Film and Television*, (Summer 1995), XXIII:2, pp. 50-55; Martin Norden, *The Cinema of Isolation*. New Brunswick: Rutgers University Press, 1995; Anne Pointon and C. Davies, *Framed: Interrogating Disability in the Media*. Bloomington: Indiana University Press, 1998; Martin F. Norden. and M. A. Cahill, "Violence, Women, and Disability in Tod Browning's 'Freaks' and 'The Devil Doll,'" *Journal of Popular Film and Television*, Summer 1998, 26:2; Anthony Enns and Chris Smit, *Screening Disability: Essays on Cinema and Disability*. Washington. D.C: University Press of America, 2001; Robin Larsen and Beth Haller, "Public Reception of Real Disability: The Case of the Film 'Freaks,'" *Journal of Popular Film and Television*, Winter 2002, 29:4; Fiona Whittington-Walsh, "From Freaks to Savants: Disability and Hegemony from 'The Hunchback of Notre Dame' (1939) to 'Sling Blade' (1997)," *Disability & Society*, 2002, 17:6, pp. 695-707; Paul K. Longmore, "The Glorious Rage of Christy Brown," in *Why I Burned My Book and Other Essays on Disability*. Philadelphia: Temple University Press, 2003; Carol Poore, "Who belongs? Disability and the German nation in postwar literature and film," *German Studies Review*, 2003, 26:1, pp. 21-42; British Film Institute, Disability Imagery: A teaching guide to disability and moving image media, 2004, bfi.org.uk/education/resources/teaching/disability/; J. D. Bellin, "Monstrous Minds: Fantasy film and mental illness" in *Framing Monsters: Fantasy Film and Social Alienation*, Carbondale, Ill.: SIU Press, 2005.

2. Martin Norden, "The Hollywood Discourse on Disability: Some Personal Reflections," in Anthony Enns and Chris Smit, *Screening Disability: Essays on Cinema and Disability*, Washington, D.C: University Press of America, 2001.

3. Colin Barnes, "Disability Studies: what's the point?" [Notes for a verbal presentation at the "Disability Studies: Theory. Policy and Practice" Conference; University of Lancaster], September 4. 2003, leeds.ac.uk/disability-studies/archiveuk/Barnes/What's%20the%20point.pdf.

4. Rachel Hurst, "Communication – The Basis of Our Liberation Struggle," International Leadership Forum for Women with Disabilities: Final Report, N.Y.: Rehabilitation International, May 1998.

5. Norden, 2001, op. cit.

6. Marc Maurer, "Of Mr. Magoo, Disney, and the National Federation of the Blind," 1998,nfb.org/legacy/bm/bm98/bm980202.htm.

7. Norden, 2001, op. cit., 26.

8. Lennard J. Davis, "Why Disability Studies Matters," Philia, A dialogue on caring citizenship, philia.ca/cms_en/page1315.cfm.

9. Academy of Motion Picture Arts and Sciences, "The Official Academy Awards Database" Mar. 12, 2005, oscars.org/awardsdatabase/.

10. NPR, "Daniel Day-Lewis: 'Nine' Lives, One Way Of Living," Dec. 7, 2009, npr.org/templates/story/story.php?storyId=121533507.

11. David Jones, "Did Dustin Hoffman exploit the Rain Man? *The Daily Mail*, Dec. 27, 2009, dailymail.co.uk/tvshowbiz/article-1238386/Did-Dustin-Hoffman-exploit-rainman-After-death-week-father-makes-startling-accusation.html.

12. Norden, 2001, op. cit.

13. Not Dead Yet, Press Release, Jan. 14, 2005, notdeadyet.org/docs/bigotpr.html.

14. Not Dead Yet, 2005, op. cit.

15. National Spinal Cord Injury Association, "Eastwood continues disability vendetta with 'Million Dollar Baby,'" Press Release, Feb. 9, 2005, spinalcord.org/news.php?dep=1&page=0&list=281.

16. Mary Johnson, *Make Them Go Away: Clint Eastwood, Christopher Reeve and The Case Against Disability Rights*. Louisville, Ky.: Advocado Press, 2003.

17. Sharon Waxman, "Groups criticize Baby for message on suicide," *The New York Times*, Jan. 31, 2005, p. E1.

18. F. X. Toole, *Rope Burns: Stories from the Corner*. N.Y.: HarperCollins, 2001.

19. J. Caskey, "'Million Dollar Baby' in Review", in "Responding to 'Million Dollar Baby': A Forum," *Disability Studies Quarterly*, Summer 2005, dsq-sds.org/_articles_html/2005/summer/m$b_forum.asp.

20. Joy Weeber, "What could I know of racism?" *Journal of Counseling & Development*, 1999, 77, p. 20.

21. Ragged Edge Online, "Why Disability Rights Activists Oppose Physician Assisted Suicide," Jan. 18, 2006, raggededgemagazine.com/departments/closerlook/000749.html.

22. Christopher Reeve, *Still Me*. N.Y.: Ballantine Books, 1999.

23. A. Nash, "Going the distance," *Reader's Digest*, Oct. 2004, pp. 108-114.

24. Reeve, op. cit.

25. Nash, op. cit.

26. William G. Stothers, "Death and Life – it's time to choose up sides," *Mainstream*, Feb. 1996, p. 42.

27. Pew Research Center for the People and the Press, "Strong Public Support for Right to Die," Jan. 5, 2006, people-press.org/report/266/strong-public-support-for-right-to-die.

28. For a roundup of links to many of the articles written about the film, visit patriciaebauer.com.

29. The Arc of Northern Virginia, "Respect," [PSA], 2008, youtube.com/watch?v=gM96e0yWjhI; The Arc of the United States, "Rally for Respect Campaign," 2008, thearc.org/NetCommunity/

Page.aspx?pid=183&srcid=-2; Haller, B. "The latest in anti-R-word fashion," Media dis&dat blog, Aug. 12, 2008, media-dis-n-dat.blogspot.com/2008/08/latest-in-anti-r-word-fashion.html.

30. Timothy Shriver, "The bigotry behind the word 'retard,'" *The Washington Post*, Feb. 15, 2010, washingtonpost.com/wp-dyn/content//article/2010/02/14/AR2010021402893. html?hpid=opinionsbox1.

31. Lawrence Carter-Long, "'Tropic Thunder' – Hollywood still doesn't get it," Disaboom.com Living section, 2008, disaboom.com/Living/movies/quot-tropic-thunder-hollywood-still-doesn-t-get-it.aspx.

32. Neda Ulaby, "Rethinking 'Retarded': Should It Leave The Lexicon?" NPR, Sept. 8, 2009, npr. org/templates/story/story.php?storyId=112479383.

33. Ulaby, op. cit.

34. Peter Wallstein, "Chief of Staff Draws Fire from Left as Obama Falters," *The Wall Street Journal*, Jan. 26, 2010, online.wsj.com/article/SB20001424052748703808904575025030384695158.html.

35. David Jackson, "Emanuel apologizes for using the 'R-word,'" *USA Today's* The Oval blog, Feb. 3, 2010, content.usatoday.com/communities/theoval/post/2010/02/emanuel-apologizes-for-using-the-r-word/1.

36. AP story reprinted at Media dis&dat blog, "End the R-word campaign spreads nationally," Apr. 1, 2009, media-dis-n-dat.blogspot.com/2009/04/end-r-word-campaign-spreads-nationally. html.

37. Michael Alison Chandler, "Mentally disabled 'self-advocates' oppose use of word 'retarded,'" *The Washington Post*, Feb. 5, 2010, washingtonpost.com/wp-dyn/content/article/2010/02/04/AR2010020402602.html.

38. National Federation of the Blind, "National Federation of the Blind Condemns and Deplores the Movie Blindness," Press Release, Sept. 30, 2008, nfb.org/nfb/NewsBot.asp?MODE=VIEW&ID=368&SnID=193212764.

39. Beth A. Haller, "My review: 'Blindness' the movie is boring," Media dis&dat blog, Oct. 2, 2008, media-dis-n-dat.blogspot.com/2008/10/my-review-blindness-movie-is-boring.html.

40. BBC News, "Avatar overtakes Titanic as top-grossing film ever," Jan. 27, 2010, news.bbc.co.uk/2/hi/8482058.stm.

41. Alison Wilde, "Alison Wilde reviews Avatar - the most expensive film yet made," Disability Arts online, Jan. 14, 2010, disabilityarts.org/?location_id=1077&item=526.

42. Charlie Jane Anders, "20 Science Fiction Characters Who Got Their Legs Back," io9.com, Dec. 23, 2009, io9.com/5431416/20-science-fiction-characters-who-got-their-legs-back.

43. Michael Peterson, Laurie Beth Clark, and Lisa Nakamura, "'I See You?': Gender and Disability in Avatar," Flow TV, Feb. 5, 2010, flowtv.org/?p=4784.

44. Lauren Cox, "'Avatar' Gets Mixed Praise from Paraplegics," ABC News, Jan. 8, 2010, abcnews. go.com/Health/WellnessNews/wheelchair-users-applaud-avatars-parapalegic-character/story?id=9505175&page=1.

10.

Advertising boldly moves disability images forward

dvertisements featuring disabled people have become more noticeable in the U.S. in the last few years, according to the many articles about this phenomenon in the business press.[1] Anecdotally, some of this visibility probably comes from the growing media coverage and awareness of disabled athletes participating in the Paralympics since the Atlanta games in 1996. Every four years, more disabled people are featured in ads after that event for elite disabled athletes. In the summer of 2005, for example, quadriplegic rugby player and star of the 2005 documentary "Murderball" Mark Zupan appeared on billboards in New York City and Los Angeles as a model for Reebok's "I am what I am" worldwide advertising campaign.[2] In 2005 Paralympian runner April Holmes became the first woman and first disabled person to represent the Air Jordan athletic shoe brand; in 2009 her blade running technique inspired new technology to be included in the shoes.[3]

However, a difficulty exists in studying these advertising images of disabled people: The biggest problem has been finding them. The "methodology" developed to locate these ads was to do searches of business press articles about people with disabilities in ads. Because the business press sees an ad campaign featuring a disabled person as "news," a search of business publications turned up articles about companies using disabled people in their campaigns.[4] Clearly, disabled models and spokespeople do not dominate advertising in the U.S., but they are there, and they are becoming slightly more visible in print and on television. This chapter looks at a selection of these advertisements since 1999 to understand the ways in which disability is currently being used within advertising messages.

Some might argue that advertising is just a necessary evil in consumer-oriented American society, and has little impact on societal perceptions of people with disabilities because ads usually convey no information about disability issues. But ads do tell us much about the kinds of people businesses believe will sell products or have resonance in U.S. culture. Hogan argues that advertisements persuade "through their symbolic articulation of a society's ideas and desires."[5] Advertisements manifest our capitalist society's central value – consumption, Schudson says.[6] Disability, like ethnicity,[7] gender, sexual orientation,[8] national origin, and national identity,[9] is one of the many types of cultural information advertising helps to construct. So advertising may have a major role to play in raising public awareness of disabled people.

A few studies have undertaken quantitative content analyses of advertising images of disability, but these have illustrated the inefficiency of quantitative methods in analyzing such a tiny segment of U.S. advertising content.[10]

Previous research[11] has shown that advertisements that use disability images have moved away from traditional pity narratives associated with charity appeals and toward images that show disabled people's integration in society, as part of a movement by U.S. companies to feature more diversity. That research also illustrated that businesses probably were incorporating disability images into their advertising for "cosmetic" reasons – to better represent the diversity of the U.S. society, which, in turn, businesses hope will increase sales and profits.

This chapter discusses the messages and themes imbedded within advertisements that feature people with visible disabilities. The goal was to determine whether advertising images are remaining static in their messages (featuring disabled people in the ads solely for diversity reasons) or are expanding their ad messages to show a variety of disability images.

Methodologically, the ads in this chapter were subjected to qualitative assessment[12] to illustrate the media frames and themes used to characterize disabled people in recent advertisements featuring them. As Altheide says, this type of analysis documents and illuminates the communication of meaning between the media text and a culture. These ads can give us a window into U.S. culture to help assess if, even in the capitalistic pursuit of advertising, imagery is reflecting a more inclusive U.S. society.

Advertisements lend themselves perfectly to a qualitative approach because of the interplay among visual images, words, and the overt persuasive message involved. In looking at visual images, Knoll developed 83 interpretive categories in 1987 for use in assessing photos of disabled people in a qualitative way. Based on Knoll's criteria, one might look for whether the disabled person is shown as a charity case in the advertisements or whether the disabled person is shown as "one of the gang," interacting equally with others.[13] Disability studies scholar Rosemarie Garland Thomson in 2001 proposed a taxonomy of visual rhetorics of disability: the wonderous (supercrip images), the sentimental (telethon and charity images), the exotic (early freak photography), and the realistic (documentary photography). She says, "the conventions of realism govern the images of disabled figures in the world of commerce, the visual component of which is advertising. . . . contemporary advertising casts disabled people as simply one of the many variations that compose the market to which they appeal."[14]

It is important to contextualize a societal understanding of disability images within advertising. Historically, advertising's emphasis on beauty and bodily perfection led to exclusion of disabled people from the images, according to disability studies scholar Harlan Hahn.[15] Concerns that images of disabled people would trigger the nondisabled audience members' fears of becoming disabled meant businesses were hesitant to used disabled people as models. Hahn says that disabled people's "inability" to ever fit within a context of beautiful bodies rendered them invisible. Hahn explains that advertising promotes a specific "acceptable physical appearance" that it itself then reinforces. These advertising images tell society who is acceptable in terms of appearance, and that attitude transfers to whom it is acceptable to employ, associate with, communicate with, and, in general, to value.

However, Hahn, even in 1987, saw signs of hope in changing societal perceptions of disabled people through advertising and other forms of mass communication. He cites many historical examples in which societal perceptions of physical appearances/attributes changed over time. Therefore, because of the modern understanding of diversity as a profitable undertaking for businesses, the cultural meaning of disability imagery in advertising has been changing for the better.[16] As Hahn predicted, some social attitudes changed, and advertising featuring disabled people became associated with profitability because of the audience's desire to see "real life" in images. *American Demographics* reported that households both with (49%) and without a disabled person (35%) valued accurate advertising images of disabled people, and these household members said they were likely to buy products and services that showed sensitivity to disabled people's needs.[17]

Analysis of selected ads using disabled people

Cingular Wireless

This ad was shown during the 2001 Super Bowl. As most Americans know, the TV airing of the Super Bowl football game is *the* place to have a company's advertising spot. They are the most costly and the most visible TV ad spots of the year. A popular-culture critic at the *San Francisco Chronicle* even suggests Super Bowl ads have become such a part of U.S. history that maybe the ads should be taught in schools.[18] Therefore, the significance of the Cingular Super Bowl ad should not be discounted.

The ad begins with an image of artist Dan Keplinger, who has a severe form of cerebral palsy that affects his speech and mobility, painting on a canvas on the floor with a paintbrush in his headstick. Religious choral music plays in the background throughout. The advertisement mimics the communication style of the 2000 Academy Award-winning documentary on Keplinger, "King Gimp," by running subtitles for Keplinger's words in Courier typeface across the bottom of the screen. Caption one says: "There is an intelligent person inside this body." Caption two says: "Art gives me a way to express myself." The ad flashes to more shots of Keplinger continuing to paint with his headstick, and then to a head shot of Keplinger in front of one of his paintings, making it clear it is a self-portrait. Caption three, which is under a split shot of Keplinger painting and his brush alone moving on the canvas, says: "Most people think 'gimp' means lame walk." Caption four then says: "Gimp also means fighting spirit," which is under a split screen of an overhead long shot of him painting a large canvas and a close-up of him moving his head and brush. Keplinger then rolls his wheelchair through the studio with a joyful smile on his face, and the ad cuts to shots of his paintings, which feature smiling faces. Caption five reads: "I am an artist" and is placed under an image of him sitting in his wheelchair in front of four of his paintings. It is shot from below and transitions to an eye-level shot. The next image provides the advertising message: "There is no force more powerful . . . [next shot] or beautiful than self expression." The last two shots are a split screen of Keplinger's clasped hands and a head shot, as he speaks the words: "I'm unbelievably lucky." The words are typed out as he says them. The final ad message reads: "What do you have to say?" and the logo for Cingular Wireless appears.[19]

The theme of this ad is empowerment. The use of Keplinger was a brave step for Cingular Wireless and moved forward the images of disabled people in advertising. Keplinger is not a typical disabled model, because traditionally advertisers choose disabled people whose bodies are not perceived to be upsetting to the audience. So the spot begins by confronting the audience's mistaken impression of Keplinger and his abilities. The words Keplinger uses in the ad are crucial because they confront those who would dismiss him because of his disability. For example, after illustrating his talents as a painter in the ad, he says with gusto: "I'm unbelievably lucky." With this, he challenges those who would pity him. A severely disabled person has told one of the largest TV audiences of the year he feels lucky, happy, and proud of who he is. The ad has the potential to shake the worldview of many nondisabled people who believe disability is a pitiable millstone hanging around someone's neck. Keplinger's image and words construct an alternative belief pattern. "Too often the media depict people with disabilities as a disability, not a person," said Keplinger in Cingular press materials. "The Cingular ad, however, is about me as an artist and that's who I am."[20]

Keplinger's message, embraced by many in the U.S. disability community, is not about changing who he is, but reveling in how fortunate he feels. "There are just so many things this ad does for us – but the most important is to show that disability in and of itself is not bad," says Cyndi Jones, a wheelchair user who is director of the Center for an Accessible Society in San Diego. "After all – I *am* unbelievably lucky."[21] This ad illustrates that some advertisers are willing to show the diversity of human bodies. It showed millions of TV viewers that accurately depicting the human spirit as joyful and creative is the best advertising image of all.

However, even with all the positive implications of the Cingular ad, it is still "using" a disabled person to draw audience attention, and it should be noted that if an ad featured a nondisabled person, it would never have a statement such as "There is an intelligent person inside this body." Although the ad is playing off the stereotypes of disabled people that it knows the nondisabled audience has, it is also embracing a potentially "supercrip" message by emphasizing Keplinger's "fighting spirit" and artistic accomplishments. The problem with the supercrip message is that people with disabilities are put on pedestals because of their perceived inspirational quality in doing ordinary things, which is actually a patronizing way to laud people. Presenting someone as inspirational is just another way of pitying them for the "tragedy of their fate."

Nuveen & HealthExtras

The TV ad for Nuveen, an investment management company, aired during the Super Bowl in 2000 with Christopher Reeve (the actor known for playing Superman before he was paralyzed in an equestrian accident in 1995). In the ad, Reeve is shown as cured of his spinal injury. The scene is set in an auditorium of the future and a group is assembled for a ceremony. The paralyzed actor rises up from his wheelchair and walks across the stage to present an award for research that cures spinal cord injury. His ability to walk was made possible using computer animation: Reeve's head was placed on the body of a man wearing a tuxedo. The narrator states: "In the future, so many amazing things will happen in the world."[22]

The theme of this ad is "disabled equals broken." In this controversial Nuveen ad, the problems caused by trading on tragedy can be seen as dangerously misrepresentative and off-putting. Although, accordiing to Chris Allen of Nuveen, the message of the ad was "to inspire a dialogue on money, to have a new dialogue and get away from buying bigger boats and bigger cars and think about the impact that money can have on the future,"[23] many people around the world misunderstood the Nuveen ad and thought spinal cord injury had been cured when they saw Reeve "walk."

The executive director of the U.S. Spinal Cord Injury Foundation said the organization received numerous calls from paralyzed people and their loved ones who wanted to know how to be cured like Reeve in the ad. The ad inspired a false hope of a quick cure for spinal cord injury. "When you go out with an advertisement like that, you tread a very, very narrow line between trying to be creative – and being misleading," he said.[24] Reeve responded to criticism of the ad with his same rhetoric of hope that a cure will be available if enough time and money are spent. Many disabled people criticized Reeve's singular focus on a cure. As William Stothers, a wheelchair user and deputy director of the Center for an Accessible Society, said of Reeve's quest:

> I don't object to research to find ways to restore damaged spinal cords or causes of other diseases. But I am deeply offended by any implication that disability is an abnormal condition removed from the reality of the human condition. Human beings come in an immense variety of sizes, shapes, talents, and functional abilities. We're all over the map in differences in what we can and cannot do. The limits in what we can do

are often found in obstacles and barriers created in and by the environment, natural, built and attitudinal. Finding a cure for those barriers, now that I can buy into.[25]

Reeve also starred in a series of ads for a disability insurance provider, Health-Extras, which emphasized the personal tragedy idea. The spots have more validity because of their connection to disability insurance; however, they teeter on the edge of using scare tactics, underlining for viewers that what happened to Reeve could happen to anyone. The industry publication *Advertising Age* criticized Reeve and the ads, saying Reeve's "victimhood is for rent" and calling the ads "the commercialization of personal tragedy."[26] Reeve was a good-looking, wealthy actor who probably shared little similarity to the ad's audience. but with his actor training he had a "command of tone and expression to charm, to touch. To persuade," *Advertising Age* explains.[27] To continue to use the personal tragedies of disabled celebrities is a particularly offensive direction for advertising to take in selling products, *Advertising Age* says.

Doritos

This ad begins with two young men playing an aggressive game of one-on-one basketball on a park's basketball court. Matched in height, both are wearing shorts, and one is African American, the other Caucasian. The shot begins from above and then takes on the perspective of one of the players and then the other. The shots cut to their legs often, revealing that the Caucasian man has a prosthetic leg. The legs all appear equal in the shots, i.e., the prosthetic leg is shown as equal to the young man's other leg and those of his opponent. After a few seconds of play, the ad cuts to a British gentleman standing next to a desk outside. His voiceover states: "Yes, my friend, you are bold, but are you daring?" which related to a pitch for Doritos corn chips: "for the bold and daring." The British gentleman then crunches a Dorito his mouth and the ad cuts back to the young men playing basketball. The African American man prepares to shoot a basket and then he arches and shoots. The camera cuts to the basket as the ball approaches, then out of the corner of the shot comes the prosthetic leg being held in the Caucasian man's hand as he uses it to block the ball from going into the basket. The British gentleman's voiceover says: "New Doritos extreme, a bigger chip with an extreme taste. Only for the bold and the daring." In the final scene, the Caucasian man is shaking hands with the British gentleman and has his prosthetic leg on the basketball. Clapping can be heard in the background as if to indicate that the young man has passed the test for being bold and daring.[28]

The theme in this ad is disability cool/disability pride. Casey Pieretti, the amputee in the ad, is a well-known inline skater who lost his leg after being hit by a drunk driver while in college. This ad, showing a vigorous disabled person, sends a strong message of pride. Pieretti is competing equally on the basketball court and in fact actually has an advantage, as is shown in the last scene when he uses his prosthetic leg to block a shot. Although focused on a sports theme, the ad does not turn Pieretti into a supercrip. All the shots show his prosthetic leg to be the equal of the other legs on the court. His aggressive play in the one-on-one game makes him seem "cool," not as if he is succeeding "in spite of" his leg. His leg is actually the star of the ad as it helps him use a unique tactic in the basketball game. His prosthesis allows him to achieve the goal of both "bold and daring" that the Doritos slogan is asking all to aspire to.

Pieretti is an interesting case study as a disabled athlete who eschews the supercrip label. In a profile of him, Joe Clark, a Canadian journalist and author who also researches accessibility issues, writes: "Disabled athletes are not always 'inspiring' or 'courageous.' Sometimes they are just heeding a call – a call that differs only in tenor, not in kind, from that which beckons nondisabled jocks. Being disabled can be a drag sometimes, but it can also act as a catalyst. Case(y) in point: Casey Pieretti, amputee skater."

Pieretti has always been an athlete, as a basketball player before his accident and as a triathlete for a time after the loss of his leg. His perspective: "once a jock, always a jock." He regularly states that the trauma of losing his leg was miniscule compared to the deaths of his father and brother due to a drunk driver several years before his accident. As an inline skater and motivational speaker, Pieretti tries not to reinforce a supercrip status and he adds, "I've had my share of being discriminated against, most definitely."[29] The problem caused by the supercrip image is that "focusing on the Herculean achievements of a few very fit disabled people obscures the day-to-day needs of the disabled majority – a barrier-free environment, an end to job discrimination, and at the most fundamental level, simply being thought of as human beings."[30] Pieretti skirts around the supercrip label to one of disability pride, especially because he rarely hides his prosthetic leg. "Pieretti's greatest contribution to disability awareness may be his willingness to walk around wearing shorts, showing off what he calls his Terminator leg," Clark writes.[31]

Bank of America

The ad opens with a long shot of a woman warming up for martial arts in a studio. The camera cuts to a close-up of her face. Her eyes are closed, and she is breathing evenly in preparation for the contest. An Asian male prepares to attack. There is a close-up of his face with his eyes wide open as he prepares to move in on the woman. Her hands fly, and she stops his attack. The camera moves to a long shot with the woman in the center of the shot with male opponents on either side. Both men are in a state of readiness to attack, and she in a position to defend. One of the men lunges and misses. She turns toward the other man, kicks and scores a direct hit. Accompanying the image of the woman "throwing" her male opponent, a voiceover asks the question, "What is possible?" A close-up shot of the woman in a resting position is shown. The next shot shows the woman leaving the studio and walking towards the camera out into the street. As she exits, she unfolds a white cane. This is the first indication that she is blind. The voice over this image says, "Does achievement discriminate? Or does it open its doors to everyone?" The final shot shows the back of the woman walking confidently down the street, the white cane stretched out in front of her. She is dressed in a sweat suit, sneakers, and carrying a sports bag over her shoulder. The caption "Talking ATMs for the visually impaired. Bank of America: Embracing ingenuity" is placed over this shot. All the shots of this woman suggest she is intelligent and has great skill in the martial arts, executing moves with strength, accuracy, and grace, with the resting shot indicating her knowledge of the etiquette of the art.

The theme of this ad is "We want your business, supercrip." This ad, entitled "Sparring," "demonstrates the company's success in breaking through societal limitations – and creating new banking experiences for sight-impaired customers" and delivers a brand promise: "To be the people who make banking work for customers and clients in ways it never has before," according to company press materials.[32] Bank of America had been providing innovative and accessible services for blind customers for awhile when it began installing thousands of talking ATMs throughout its branches.[33]

However, this ad rightfully attracted criticism. *Advertising Age* said what the Bank of America wants is everybody's money, even blind people's.[34] and that the ad smacks of pity in an effort to attract nondisabled customers to its "worthy" efforts on behalf of disabled people, trying to woo disabled people and their money with its "supercrip" blind woman. "What message do we send the disabled – to say nothing of the able-bodied – with our insistence on viewing them as pitiful wretches unless riding a unicycle on a tightrope with a piano balanced on each knee?" it questions.[35] With these types of supercrip images, in which a blind woman beats three Asian men in a martial arts competition, the ad is sending an insulting message. An *Advertising Age* article favors mainstreaming disabled people into advertising but says the medium should be accessible to them.[36] The irony of the Bank of America TV ad is that it actually does little to inform blind people about talking ATMs because it uses captions instead of voiceover.

The ad on its surface seems inclusive. It does show a blind woman being independent, following her interest in the martial arts, traveling on her own, being a high achiever in her chosen sport. The ad goes for a big impact, but by using her blindness as a surprise, it cheapens her independence. Is she best in her sport because she is a woman or because she is blind? The audience is suddenly confused. Is she showing greater skills of movement or is the message really the improbability of a blind woman (no matter how excellent at martial arts) actually beating three others? The overall theme of the ad pushes inclusion to the background and sends the resounding image of a supercrip, with all the condescension that implies.

Conclusions

Previous research found that disability advertising images focused primarily on two impairments: wheelchair use and deafness.[37] This appears to be changing some. Although there is still much emphasis placed on wheelchair users, now prosthetic limbs, missing limbs, white canes, and more severe impairments associated with cerebral palsy also provide the visual cues that advertisers need to denote disability. This qualitative analysis of ads featuring disabled people illustrates that disabled people are representing explicit advertising messages, as well as denoting themes about the current place of disabled people in U.S. society. As a disabled screenwriter explained, "with varying degrees of finesse, [advertisers] juggle two points: Their products or services are worthy, and so are people who can't walk."[38]

Of course, as with much advertising, only attractive people typically become models. Still, as one disabled actor said, "the Adonis in a wheelchair is better than the whimpering victim in a corner."[39] However, this study shows that recent advertisements are taking more risk when they show disability. Keplinger in the Cingular ad has severe cerebral palsy and is difficult to understand, but that makes his message of self expression for the cell phone company even more powerful. And Pieretti does not hide his prosthetic leg; in fact, it is the star of the Doritos commercial. These more risky disability images have the potential to send an empowering media message about disability to audiences who see them and, according to several scholars, this has the potential for attitude changes towards disabled people.[40]

Though still relatively rare, ads featuring disabled people seem to be increasing in the U.S.. Making money, of course, is the reason companies advertise. "The implication of the images produced in these advertisements is that advertising not only includes disabled people for capitalistic reasons, but realizes these must be accurate images to earn any profit from their use."[41] The positive impact of appealing to disabled consumers' wallets has long been documented.[42] Despite the ad being poorly done, Bank of America has recognized the potential of a large untapped source of customers – visually impaired people – and has begun nationwide installation of talking ATMs. Some ads analyzed presented this very straightforward capitalistic theme of "we want your business." This same theme existed in previous analyses of advertising images of disability.[43]

The goal of this ad analysis was to investigate whether advertising images remained static in their messages (focusing solely on integration) or were expanding their messages to show a variety of disability images. The findings from the analysis of a few selected ads revealed that some improvements have occurred in advertising images of disability, such as the themes of empowerment (Cingular) and the themes of disability pride and inclusion (Doritos). However, several ads still embrace antiquated themes that continue to stigmatize disabled people: Nuveen, HealthExtras, and Bank of America. These ads' themes convey underlying messages that disabled people are broken and in need of repair, are awash in tragedy, or are supercrips, who are presented as inspirational just by living their lives. The advertising images analyzed fit with two categories of Thomson's 2001 taxonomy of visual rhetorics of disability: the wondrous (supercrip images) and the realistic.[44] In what may be a positive trend, Thomson's other two categories (sentimental and exotic) seem to meet with rejection. Although the sample of ads is very small, the study reviewed several dozen ads that featured people with disabilities. Hopefully, the more enlightened of the ad campaigns illustrate an ongoing trend that the pity-filled, sentimental images represented by telethons and charities and the exotic im-

ages of disabled people as freaks are no longer appropriate in 21st-century societies that are trying to restructure themselves so disabled people can compete
equally in all facets of life.

Notes

This chapter is adapted from "Are Disability Images in Advertising Becoming Bold and Daring? An
Analysis of Prominent Themes in US and UK Campaigns" by Beth Haller and Sue Ralph, *Disability
Studies Quarterly*, Summer 2006, www.sds-dsq.org.

1. Beth Haller and Sue Ralph, "Profitability, Diversity, and Disability Images in Advertising in the
United States and Great Britain," *Disability Studies Quarterly*, Spring 2001, 21:2.

2. Alan Krawitz, "Wheelchair warriors," *Newsday*, July 31, 2001, p. G2.

3. "April Holmes Inspires New Technology Included in Air Jordan 2009; Shoe Launches
Nationwide on February 14." U.S. Paralympics Web site, Feb. 3, 2009, usparalympics.org/news/
article/9439.

4. Judy Quinn, "Able to buy," *Incentive*, 1995, 169:9, p. 80; Candy Sagon, "Retailers reach to the
disabled; Stores see profit in undeserved market," *The Washington Post*, December 19, 1991, p. B10;
Joan Voight, "Accessibility of disability," *Adweek*, March 27, 2006, adweek.com; Joshua H. Prager,
"People with disabilities are next consumer niche – companies see a market ripe for all-terrain
wheelchairs, computers with 'sticky keys,'" *The Wall Street Journal*, December 15, 1999, p. B1, 2.

5. Jackie Hogan, "The construction of gendered national identities in the television advertisements
of Japan and Australia," *Media, Culture, & Society*, 1999, 21, pp. 743-758.

6. Michael Schudson, *Advertising, the Uneasy Persuasion: Its Dubious Impact on American Society*. N.Y.:
Basic Books, 1984.

7. William O'Barr, *Culture and the Ad: Exploring otherness in the world of advertising*. Boulder, Colo.:
Westview Press, 1994.

8. Alexandra Chasin, *Selling out: The gay and lesbian movement goes to market*. N.Y.: Palgrave, 2000.

9. Hogan, 1999, op. cit.; S. Hall, "The question of cultural identity," in Stuart Hall, D. Held, and
T. McGrew, eds., *Modernity and its Futures*. Cambridge: Polity Press, 1992.

10. Dennis J. Ganahl, "Creating a virtual television culture: Using actors and models to reflect
desired perceptions in primetime television advertising." Paper presented at the annual meeting
of the Association for Education in Journalism and Mass Communication, Washington, D.C.,
Aug. 2001; Dennis J. Ganahl, and Mark Arbuckle, "The exclusion of persons with physical disabilities from prime time television advertising: A two year quantitative analysis," *Disability Studies
Quarterly*, Spring 2001, 21:2; Dennis J. Ganahl and Jeff Kallem, "Physiographic aggregation and
segmentation: Inclusion of visually-detected physically impaired role models in advertisements."

Paper presented at the annual meeting of the Association for Education in Journalism and Mass Communication, Baltimore, Md., Aug. 1997.

11. Haller and Ralph, 2001, op. cit.

12. David L. Altheide, *Qualitative media analysis.* Thousand Oaks, Calif.: Sage, 1996; K.B. Jensen, "Introduction: The qualitative turn," in K.B. Jensen and N.W. Jankowski, eds, *A Handbook of Qualitative Research Methods for Mass Communication Research.* London: Routledge, 1991, pp. 1-12; Clifford Christians, and James Carey, "The logic and aims of qualitative research," in G.H. Stempel and B.H. Westley, eds., *Research Methods in Mass Communication.* Englewood Cliffs, N.J.: Prentice-Hall, 1981, pp. 342-362.

13. James A. Knoll, *Through a glass, darkly: The photographic image of people with a disability.* Unpublished doctoral dissertation, Syracuse University, 1987.

14. Rosemarie G. Thomson, "Seeing the disabled: Visual rhetorics of disability in popular photography," in Paul K. Longmore and Lauri Umansky, eds., *The New Disability History.* N.Y.: NYU Press, 2001, p. 368.

15. Harlan Hahn, "Advertising the acceptably employable image: Disability and capitalism," *Policy Studies Journal,* Mar. 1987, 15:3, pp. 551-570.

16. Haller and Ralph, 2001, op. cit.

17. Rachel J. Dickinson, "The power of the paralympics." *American Demographics,* May 15, 1996, p. 15.

18. Peter Hartlaub, "Sorting through the history of Super Bowl ads," *San Francisco Chronicle,* Feb. 1, 2008, sfgate.com/cgi-bin/article.cgi?f=/c/a/2008/01/31/DD3GUNQ39.DTL.

19. Cingular Wireless, "I'm unbelievably lucky," Television advertisement , 2001.

20. Cingular Wireless. "Cingular Wireless Super Bowl ads showcase self-expression in unexpected ways," Company press release, Jan. 28, 2001.

21. Beth Haller, "Disability and advertising," *The Baltimore Sun,* Feb. 18, 2001, p. 4C.

22. Emily Farache, "Reeve ad under fire." E! online, Feb. 2, 2000, eonline.com/News/Items/0,1,5954,00.html.

23. Jim Fitzgerald, "Superman 'walks' in TV commercial," *The Guardian,* 2000, guardian.co.uk/Archive/Article/0,4273,3958332,00.html.

24, Fitzgerald, 2000, op. cit.

25. William Stothers, "Sometimes Reeve makes me want to heave." *Mainstream,* Mar. 7, 2002, mainstream-mag.com/.

26. Bob Garfield, "Christopher Reeve's credibility connects for disability insurer," *Advertising Age,* Apr. 24, 2000, p. 101.

27. Garfield, 2000, p. 101, op. cit.

28. Doritos Web page. Basketball commercial, 2002, doritos.com/watchthetv/watchthetv.cfm.

29. Joe Clark, "A leg to stand on," Feb. 22, 2002, joeclark.org/caseypieretti.html.

30. Clark, 2002, op. cit.

31. Clark, 2002, op. cit.

32. Scott Scredon and Joby Humphrey, "Bank of America launches new brand ads," Bank of America press release, August 13, 2001, bankofamerica.com/newsroom/press/.

33. Disability Rights Education and Defense Fund (DREDF), "California, Florida to get first Bank of America talking ATMs," Press release, March 15, 2000, dredf.org/press_releases/newatms.html.

34. Bob Garfield, "Condescension lies hidden in Bank of America's blind spot," *Advertising Age,* Sept. 10, 2001 p. 73.

35. Garfield, 2001, op. cit., p. 73.

36. Garfield, 2001, op. cit.

37. Haller and Ralph, 2001, op. cit.

38. Marc J. Moss, "The disabled 'discovered,'" *The Wall Street Journal,* June 19, 1992, p. 19.

39. Patricia McLaughlin, "Roll models," *The Philadelphia Inquirer,* Aug. 22, 1993, p.31.

40. Olan Farnall and Kimberly A. Smith, "Reactions to people with disabilities: personal contact versus viewing of specific media portrayals," *Journalism and Mass Communication Quarterly,* 1999, 76:4, pp. 659-672; Olan Farnall, "Positive images of the disabled in television advertising: Effects on attitude toward the disabled." Paper presented at the annual meeting of the Association for Education in Journalism and Mass Communication, Anaheim, Calif., 1996; and Z. Panol and M. McBride, "Print advertising images of the disabled: Exploring the impact on nondisabled consumer attitudes." Paper presented at the Association for Education in Journalism and Mass Communication annual conference, New Orleans, La, 1999.

42. Haller and Ralph, 2001, op. cit.

42. John M. Williams, "Disabled people work their way up to TV ads," *Advertising Age,* Aug. 16, 1999, p. 30.

43. Haller and Ralph, 2001, op. cit.

44. Thomson, 2001, op. cit.

Index

Also available from The Advocado Press:

Disability Awareness – Do It Right!
Your all-in-one how-to guide: Tips, techniques, and handouts for a successful Awareness Day from the Ragged Edge Online community (2006) – $19.95

Disability Rag COMPLETE ARCHIVES 1980-1996
Complete text version on fully-searchable CD-ROM – $299.00

Getting Life
Fiction by Julie Shaw Cole (2000) – $16.00

Make Them Go Away: Clint Eastwood, Christopher Reeve & the Case Against Disability Rights
by Mary Johnson (2003) – $16.95

Making News: How to Get News Coverage of Disability Rights Issues
by Tari Susan Hartman and Mary Johnson (1993) – $10.95

Safely Home: A Profile of a Futures Planning Group
Edited by Julie Shaw Cole (2008) – $20.00

The Ragged Edge: The Disability Experience from the Pages of the First Fifteen Years of The Disability Rag
Edited by Barrett Shaw (1994) – $18.95

To Ride the Public's Buses: The Fight That Built a Movement
Edited by Mary Johnson and Barrett Shaw, photos by Tom Olin, foreword by Stephanie Thomas (2001) – $17.95

All books available for purchase at www.advocadopress.org